How
to
Kill
a
Unicorn

AND BUILD BOLD IDEAS THAT

MAKE IT TO MARKET, TRANSFORM

INDUSTRIES, AND DELIVER GROWTH

MARK PAYNE

NICHOLAS BREALEY
PUBLISHING

London · Boston

First published in Great Britain by
Nicholas Brealey Publishing in 2014

3–5 Spafield Street
Clerkenwell, London
EC1R 4QB, UK
Tel: +44 (0)20 7239 0360
Fax: +44 (0)20 7239 0370

20 Park Plaza
Boston
MA 02116, USA
Tel: (888) BREALEY
Fax: (617) 523 3708

www.nicholasbrealey.com
www.howtokillaunicorn.com

ISBN: 978-1-85788-628-3
eISBN: 978-1-85788-947-5

British Library Cataloguing in Publication Data
A catalogue record for this book is available from the
British Library.

Book design by Donna Sinisgalli
Jacket photograph Chris Cook

Printed in Finland by Bookwell.

How
to
Kill
a
Unicorn

Contents

This is dedicated to anyone who ever reached, stretched,
dreamed, wondered, tried, tried again, and finally
found a way to push the boundaries of possibility.

To restless thinkers and tinkerers like John Lee Love,
whose invention of the portable pencil sharpener in
1897 saved this book from being overly blunt, and
Hymen Lipman, for the tender mercies of the eraser in 1857.

To my past and present colleagues at Fahrenheit 212, the
spectacular band of brothers and sisters who amaze me daily.

But above all, and with all my heart, this is
dedicated to my remarkable family.

To Elizabeth and Jacob, my brilliant, loving wife and incredible
son, your imagination, puns, and patience have inspired
me beyond measure. Neither the journey in these pages
nor the harvesting of its lessons could have ever happened
without the light you bring to my days and my spirit.

Todd, you filled my life with music.
Mom, you showed me the joyful rhythm of a phrase well turned.
Dad, you taught me the immense satisfaction of a job well done.

Foreplay

As innovators, we are powered by inspiration,
but measured in realization.

No unicorns were harmed in the making of this book.

Unicorns aren't real.

Chapter 1

Seeing Through It

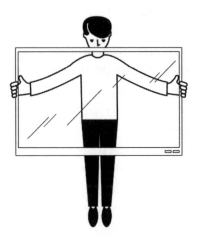

It's Cool, but So What?

It just might be the coolest technology we've ever seen.

We're sitting in Fahrenheit 212's offices, watching as grainy You-Tube clips roll by, one after the other. In a rapid-fire montage of short video reports, a string of tech reporters from various corners of the globe sound as breathless as kids on Christmas morning.

The object of their awed fascination is a new translucent LCD screen technology Samsung has unveiled at the Consumer Electronics Show in Las Vegas. Showcased on a sleek fourteen-inch laptop, the translucent screens cause a feeding frenzy among the tech paparazzi working the floor. Shooting video for their audiences back home, the reporters can't resist waving their hands behind the see-through screen as they proclaim it to be the most amazing thing they've seen in ages.

Welcome to another Fahrenheit 212 project briefing. On a crisp June afternoon, a dozen of us on Fahrenheit 212's Samsung team—an amalgam of strategists, analysts, financial black belts, writers, designers, architects, film producers, and conceptual thinkers, are gathered around the back bar of our office in Manhattan's West Village. In aggregate, the team spans what we call the Money and the Magic. They make up the two sides of our philosophy, our team structure, and our model for developing high-impact innovation solutions. It is the way we create new strategies, ideas, products, categories, and businesses.

The Money & Magic model is in essence an innovation aimed at innovation. Its purpose is to turn the pursuit of breakthrough ideas from a hopeful hit-or-miss rain dance in search of random lightning strikes, into the reliable growth engine modern business needs innovation to be. Money & Magic does this by forcing the collision of two power sources that have traditionally been kept apart—user-centered creativity and outcome-driven commercial grunt. The two forces are joined at the hip in full-bore end-to-end collaboration. Each side of the business comes to a project with equal intensity, equal influence, and equal accountability in shaping high-impact innovation solutions.

Embedded in our approach to new ideas are hard-earned lessons about what separates innovations that work from those that don't. The ones that work make it to market and make good money. The ones that don't are what we call unicorns—ideas that are lovely to think about but don't become real. The lessons here are designed to help any innovator—from the Fortune 500 C-suite exec to the startup entrepreneur to your next-door neighbor tinkering in his garage to your cousin building apps in his dorm room—turn ambition, sweat, and the alchemy of human imagination into real products and businesses that change people's lives.

My colleagues and I gather for project briefings like this kickoff for Samsung's translucent screens around this same worktable every week. As kids kick balls around the park below us, we kick around visions of the future up here. Many of the world's great companies invite us to help crack their most strategically important, commercially critical innovation challenges across a spectrum of businesses. From software to soft drinks. Money to music. E-commerce to eco-packaging. Hotels to haute jewels. Wellness to whiskey. Microchips to potato chips. Resorts to retail. Fashion to factory equipment. Productivity tools to perfume. Textiles to high-tech manufacturing systems. Lipstick to life insurance. And literally soup to nuts. The running joke around the company is that we've turned ADD into a business model.

As the video clips run and the buzz builds, project point man Jon Crawford-Phillips has seen enough. An eloquent pragmatist of British upbringing, Crawford-Phillips is an embodiment of Money & Magic. He hops off his bar stool and shuts down the video feed. In the silence that follows, he walks to the glass wall in front of the back bar where we jot down ideas, grabs a marker, and writes five words.

It's cool. But so what?

Pointing at the words on the wall, he turns toward the rest of the group. *"That's the question Samsung has asked us to answer. We have four months to solve it."*

What Jon means is that our assignment is to help Samsung turn this cool technology from something interesting into something valuable. What lies ahead is a rapid march through a gauntlet of high-stakes questions. For starters, where should Samsung point this amazing technology? Dozens of industries are fair game. Within any of them, what pain points and unmet needs would translucent LCD address and for whom? What new user experiences, benefits, business models, revenue streams, and competitive advantages would it ignite? What would it replace? What specific products would be the door kickers to begin a revolution? What would those products do and how would they work? And in a technology sector that moves at light speed, how could Samsung get to this bold see-through future faster than competitors who might be chasing similar science?

Solving an innovation challenge like this is a bit like wrestling an octopus. Pin down one arm and another wriggles loose. Before diving into the variables we have to start with the few fixed parameters we have. In this case there are just two: the technology itself and the capabilities of the company behind it.

Jon reaches under the table and pulls out an early prototype Samsung has built for us to play with. It's a TLCD screen mounted into a monitor. He flips it on and talks us through the nuts and bolts. Translucent LCD is a see-through glass panel with the ability to deliver digital content while allowing a viewer to see whatever lies behind or beyond the screen. Long the stuff of futurist films like *Minority Report*, it's a piece of the future seemingly teleported into the here and now.

The technology is impressive. Samsung's engineers have handed us a seemingly miraculous way to deliver imagery onto a piece of glass without the typical backlight and solid back panel that make today's LCDs work, and without any external projection mechanism. It does this in part by recycling the ambient light around the screen and repurposing it for image creation. Eliminating the backlight has a number of positive side effects, including reduced weight, energy consumption, and cost.

Cool, cool, and cooler.

But at the back of our minds is Jon's nagging question. *So what?*

WHERE TO PLAY

Job one is cracking the issue of what businesses this technology should be unleashed upon. Or at least where it should start. The laptop at CES was a showpiece to get reporters talking; it was not meant for market.

From a commercial point of view, Samsung had understandably high interest in opportunities beyond existing consumer electronics markets. They were looking for ways to drive their world-leading LCD capabilities into new industries, rather than purely chasing the next upgrade cycle in current lines of business. In truth, the translucent screen could conceivably go anywhere a pane of glass could fit, electricity could flow, and added content could deliver added value. Entire cities built of LCD-skinned skyscrapers? Implausible, but not impossible.

Finding possibilities with this potentially transformative technology wouldn't be the hard part. It never is. Making decisions on which opportunities to pursue and which to jettison is the tougher task. Veteran innovators know that this kind of breadth is both a blessing and a curse. As a design researcher named Dr. Sam Ladner once put it, "There is no shortage of creative solutions to unmet needs, only a shortage of profitable ways to provide them."

Where the dazzling technology is our first killer asset in terms of identifying new product opportunities, the second is Samsung itself. Samsung isn't just one of the world's biggest technology companies, it's one of the smartest and nimblest. The company's scale is mindboggling. With 2013 global revenues of $268 billion, Samsung is the world's tenth-largest company. We've worked with them on many innovation challenges and have consistently been amazed by their ability to execute with brilliance and speed against the things they consider important. Most businesses reaching that kind of scale are slow to spot new opportunities and act on them. But Samsung keeps charging forward.

Fast Company magazine recently celebrated Samsung as one of the world's most innovative companies. Two of the four innovations that were cited were ideas we'd helped shape with their world-class innovation teams. In an age where every company talks incessantly about innovation, Samsung lives it, moving with remarkable speed and decisiveness. They have an unusual ability to simultaneously jump on near-term opportunities and keep their gaze on the long-term horizon. For all the headlines Apple has commanded, Samsung has earned global market leadership in smartphones, and transformed itself from what was once a primarily industrial company into a top-tier global consumer electronics brand, achieving most of that transformation inside of twenty years.

As a more vertically integrated business than most of its peers, Samsung invests heavily in raw component innovations like memory technologies and next-generation screen components, which they sell to other Samsung divisions and to other big-name companies in consumer electronics. If the history of Samsung's prior LCD innovations offers any indication, the products using this translucent LCD technology are as likely to go to market under other companies' names as under Samsung's. This is exciting as it opens up businesses beyond Samsung's category footprint. But it is also a challenge. It means we don't just need to invent products that use the new screen; we also need to fashion the ecosystems around them, creating value propositions capable of attracting other players Samsung may not be doing business with today.

The skill set required to handle this kind of multifaceted challenge is decidedly bipolar. It demands equal doses of inventive imagination and hard-nosed strategic and financial skill. We would have to generate compelling product options, and give those fledgling ideas enough specificity to be able to levy judgment on their feasibility and potential and assess their economic value.

DEBATING DEBATE

Anyone who has bought into the happy-go-lucky myths about what a great creative process feels like would be puzzled by the way we come at it, if not outright mortified. Joyful romps where every idea is celebrated tend to fill rooms with Post-it notes rather than real value, so you won't find them here. It's more intense than that. The players on the team are sent off their separate ways to think independently about the problem on the table, and then regroup to fire ideas at one another and debate their merits. Ideas are treated not as precious pearls to be polished, but as sparks born of friction. They ignite heat, iterations, and tough questions that propel and shape them further. It's not an inquisition. Irreverent jibing peppers the conversations. But it's exploration by interrogation. In the weeks ahead, we'll synthesize and shape big ideas, but won't stop until we've run them through an intense internal gauntlet. Experience has taught us what the geologists learned long ago: it takes pressure to make diamonds.

Exposing fledgling innovation ideas to the tough love of tough questions—like how could that actually be made with today's technologies, where's the competitive advantage, what's the business model, and how could that ever be profitable—ensures those ideas can survive in the real world of real companies placing real bets with real money. Friday afternoon fantasies have to endure the harsh light of the Monday morning reality check.

We work this way not because we like debate for debate's sake, but because it's more effective at generating a greater proliferation of ideas and sharper, more valuable thinking than the artificial coddling that goes on in typical ideation methodologies. Former *New Yorker* columnist Jonah Lehrer wrote an interesting piece on how the myth of brainstorming's potency took hold, and how it's subsequently been debunked by a growing body of scientific evidence. Brainstorming as the world knows it, wrapped in the gauzy belief that every idea deserves a trophy, traces back to adman Alex Osborn's 1948 book, *Your*

Creative Power. In it, Osborn says, *"Creativity is so delicate a flower that praise tends to make it bloom while discouragement often nips it in the bud. . . . Forget quality; aim now to get a quantity of answers. When you're through, your sheet of paper may be so full of ridiculous nonsense that you'll be disgusted. Never mind. You're loosening up your unfettered imagination—making your mind deliver."* Brainstorming's core underlying tenet, a belief that the key to unleashing creativity is the creation of a judgment-free zone for the development of ideas, was taken as a given and widely propagated. We initially bought into it, too.

At Fahrenheit 212 we got to a debate-centric way of building ideas not by conscious choice, but as an accidental side effect of hiring a lot of restlessly curious alpha personalities and feeding them too much good coffee. We had no inkling of the science behind it. But a deeper look at the science has painted a clear picture of why our seemingly tough method has delivered a higher hit rate than more common methods. While brainstorming works better than having no method at all, recent research shows that debate-centric idea development is far more effective, not despite brainstorming's judgment-free model, but because of it. In 2003, Charlan Nemeth at the University of California, Berkeley, ran a creative problem solving study where 265 students were put into teams and asked to come up with creative ideas to alleviate traffic problems in San Francisco. The teams were given the same problem—"How can traffic congestion be reduced in the San Francisco Bay Area?" Each team was assigned one of three conditions. One got the standard brainstorming playbook, which included the no-criticism ground rules. One got what Nemeth called the "debate" condition, where team members could freely debate, criticize, and challenge one another's ideas. The third got no instructions whatsoever, leaving team members free to come up with ideas in whatever way they wanted. Each of the teams was given twenty minutes to come up with as many solutions as possible.

The results? The brainstorming teams slightly outperformed the team that was given no instructions at all. But teams that debated and criticized ideas were far and away the most creative. "While the instruction 'Do not criticize' is often cited as the important instruction in brainstorming," Nemeth says, "this appears to be a counterproductive strategy. Our findings show that debate and criticism do not inhibit ideas but, rather, stimulate them relative to every other condition."

In other words, unless you're 3M, you're not in the Post-it note business. Every idea isn't worth writing down and spending time on. Failing to strengthen an idea by throwing tough questions at it is a disservice to creativity.

As we start riffing on the Samsung challenge, there's an energized positive tension in the room. The group has no hesitation to lob judgment at a fledgling thought or suggestion, but it's done through a positive lens. The key question posed over and over is "Okay, but what must be true for that to work?" It's a powerful question, one that quickly separates high-potential ideas from the blizzard of distracting ideas that can result in lost traction. If that list of "what must be true?" is kind of long, the idea may be a long shot. If it's extremely long and laden with monumental barriers, we label that idea a "unicorn": lovely to think about, but doable and profitable only in an imaginary world. We're out to build big ideas and make them real. Big and absolutely impossible isn't big. One of our important steps to success, in other words, is to kill off the unicorns, or at least cordon them off in their own private pasture.

Within this rapid-fire process, creativity and critique play off each other like melody and rhythm in a Coltrane tune. The Money & Magic players on the Fahrenheit 212 team each represent their own epicenter. Magic gets out of bed each morning to solve for the needs of the consumer. Money comes to work to solve the business questions—the strategic, operational, commercial, and financial needs of the company that's paying us to help crack their problem. Money & Magic work together in lockstep through every step of the process. This too is a break from prevailing orthodoxy in the world of innovation, which says thinking about how money can be made from an idea is toxic to creativity until a consumer solution has been defined. For us, the electricity and riffing back and forth between the Money & Magic folks in these sessions is living proof that the orthodoxy is off base.

DAY TWO

Back in the Samsung team, the euphoria of day one has given way to the hard work of getting under way. Day two on most projects is focused on organizing a rapid two-track learning curve, with a Magic work stream aimed at uncovering consumer pain points, tensions, and aspirations in a given category, and a parallel Money work stream aimed at interrogating the assets, pain points, needs, and opportunities of the business. The Magic side is familiar to anyone versed in user-centered innovation, but the Money side is not. The latter is a sort of ethnography on the business, unearthing commercial insights, strategic challenges, competitive threats, financial performance, leverageable operational assets, and management priorities. A business needs to be actively and aggressively dissected, from its strategic imperatives to its financial metrics, its leverageable assets to its operational capabilities, its brand equities to its competitive landscape.

The front end on the Samsung project is unusually complex, as the array of potential industries that could be transformed by the translucent LCD technology is vast. Analyzing every potential addressable market would take months or years. It was time we didn't have. Do we research the needs of architects and engineers? Laptop buyers or car designers? Instrument display specialists or surgeons who rely on enhanced optics? Military contractors, gamers, or gadget freaks looking for the next cool thing? At this point they were all in the mix. The risk of a rival beating us to market mandated speed. We had to find a smart and efficient way to narrow the playing field.

To go narrow, you have to start broad. You need to pin the out-lier dots on the map to know you've set the borders of the opportunity in the right place. Then you work your way inward, vetting and honing your way to the hottest epicenters. With this project's unusual convergence of breadth and an acute need for speed, we had to quickly bring together imagination, hard data points, strategic and commercial considerations, technical limitations, and healthy doses of instinct. In *Blink*, Malcolm Gladwell writes that 90 percent of decisions are based on the first 10 percent of information that's available. It's a marriage of intuition, a handful of data points, and institutional knowledge. That's what we had to do here.

The journey begins with a hunt for gaps in the world that this technology might fill. It takes mental gymnastics. All seasoned innovators know the value of watching, listening, and observing what's out there. And that's very powerful, as far as it goes. But here we have to look for something deeper. We observe what *isn't* there. We look for situations and experiences where what's observable is in some way inadequate. The people involved often have no idea what they're missing. They accept current reality at face value. We are charged with spotting the gaps hidden in plain view, apparent to us only because we have a piece of the future in our pocket called translucent LCD. The vantage point of the future lets us look retrospectively at the present, spot its shortcomings, and uncover hidden needs we can address.

PEELING BACK THE LAYERS

Every hunt needs a compass. In this case, true north lies in the fundamental truth about the technology. Where conventional backlit LCD screens deliver self-contained images, TLCD is different. At its core, it's a way of delivering layered information to a human eye. The foreground layer is what we'd call *controllable* content of any variety a screen could handle, from information to moving imagery to entertainment. The background layer we call *uncontrollable* content, which is entirely a function of where the screen is placed. Used as a computer monitor, for instance, the view would include the chair across from your desk or the view out the window. We're realizing that being see-through is a double-edged sword—on one hand, a big cool factor that got the tech reporters on YouTube so fired up, but also a constraining performance challenge with big implications for what markets would make sense. In a tech world with an unquenchable thirst for higher and higher definition imagery, we don't want to see Pixar's latest hi-res visualization of goose bumps on a lizard's eyelid compromised in any way. Blue paint on the wall behind a TLCD TV set might mean blue iguanas.

There are privacy factors to solve for as well. If you can see out through the screen to whatever surrounds you, anyone passing by can see into the screen in front of you, albeit in reverse.

MAKING MARKETS

We have to come up with applications where this layering will be a valuable thing rather than a compromise. We spend some time pondering the plight of the microsurgeon, who always needs more information than his or her eyes can gather in any single plane of vision. Bringing together multiple layers of visual information could save lives. Magnifying the area of surgery while allowing hand movements behind the screen to be seen in real time and scale, and overlaying monitoring data that could otherwise be seen only by looking away, might be a way to improve the accuracy of delicate procedures. This dynamic of helping doctors see what otherwise can't be seen has spawned advances from the X-ray to MRI to ultrasound to scope-based surgery. Could translucent LCD be the next advancement in seeing the unseeable?

Other opportunities rapidly came into view. Could translucency open up new locations in our homes or professional environments where traditional "black rectangle" devices might be aesthetically unwelcome? Other gaps were spotted in the rhythms and routines of everyday life.

One technique we frequently use is giving ourselves a specific new lens to bring to bear on the everyday life experiences of our team to see what jumps into view. What we urge Fahrenheit 212 innovators and anyone else to do is use your eyes and ears as much as you use field research. Your own observations on the way to work can spot an opportunity every bit as effectively as months of expensive research if you bring the right perspective. You can always go back later and validate your hunches. Knowing that translucent LCD was in simplest terms a see-through glass panel with new functionality, we have every member of our team spend a few days taking inventory of all their daily encounters with any form of glass panel, in a machine, a building, a device, or any other physical object. When we regroup to tally up what surfaced, the daily incidence of glass panel encounters proves massive. From that first glance out the window in the morning to peek at the weather, to glancing at shop windows, waiting at a bus shelter, glancing out of a moving vehicle, panning across thousands of glass panels that make up the city skyline, or even writing the notes of the exploration on the glass walls in our office. (In designing our workspace as a collaborative idea factory, we built the walls out of glass panels, so impromptu hallway conversations can be captured by scribbling with a marker on whatever wall is behind you.) One of the firm's partners, Rony Zibara, a Lebanese-born innovation lifer and a hard-core foodie, noted two dozen encounters with glass panels in a single lap around the grocery store. Retail environments hadn't really been on our radar until we started investigating our own lives. Once again, we found opportunity areas that were, like so many others in life, hidden in plain view.

In just two weeks we defined and did a first-cut assessment of about twenty plausible markets this technology could potentially create, disrupt, or transform. Some were consumer electronics markets where the arrival of translucent LCD could ignite new performance characteristics. Others represented entirely new or fringe businesses where there was no obvious competitive set or business model to plug into, like the fledgling augmented-reality business, where devices let consumers digitally see virtual objects in real-world environments. Between these bookends were an array of established industries where LCD technologies were not currently used, but where translucent LCD's arrival could create new value and new competitive advantage for whichever incumbent players unleashed the technology. Selling TLCD into the business of bus shelter–based media companies was an example of this.

With the range of possibilities defined, we now kick into filtering mode. Based on available knowledge, we build a visual plot that allows the opportunities to be compared, contrasted, and clustered.

In this case, we use a very simple filtering tool we developed that we call the BFD Map. BFD is short for "Big Fast Doable." The axis labeled "Big" reflects our early-stage sense of the relative size and strategic value of each of the opportunities we're considering. Scale is self-explanatory, though tricky for those opportunities that represent new-to-world businesses. Strategic value is specific to the product. Some opportunities have relatively small commercial value but huge strategic value, and vice versa. An application in a small product category that is an attention-getter that opens the door for more lucrative subsequent applications may rank higher on "Big" than its size alone would warrant. A technology like Kevlar, for instance, has been used in dozens of industries, from bridge construction to fiber optic cable protection to drumheads and even Nike LeBron basketball shoes. But it cemented its reputation for toughness through its use in bulletproof vests. Applications showcasing its incredible strength-to-weight ratio would have ranked "big" on this scale, even if they had limited revenue potential. Like so many things in innovation's fuzzy front end, evaluating how big a given idea is requires art and science in equal measure. Money & Magic capabilities pushing one another onward in real time makes it work.

The other axis is labeled "Fast & Doable." This blends considerations like technical feasibility, relative complexity of the potential business system, near-term manufacturing capacity, existence of a robust supply chain, clarity of route to market, and whether we would expect it to scale up quickly or gradually over a number of years. Where two ideas seem equally doable, the one that is more likely to happen quickly—perhaps because it can be produced using existing manufacturing capacity or has relatively few technical hurdles to clear—gets higher placement on the map. Applications in the medical and military markets, for example, might sit high on the Big axis, but lower on Fast & Doable, as they involve issues of life and death, years of safety testing, complex regulatory environments, and elaborate, slow procurement systems. The point is not to say no to opportunities like these, but to separate lead opportunities from things that are likely to happen much more slowly.

This simple BFD map creates separation between top-tier opportunities, and other ideas that should go on the back burner or be killed off. It's hard to let go of fledgling ideas, and you shouldn't until you've kicked the tires on them and explored their potential. But focus, we've found, is our friend. By nature of our line of work, and our healthy obsession with concrete outcomes, we have no choice but to sideline or kill off more great ideas in a week than a lot of highly successful businesses may conceive in a year. At least it feels that way. True or not, it's a healthy sign of the need for hard-core filtering and focus on the big, rather than the merely interesting. Too many innovation methodologies emphasize the sheer quantity of ideas generated, failing to recognize that the allocation of a team's time, energy, and attention is a zero-sum game. Time is the only

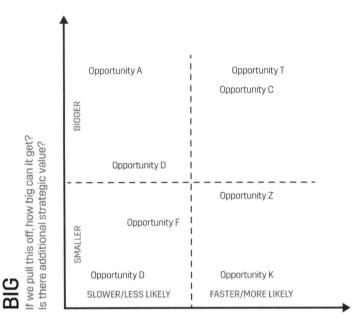

investment you can never get back, no matter how good your exit strategy may be. There's a sweet spot where broad enough is broad enough.

As helpful as the map itself can be, the process of building it unlocks tremendous value in its own right. The cross fire of consumer and commercial perspectives ignites a mix of both objective and instinctive arguments about why a given idea is bigger or more doable than another. With amazing speed, this highly charged, structured debate cuts through the untilled ground like a supercharged titanium plow, uncovering otherwise buried issues and hidden assumptions that might kill off an idea down the road. It also works like a fast-forward button on the work to come, turning lead ideas from hunches to compelling consumer and commercial propositions.

What emerges from this gauntlet is a handful of priority opportunities, and a batting order of second- and third-tier opportunities to deploy over time. Those ideas we labeled unicorns may show up here as very remote long-term long shots, worth a few minutes' conversation before parking for five or ten years until technologies or businesses can be marshaled to make them workable. But for now they're killed from the consideration set for the duration of the project at hand. (LCD-skinned skyscrapers, for one, are solidly in the unicorn camp, requiring dozens of things to be true to make a big, profitable business in that space, from climate-proofing the technology to needing thirty-plus years of durability to competing in the fragmented building design and construction industry to lacking a route to market to overcoming the omnipresent belief that a better technology is always just a few years away, to name a few.)

Armed with the insights we've identified so far, we meet with the Samsung team to share our thinking, and engage with them in the same kind of healthy two-track debates that we worked through internally. We riff on the core insights, talk about technical assumptions, discuss the market ecosystems each idea unlocks, and get a collective view of the landscape. We also push ourselves to see if there's unexplored terrain worth further tilling. As with all our best clients, we push the Samsung team's perspective on the opportunity, and they push ours. 1 + 1 = 11.

The top-tier opportunities over the weeks ahead would be rapidly transformed from what we call ideas to solutions. To us, there's a world of difference. And that difference is a big reason why we've been able to achieve inordinately high rates of projects successfully delivering products into our clients' pipelines. An idea is a powerful thing—but it's just an idea. It's like a sketch before the painting. If it's a big idea, it should have big insight behind it, big benefits in its realization, and a compelling experience to deliver those benefits. But the truth is that an idea is rarely an answer. It's usually a hunch wrapped in a bundle of unanswered strategic, operational, technical, and financial questions. What we call a two-sided solution involving both the Money and the Magic sides of the equation doesn't make all those questions go away. But it's a quantum leap beyond the loose hunches that too many innovation practitioners consider the end-point of a job well done.

The months ahead would see us, in partnership with the Samsung team, define our top-priority markets for entry, assemble data points and strategic rationale supporting the attractiveness of these markets, build indicative product specifications for technical and financial assessment, create initial product designs and animations to bring realism to the vision, and distill the strategic story of each idea into a three-minute video prototype, making the vision for each idea readily understandable and self-contained for any senior executives looking in on the project for the first time.

By the end of the four-month collaboration that kicked off that day spent watching video of the debut of the translucent LCD technology, Jon's challenge of *It's cool, but so what?* had been answered in spades, both in vivid dimension and in dollar signs, giving Samsung a clear vision of both its first moves and those that it would deploy in subsequent years.

OPENING THE DOOR

Just nine months after that June briefing, working prototypes of the first market-bound translucent LCD products were unveiled to the world at trade shows in Europe. The unexpected lead horse that had emerged was a play in the commercial refrigeration business. It was born at the intersection of unmet needs of consumers and companies in the food and beverage business, where products sold in refrigerated and frozen form typically command premium margins, but impose a barrier between the product and the consumer. The glass on the beverage fridge or the grocery freezer obscures the products behind it, making it hard for consumers walking through the store

to find the products they're after. It also makes it harder for manufacturers of those glass-enclosed products to ensure their products
get noticed. The solution we offered Samsung opened the door, quite
literally, to creating significant benefits for every player in the commercial refrigeration ecosystem. It all started by simply replacing
the conventional glass in commercial fridges and freezers with a
translucent LCD panel.

For consumers, the information, context, and imagery that
TLCD made possible meant new ease of finding what they were after
in a cluttered grocery environment. They could see what was new,
or get more information about a product with just a tap on the glass
instead of squinting at incomprehensible back panels and letting the
cold air out. Refrigeration equipment makers, whose biggest customer base is large-format food retailers and big beverage companies, suddenly had a way to disrupt the long upgrade cycle. Instead
of waiting for old equipment to break down, retailers now had motivation to leap to the next-generation equipment and the new benefits
it offered. For the first time, food and beverage manufacturers could
call attention to their products in the cooler as effectively as they
could in every other aisle of the store. Retailers suddenly had a new
revenue stream by selling marketing time on the door of the fridge,
as well as a new vehicle for promoting house brands, and a new tool
for cross-promoting different categories in the store. For a consumer
buying a frozen pizza, up pops a message about the specials on beer
in aisle nine.

The value propositions were so clearly defined that Samsung
was able to write big deals with equipment and food companies a
year before the manufacturing facilities were even operational.

As the lead play in commercial refrigeration was being created,
a second TLCD business followed in its wake: smart shop windows.
Here conventional retail window glass would be replaced by TLCD
panels, allowing window displays to be augmented with multi-
media overlays, enticing video content or dynamic information about

the featured products. Samsung's smart-window concept went on to sweep Best Innovation in Show prizes at the Consumer Electronics Show in 2012. By now Samsung is well on its way to leading the category in translucent LCD. The transformation from cool to highly valuable is under way.

SO WHAT?

In the bigger context of the mission around which Fahrenheit 212 was formed—to find a way to turn breakthrough innovation from a hopeful hit-and-miss rain dance into a more reliable growth engine—Jon's impromptu scrawl at the kickoff session hits at a far bigger point. *It's cool but so what?* is a telling commentary on modern innovation practice, and on the conventional wisdom that permeates it.

Innovation methodologies have been evangelized and adopted with an extreme bias toward the merely interesting, new, and novel in isolation from *commercial* factors. In other words, innovation teams are not being taught to pour adequate sweat and inspiration into the things that in the end really drive adoption, impact, scale, speed to market, and return on investment of cash, talent, and time. In a way, these methods have proved to be unicorns in their own right—promising great things but too often culminating in something ethereal rather than tangible.

This has contributed to innovation project failure becoming not only irrationally common, but something seen as normal and natural—shrugged off with no more alarm than an ice cream cone melting on a sunny day.

This has happened even as most markets have approached saturation, with the low-hanging fruit already plucked and pureed into prior years' earnings, creating a growing need for innovation to spur the top-line growth that investors, CEOs, entrepreneurs, and global powerhouses require.

Measured from the front of the innovation pipeline, from the day

a project team transforms a blank page and an ambition into ideas—
the odds of an innovation team's good intentions coming to fruition
are exceedingly slim. With innovation's soaring importance to companies' growth agendas, this is unacceptable. But even more surprising to me than the failure rate is the complacency that surrounds
it. Failed innovation projects don't just waste cash, time, impetus,
and sparks of human imagination; they somehow manage to do so
without upsetting anyone—from the project manager to the C-suite
sponsor, from the CFO who writes the big checks to fund innovation
efforts that don't deliver top-line growth and return on investment,
to the creative visionary whose groundbreaking ideas die on the
vine. It's the train wreck no one is talking about.

One night a few months before we decided to roll the dice and
start Fahrenheit 212, I was sharing a beer with our fledgling team,
contemplating our mission of finding a more reliable way to make
innovation work. Why wasn't corporate America complaining? Why
the profound silence on the subject? Then it hit me. I wondered out
loud to Jon Crawford-Phillips, who is now a ten-year veteran of the
firm, a partner, and our COO, "Jon, when was the last time we heard
someone bitch about how intolerable gravity is?"

The answer of course was never.

Human nature tells us not to waste our energy getting wound up
about things that just are the way they are and can't ever be changed.
No one's ranting about rate of failure in innovation because everyone's been conditioned to think that high rates of failure are an irre-
versible fact of life. It's like gravity. People don't rant about it because
they think it will always be exactly the way it is now.

There is of course a healthy kind of failure that throws off opportunities for iteration as a stepping-stone to success. But that's
not what we were talking about that night. We were talking about
the parade of expensive projects that deliver nothing but a pile of
Post-it notes, a big research bill, an occasional Friday afternoon
goose bump, a splitting Monday morning headache, and no tangible

returns. Depending on the cited source, the prevailing rate at which innovation projects fail to bear fruit is somewhere between 85 and 95 percent. It's staggeringly high.

We were either crazy enough or ambitious enough to believe that this seemingly inevitable gravitational pull toward failure was something that not only *should* be mitigated, but *could*. The answer to how to pull that off wouldn't be clear to us for a few years, but our intent was unambiguous. We wrote it down and stuck it on the wall. It defines the reason we get out of bed every morning. And it is as true today as it was on day one.

The years between the moment when our purpose was first taped to the wall and that highly energized Samsung briefing would generate a vast and valuable set of insights and lessons on how to innovate successfully. We treated the triumphs and failures along the way as equally helpful markers and data points toward cracking the innate code, fueling the restless experimentation and course correction that culminated in Fahrenheit 212's Money & Magic methodology.

To get it right, we would first get it wildly wrong.

In our early days, we drank the Kool-Aid of conventional wisdom—brilliant thinkers like Edward de Bono and leaders in the design thinking movement who believed that human-centered creativity was innovation's missing link. As de Bono eloquently put it, companies struggled at innovation for the simple reason that the future cannot be analyzed. Designers told companies to stop thinking about products and profits and start focusing on people. These ideas resonated with us and fed our desire to be change agents.

Starting our firm with little more than hot coffee and a hunch, we took it all at face value and applied it, moving the creativity that had historically been applied to innovation at the go-to-market stage, all the way to the front end of the innovation process, where the page is blank and the possibilities are vast.

But over time, we came to the unavoidable realization that

user-centered creativity on its own was capable of many big things, but moving the needle on innovation success rates wasn't one of them.

We realized that what too often comes from a conventional user-centered innovation process, even in partnership with some of the greatest companies on earth, is unicorns: ideas that are beautiful to think about and highly interesting, but that will never appear in the marketplace or your backyard, because they're conceived in blin-kered isolation from the myriad of things that actually determine what makes it to market and what doesn't.

In the end, there was a certain freedom that came with being beholden to no particular orthodoxy, other than a product or idea's impact upon the market, consumers' lives, and the business it's meant to grow. It let us stumble and solve our way through our white-knuckled startup days to a model that seems, having been field-tested across scores of innovation challenges in dozens of industries, to be capable of doing the thing we set out to do: to make innovation the reliable source of growth that businesses now need it to be. I would like to share that model with you.

Chapter 2

The Two-Sided Problem

It was a day of stark contrasts.

A team from Fahrenheit 212 has spent the afternoon pounding the pavement in the 118-degree heat of the Dubai streets, squinting through the dust and their own rolling sweat, looking for clues and insights to ignite a revolution in the way banks grow their businesses.

While the day of fieldwork ended just an hour ago, it seems like ancient history, far removed from the creature comforts of a buzzing restaurant in one of Dubai's soaring towers. The blistering heat's been replaced by overtorqued air-conditioning, our scorching thirst by a cool drink, the team's street-level granularity by the macro view from this perch a thousand feet up.

The restaurant is another study in contrast, a sleek modern interpretation of the ancient mosaics that define the region's architectural legacy. It offers one experience up close, where the hand of the artisan is vested in each textured seam, and another from a distance, as the full-scale image emerges from the pixilated tiles.

Led by partners Pete Maulik from the Money side and Rony Zibara from Magic, the Fahrenheit team debriefs over dinner on the day's discoveries. The operating styles of these two seasoned innovators could not be more different or complementary. Raised in Beirut (the Paris of the Middle East) and Paris itself, Rony sees innovation as a hunt for hidden codes, deep human truths, and elegant solutions that have to be coaxed out and carefully honed. A product of tough Minnesota winters, Harvard College, and Columbia Business

School, Pete treats an innovation challenge as a series of barriers to be overcome, not unlike the Yale running backs he took down as a Harvard nose tackle.

As they reflect on the day, this theme of contrasts peppers the conversation. It's fitting, given that we believe the best way to get to successful innovation outcomes is by approaching innovation as a two-sided problem.

To make the leap from the Post-it note to the balance sheet, an innovation has to succeed in two completely different worlds—the world of consumers and the very different world of the business that's out to serve them. Each of those worlds holds its own set of challenges.

The Fahrenheit 212 team has come to Dubai at the invitation of a big private bank in the United Arab Emirates. The bank's president has asked us for help on a challenge that, like many innovation tasks, appears straightforward on the flight over, but less so on closer inspection. We're to help them build innovations capable of getting more consumers to buy more broadly into the range of products the bank offers. If the average customer today has two of their products, say a mortgage and a credit card, our mission is to create innovations that ignite a broader and deeper relationship, driving average products per customer up from two to three. Getting existing customers to participate more broadly across the product portfolio is one of the most powerful profit levers any retail bank can move. The financial impact of moving the needle is easy to model and sexy to look at. The question is how to make it happen.

As we head into our fieldwork, the assumption is that there's probably a product issue—some readily fixable flaw in the bank's menu of offerings. But after kicking the tires, we know that's not the case. They have a deep, well-conceived product portfolio from checking to car loans, credit cards to savings accounts, time deposits to private banking services. But for reasons unknown, fewer customers than expected are participating broadly across the product range.

Around the world, the way most banks drive customers across their product portfolio is through a combination of opportunistic selling by customer service when they spot a client need, and rate-driven promotions. But faithful use of these tools over a number of years hasn't had the impact the bank's growth goals require. The bank's president and his team want to find a new approach, so they called us in to see if together we could find the missing link.

The work of the team on that hot Dubai afternoon and over the weeks ahead is a two-track effort yo-yoing back and forth between customers and bankers, hunting for insights around which game-changing innovations would be constructed. What becomes apparent is that successfully solving the adoption problem will require cracking not one problem, but two: the consumer problem and the business problem. As is so often the case, these two problems have remarkably little to do with each other, other than one huge thing: neither problem can be solved without also solving the other.

To get to the core of the customer problem, we have to get deep inside the lives of the hardworking Asian expatriates who make up the majority of Dubai's workforce and the bank's customer base. But there is just as much digging for us to do within the bank itself, to understand the relationship between the structures, systems, technologies, products, personnel, programs, and processes that will underpin, or potentially impede, greater customer adoption.

During the 2012 U.S. presidential campaign, Mitt Romney shot himself in the foot with a flippant comment that "corporations are people, too." In a time of economic hardship, it cost him votes. But leaving the politics out of it, there's an innovation analogue here in thinking of businesses as individuals. To drive up the odds of creating innovation solutions that make it to market and thrive, you have to treat the interrogation of the business with the same intensity you pour into understanding the people on the street. Design thinking orthodoxy tells designers to just worry about understanding the needs of the end users. Obsessing over end users is vital, but the needs of the business need equal attention, or you leave precarious gaps in understanding a business proper. For every hour our team would spend observing and interviewing bank customers, trying to decode the motivations, tensions, and rhythms of life that were influencing their financial behavior, we would spend another hour examining the strategies, behaviors, attitudes, and systems in play within the bank itself.

On the consumer track, the findings that leap out are fascinating. The desire to build better lives for our families is a fundamental human drive that transcends geographies and social strata. But here we're picking up important nuances. One is a cultural tendency to think differently about time. In many parts of the world, consumer conversations about finance tend to be all about the future. But in the cultural context of the Emirates, what consumers are describing is a sense that the past, present, and future are inseparable parts of a continuum. Financial well-being is a progression, spanning generations of a family, the aggregated effect of small decisions and big ones, and all the connections between them. Working in from this macro view, we begin to examine how these customers have chosen the array of financial products they have. Surprisingly, they talk about them as a series of one-off decisions, each triggered by an immediate need or promotional offer. The tension is there in plain sight. They see their financial picture in terms of multiple decisions over time, but describe each individual decision as an isolated event. They're thinking one way, but acting another. We have to figure out why.

The picture gradually emerges. Consumers may think of financial products as pieces of a bigger whole, but they don't acquire them that way for one big reason: the banks themselves tend to treat each product in isolation. They've conditioned customers to look for rate offers, rather than take a deeper view of their bank relationships. There is no meaningful connective tissue between bank products. It's not a problem unique to our client's bank—it's industry-wide.

It's starting to make sense, but one more nagging inconsistency has us scratching our heads. If customer decisions were one-offs, and rate offers played such a big part, why were these consumers relatively unresponsive to the offers from the bank they already did business with? When we ask customers, the question sets them twitching. As we all know, body language often carries more insight than spoken language. Eventually, the biggest barrier to product adoption comes into view. We're fighting an unspoken fear. Bank customers in the Emirates are afraid of getting too vested in any one bank, as they think it would leave them exposed to increased risks, either by the bank falling on hard times, or changing the rules in a way that compromised their interests. Spreading their money among multiple banks, even in mundane products like checking and savings accounts, was a form of self-protection.

The implication is that regardless of how well conceived the bank's products and cross-selling efforts may be, many of our bank's customers would actually *prefer* to get their next financial product from another bank. The reasons for avoiding consolidation of their finances in a single bank may seem irrational to those in finance but are emotionally sound to the bank customers. The value of getting their next mortgage or loan or credit card from a bank they already did business with was not. Having multiple points of contact with a single bank lacked any form of strong value proposition for the customer.

Back at the restaurant, as the waiter brings entrees to the table, the depth of the challenge is sinking in. Rony looks out the window at the night sky and sums up these realizations: "Dubai may look pretty flat, but we have a mountain to climb."

Conventional innovation orthodoxy, labeled as user-centered design or design thinking, would say that this level of clarity around the consumer problem is the primary, or perhaps the only essential, input to igniting the innovation process. But we treat it as just half of the two-sided problem. The parallel work of getting to a comparable level of understanding of the business problem to solve is still under way.

Halfway across Dubai, our Money team is becoming deeply immersed in commercial and operational realities, walking the corridors at bank headquarters, talking to key stakeholders, probing to uncover commercial insights and the core business issues. We go in assuming the lack of deep customer buy-in across the bank's product portfolio isn't actually the problem—it's probably just a symptom of other problems. You don't create value by solving symptoms. You have to aim an innovation at solving the underlying causes. With the same intensity we brought to probing consumer truths, we analyze the barriers inside the bank itself.

We drill into everything from the profit-and-loss statements to the performance of individual business units to the inner workings of the bank's IT systems to daily routines of customer service reps on the floor. What we find is not particularly unique to our client, but endemic in the way banks around the world operate. Up and down the organization, we see ample good intentions and lip service paid to cross-divisional collaboration to serve customers. But nothing about the way the bank actually operates has been designed to create synergy or collective impact across the various product groups. The organization structure, built over time to accommodate the expansion of product offerings, is rigidly siloed. The separate divisions responsible for selling mortgages, credit cards, car loans, etc., are almost worlds unto themselves. Executive incentives are tied to the financial performance of the executive's individual business unit rather than the bank as a whole. There's no structural mechanism for turning a customer of one division, say a young couple who just signed their first mortgage, into a prospect for another division. In fact, an executive running the mortgage business would see little growth potential in a customer with a newly minted thirty-year mortgage. Instead, he steers his energies toward acquiring new mortgage customers, rather than cultivating existing relationships.

Reps on the branch floor, meanwhile, who often pick up anecdotal

clues that point to cross-selling opportunities, has no real tools beyond their own instincts and separate rate sheets for each type of
product.

Even the IT system, which ostensibly unified the bank's offerings, was built in a Lego-esque way with separate software supporting each product, and no real ability for product metrics to interact.
Again, these issues aren't unique. Nearly every bank on earth faces
similar challenges. But that doesn't matter. These barriers have to
be overcome to answer the innovation challenges of increasing products per customer. Customers had not found a way to fit the financial
pieces together in a coherent, meaningful, valuable way that encour-
aged them to do their banking in one place. But neither had the bank.

Taking it all in, Pete shares a confession. "To be honest, I thought
the consumer side of this equation would be the tougher one on this
project. But the internal realities may be the real game breakers.
Whatever the innovation may be or do for customers, we need to
start thinking now about how to break down all these organizational
barriers, or in the end nothing will happen."

To be successful, the innovation we're going to come up with
has to thread two needles at once. It has to transcend consumer resistance with a value proposition that makes consolidating their assets under one roof both rationally and emotionally attractive. And
it also has to thread the second needle, carving its way through the
IT systems, the siloed P&L structure of the different business units,
the executive incentives, and the realities of the bank rep on the floor.

Facing a two-sided problem, which is the norm in innovation
rather than the exception, if you look only at threading that first
needle, you can come at it from almost any angle and get through it.
But then it's left to random luck as to whether the angle you took to
get through the first loop will land you anywhere near the second.

Looking across both sides of the problem, over the coming weeks
the project team cracks the challenge wide open. The answer in the

If you're only looking at one side of an innovation challenge, the angle you take to get through the first may miss the second by a mile.

end will draw inspiration from that night in the lushly tiled restaurant a thousand feet above the streets of Dubai.

The solution was not a new product but a new system called Mosaic that delivered transformational benefits to both consumers and the bank. The idea was born at the crossroads of key insights about the consumer and the business. Consumers see their financial picture as an aggregation of many small pieces that accumulate over the years. The bank, meanwhile, if it hopes to materially drive multi-product adoption, needs to transform a silo-like business into a cohesive, synergistic whole. Through the Mosaic system, the pieces would suddenly connect in a new way. For starters, Mosaic gave consumers a new rational basis for getting their next product from our bank in a very unexpected way: adding a new product from the bank's lineup would instantly improve the terms on any and all the products that consumer *already had* with us. Adding a new checking account for instance would immediately improve the terms on the car loan they'd had for five years, dropping it to a more attractive net rate. Or the fees they paid each payday to wire money back to their families overseas would suddenly be slashed. Or the rewards program would start accumulating rewards faster. A customer walking into the branch with, say, a car loan and a checking account, looking for a new credit card to manage monthly cash flow, would suddenly see an amazing reason to get that card from our client rather than another bank.

Consumers' fears about consolidating assets at one bank had been tangible to them, while the benefits of consolidation had been amorphous. The customer-facing piece of the Mosaic system was a tablet-based tool we created (which preceded the iPad launch) making the benefits of consolidation tangible for the first time. It let a bank rep sitting with a customer pull up the customer's existing product mix and, with a few taps of a finger, show the impact adding a new product would have on the terms of the existing products. Seeing this transformation visualized before their eyes, fascinated customers instinctively asked what would happen if they added two more products, or three. Again, in just a few taps, they got their answer. The rational financial foundation of the value proposition was underpinned by the deeply emotional and culturally resonant theme of the Mosaic, which came to life in every design touch point, from the interface of the tool to the training program we created for staff.

The Mosaic theme was equally meaningful among bank

executives, symbolizing the transformation of disconnected busi-nesses and divisional customer bases and company performance into a unified whole.

The good intentions each division had toward supporting the growth of the rest of the bank suddenly had an active conduit. Each division knew they had to give something up (a small slice of the rev-enue on its products) to get something (new customer acquisitions from other divisions' customer pools), so a new executive incentive scheme was put in place to reflect the win-win culture.

Within a year of going live with Mosaic, the bank exceeded its aggressive product adoption goals. Revenue targets were exceeded by 35 percent. And an organization encumbered by disconnected ways of working had a powerful mechanism for making the whole more than the sum of the parts.

What made Mosaic possible was not the cleverness of the solution (though it was an amazing piece of work by our team of strategists, idea developers, and designers), but the philosophy and approach of coming at the challenge as a two-sided problem. The problems of the consumer and the business were completely different, but the inno-vation had to solve them both. Neither could be solved without also solving the other.

A root cause of the unacceptably high failure rates permeating modern innovation practice is a baked-in assumption that if you solve for the needs of the consumer, the needs of the business will eventually sort themselves out.

It's a bit like trying to hit a golf ball with one eye closed. The depth perception isn't there. What seems like a perfect swing or line of attack when viewed through just one eye is often well off the mark. Realizing that there are two separate sets of needs to solve for is the first step to turning the corner. With both eyes open, pure contact becomes far more likely.

Chapter 3

The Two-Sided Solution

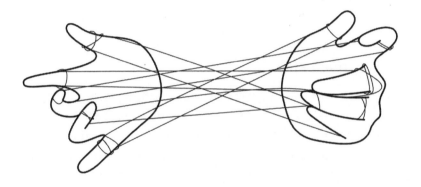

All of us involved in the practice of innovation have felt that adrenaline-laced thrill of cracking the transformational idea, and also the hollow heartbreak that kicks in when a seemingly promising idea unravels before it ever gets to market and scales up.

The causes of these derailments may vary: budget cuts ending funding before the finish line, a project sponsor leaving for a new job, an investor backing out, innovation triage favoring another program over yours, or a risk profile that spooks management and keeps them from pulling the trigger. But actually many of the meltdowns trace back to the fact that what your bosses or investors are being asked to bless is just a one-sided solution—an idea that's great for the consumer *or* the business, but not both.

In the last chapter we looked at how treating innovation as a *two-sided problem* sets you up with better odds for success. Let's go deeper now into where all this leads: *two-sided solutions* that deliver big value to the consumer and the business. We'll look at some examples of what two-sided solutions look like, then drill into why ideas built this way consistently beat the odds, make it to the street, impact people's lives, and grow businesses.

NOW THAT'S PROGRESS

Auto insurance may be unique in being something you pay a heap of money for and hope to never use. Little wonder, then, that low rates are such a dominant focal point in the industry's competitive wars. Why pay more than you should for something you hope to file away and forget? With more than $160 billion spent each year on auto insurance premiums in the United States, the battle is understandably heated, bookended by promises of better service and lower prices.

The price king is Geico. Unapologetically embracing lower rates as their reason for being, they run an operation as lean as their famous gecko to make those low price points possible. The insurance industry measures efficiency on a metric called *expense ratio*, which rolls up overheads, marketing costs, and other operating outlays and compares them to premiums collected. Despite dropping almost a billion a year in marketing, Geico is efficiency's poster child, with an expense ratio far below that of market leaders like State Farm and Allstate. That's a strong right to win on a price platform, and their share growth shows it. Geico passed Allstate to take the number two spot in market share in the first quarter of 2013. With price consciousness prodded by a tough economy and Geico's relentless hammering on saving money on your insurance, consumers' average policy costs have come down steadily since 2004.

While Geico pounds away on price, premium players like State Farm and Allstate counterpunch by warning us that accidents *do* happen, that cheap insurance will let us down in our hour of need, and that they'll go the extra mile for us. With State Farm and Allstate staking their claim on top-notch service, Geico killing it on price, and the three of them combining to own almost 50 percent market share, sitting between these three can be a precarious middle-of-the-road position. There is a lot of roadkill in the middle of the road. Parked in that position (though hardly standing still) is Progressive, a seventy-five-year-old company ranked number four in market share. Carving a path between those two value propositions, based in quality and price, is no mean feat. But what's helped Progressive more than hold its own is a string of textbook two-sided innovations—each seamlessly melding a meaningful consumer need together with a key pain point of the business, solving both in one bold move.

One of their great double plays is their online rate comparison tool. Many consumers will tell you the insurance business works in mysterious ways, using tricky sales techniques to sell them coverage they don't need, or obscuring competitive choices by comparing apples to carrots. Fine print may not have been invented by the insurance business, but it sometimes seems as if it was perfected there. As Progressive CEO and president Glenn Renwick put it, "Product design differences between auto insurance offerings are understandably obscure, and certainly less obvious than those of many consumer products."

To help consumers see through the fog, Progressive hatched an online rate comparison tool that turns a bit of customer information into a comparison of rates on similar coverage plans from multiple companies. The win for consumers is convenient, transparent one-stop shopping in an industry that lacked it before, backed by an amazing proof point of objectivity—the tool sometimes shows a competitive offering to be cheaper than Progressive. It's a big wow factor that tells consumers Progressive is a straight shooter and has their backs.

But behind this consumer proposition sits a solution to a mission-critical need of the company. Paying out big claims to risky drivers hampers both profitability and Progressive's ability to charge attractive rates to win over the safe drivers it covets. In addition to that expense ratio mentioned earlier, another closely watched performance metric for insurance companies is their loss ratio—the gap between what they collect in premiums and what they pay out in claims. Risky drivers drive up loss ratios and that's bad for insurance companies. Progressive has historically maintained a loss ratio well below industry averages by obsessing over the *quality* of its drivers, not just the quantity.

Served up in the name of transparency and empowering consumers to make smart choices—all of which it does in spades—what the online rate checker tool does from Progressive's vantage point is deliberately steer risky drivers away from Progressive to its competitors' waiting arms. Over the long term, this feeds a virtuous circle. It reduces the risk profile of Progressive's customer base, which means fewer claims, better profits, and an ability to price more competitively to attract more of the kind of drivers they want. One innovation, two pain points solved: a key need of the consumer, and a key need of the business.

But Progressive didn't stop there. Their next two-sided leap was a driver-monitoring device called Snapshot (not to be confused with the popular app Snapchat). Wrapped in the compelling consumer promise of reducing current Progressive customers' rates for safe driving behavior, the in-car gadget harvests and automatically transmits back to Progressive lots of data on drivers' actual behavior behind the wheel, from how much they drive to whether they speed. In essence it creates an individualized statistical proxy for defensive driving behavior. Progressive policy holders who agree to plug in the device are told their rates can't go up, but can go down by as much as 30 percent depending on what the data say.

While it's giving consumers a chance to save money by getting credit for how safely they actually drive (rather than hitting them with a generic rate based on the average person in their demographic), Snapshot gives Progressive something akin to the insurance industry's holy grail. It's a way to spot dangerous drivers *before* the usual clues of speeding tickets and accidents appear and, conversely, to put halos on the angels. In the process, it holds the potential to transform the mathematical premise on which the whole insurance industry is predicated—replacing aggregated pricing for wide swaths of the population with personalized pricing based on actual individual behavior.

As Renwick put it in describing the success of the program to Progressive shareholders, "'I'm a good driver so why don't I get credit for that?' 'What does my age or occupation tell you about my driving?'" Snapshot, and what is sure to follow in its evolution, is a meaningful start toward personalized insurance pricing based on real-time measurement of your driving behavior—a statistic of one. Beyond the big leap in fairness this represents for consumers, it blows apart the actuarial guesswork at the core of the insurance business model. That's a huge win-win.

These two-sided innovation solutions, and others, including a name-your-price tool—a Priceline-like policy-hunting tool that looks for policies that match a consumer's desired premium—have helped Progressive overcome what would appear at face value to be a tenuous position—being a number-four player caught in the cross fire between low price and quality service propositions. They've not only survived, but grown market share and been recognized as an innovation pacesetter.

TOUCHING DOWN

Another great two-sided solution can be found among the hangars and coat hangers at Seoul's Incheon Airport.

Asia is a big region with diverse climates. When South Koreans feel the bite of winter, they head south to Bali or the region's other tropical hot spots. They pull on a bulky down parka for the trip to the airport, and carry it everywhere they go, car to plane to taxi to beachside hotel, despite having no use for it until they leave the airport on their return home.

Two of Korea's leading airlines stepped forward with what at face value appears to be a delightful bit of customer-coddling innovation: a coat valet service. Flyers can check their coats at the gate in Seoul and collect them on return. No more schlepping of useless and unwieldy bulk to the beach.

But this innovation is actually an answer to a big operational and financial pain point. On every winter flight, travelers would tuck their carry-on bags in the overhead bins, then stuff in their bulky down coats, filling the bins prematurely, with many customers in line yet to board. The inevitable result was chaos. Stressed-out customers would move up and down the aisle hunting for overhead space, bringing the boarding process to a halt. They'd try to smash big bags into small spaces, creating tension among passengers as they crushed one another's belongings. Fighting the current of the boarding queue, flight crews would make a last-ditch attempt to rearrange bags and optimize bin space, and eventually have to carry bags off the plane.

As painful as this was for the customer experience, it was bad for the business, too. Savvy travelers keep an eye on the on-time departure rates of various airlines. Delayed departures mean lost customers, inefficient use of employees, wasted fuel in idling planes, and delays on incoming flights as outbound planes are held up and late off the gate.

Coat valet service is a brilliant two-sided solution, putting big smiles on the faces of the airlines' customers, the heads of operations, and the CFOs alike. Customers are ecstatic at being relieved of their bulky burden. The boarding process is as smooth as the beach sand in Bali. And while the first few days of the service are free, the airlines charge for extended coat storage, so they're getting paid, as well. That's the kind of win-win we all want.

MINI ME

Another great double-barreled innovation is the Mini Cooper.

Before the Mini Cooper came along, affordable efficient cars were deadly boring, devoid of fun behind the wheel and lacking any kind of bold personal statement at curbside. Enter the Mini.

Efficiency, fun, and charisma suddenly yanked open the roof with the Mini Cooper and piled in together for a happy joyride. Customers could liberally personalize their Mini with an array of paint combinations, interiors, door configurations, and special accents. Suddenly a small car was a blast to drive and could make a big personal statement, as well.

But that wasn't enough to make it a great business.

Commercial success would lie in something most customers never knew or cared about—a solution to a key pain point in the way the car business had approached serving individual customer needs.

The old automotive paradigm said that covering a broad array of consumer segments required a broad array of models—big cars, little cars, fancy ones, cheap ones, practical kid-movers for the family, and racy muscle cars for the inevitable midlife crisis. Each of those models came with its own assembly line, labor force, and massive tooling costs each time a model was updated.

Mini broke that mold. They built the proposition from the ground up to ensure that a high-level customization could be delivered on a single platform running down a single assembly line with a single set of tooling and labor costs.

Customer problem solved and business problem solved, all through one double-barreled innovation.

FREE AT LAST

To see a particularly refreshing example of what a two-sided innovation can look like, head down to your local Burger King, Wendy's, or Five Guys and look for the Coca-Cola Freestyle machine, one of the many innovations we've collaborated on with the Coca-Cola Company.

Expansion of consumer choice is a theme that comes up quite often in innovation. It's become a dominant reality of consumer expectations and the way we have to think about the innovation landscape. As consumers, we've come to expect what we want, when we want it, and breadth of choice is key to making that happen. The leap in choice over just a few decades has been pretty staggering. In the 1970s, the average American grocery store held 4,000 products. Today it holds about 40,000. The beverage category in particular has exploded over this time frame, sprouting a dizzying array of options like energy drinks, fortified waters, sports drinks, ready-to-drink coffees, new-age drinks, shots, and functional beverages that we take for granted today, but that are quite recent additions to the repertoire. To serve the explosion of choice, retailers have expanded their store sizes, and the beverage section, too. But for quick-service restaurants like Burger King, addressing the proliferation of beverage options has posed a problem. Consumers have grown accustomed to having precisely the drink they want, when they want it, and were frustrated by the narrow set of choices offered by the traditional six-spout soda fountain these restaurants relied on. Some consumers would rather go thirsty than settle for anything other than exactly what they're craving. For QSR operators, adding breadth to their beverage choices by adding refrigerators to fixed store footprints would mean taking out restaurant seats or reworking parts of the operation. It was a conundrum. Enter Coca-Cola Freestyle.

The Coca-Cola Freestyle system is an elegant two-sided solution. For consumers, it offers a choice of more than a hundred options from Coca-Cola's ever-expanding portfolio of drinks—from sparkling options including the classics and flavor variations like Strawberry Sprite that can't be had anywhere else, to emerging brands like Fuze, to sports drinks like Powerade—all with just a few taps of a touchscreen. What makes this possible is a technology that replaced the traditional bulky syrups that Coca-Cola sells to QSR chains for the old fountains with a new cartridge-based ingredient system called PurePour that can create and pour precise recipes of all these options, fresh on the spot. Suddenly no consumer walks away thirsty because a restaurant has too few beverage options. And for the restaurants and Coca-Cola, it solves the space constraints that prevented serving up the kind of variety they'd both need to offer to maximize beverage revenues. A hundred-plus choices can now be served up from the same amount of space that the old six-spout fountains occupied.

The result? Happy customers, and even happier businesses.

And it's an environmental win, as well, as the burden of shipping traditional, bulky, water-dense syrups is no longer necessary.

STARRY, STARRY NIGHT

Picture this. You're one of the top innovation people in one of the most innovative companies of the past few decades. Your CEO, the visionary founder of the company, has devoted four decades of his life to transforming and perfecting the coffee experience, a pursuit that's been rewarded with an aromatic $58 billion market cap and $13 billion in annual revenue. That's big love from bean counters and bean lovers alike, all anchored in coffee. Today you're pitching the boss an experience that pivots around a glass of wine. Good career move.

Rachel Antalek, director of New Concept Development at Starbucks, is undaunted for one simple reason. She and her team have their sights on a potent and potentially lucrative intersection between an unmet need of the business and an unmet need of Starbucks guests.

An insightful natural-born storyteller with an eye for irony, Rachel prepares to pitch CEO Howard Schultz an idea that opens a new dimension in the Starbucks experience. She knows it won't be an easy sell. Beyond the jolt of bold Sumatra, Starbucks has been propelled by its founder's unique blend of an eagerness to push the envelope and an open dislike of failure. The company tried an adult beverage play before but couldn't make it work, so this new concept has two strikes against it. It's not coffee. And it's failed before.

You might think that what comes next is the sound of a wineglass falling off a table. But that's not what happens. Because offsetting these two strikes is an elegant two-sided solution that solves a big consumer need and a big commercial need in one move. The business need is there for all to see. The consumer need is deeply hidden.

On the commercial side, the backdrop to this story is an innovation dynamic that plays out in many high-growth businesses. An entrepreneur comes up with a great product. To help that product scale up, they build assets around it, like a supply chain, a brand, or a string of stores. Eventually they hit an inflection point. The product that catalyzed all that asset creation isn't broad enough to fully leverage the assets built to serve it. Nike's a great example. Catalyzed by a better running shoe, Nike's addition of a broader array of footwear, apparel, equipment, and even digital tools wasn't just opportunistic; on some level these moves were necessary to fully leverage the value of Nike's assets, from its brand to its design capability, manufacturing, athlete relationships, and distribution. It's like a game of leapfrog. Products ignite asset creation. Asset leverage requires additional products. Repeat and repeat again. The dynamic plays out in smaller business, too, even Fahrenheit's. Our initial product was a five-month breakthrough innovation model purpose-built to transform success rates on the most complex and disruptive innovation challenges. That's a very narrow but lucrative market of high-risk, high-reward initiatives that represent only 5 percent of most companies' innovation activity. Nailing and scaling that required creating assets: a methodology, a new kind of team, a brand, and relationships with visionary clients. Inevitably, the value of the assets outgrew the initial product. A wider spectrum of innovation services would follow, spanning strategic consulting, closer-in innovation efforts, and implementation, which deliver about half our revenue today. Pick any industry and you'll see this leapfrog dynamic playing out, consciously or organically, in a progression from one opportunity to the next. Look for these inflection points as your own business grows, and big opportunities will come into view for you.

Back at the coffeehouse, Starbucks' spectacular ascent can be seen as several cycles of this product/asset leapfrog. Unleashing the value of Howard Schultz's advances in coffee sourcing and roasting required giving his products a worthy experiential home in a new breed of coffeehouse. Leveraging the coffeehouse in turn demanded a broader set of beverage products to address individual tastes and drive frequency. Adding more shops and entering retail were then necessary to fully leverage the appeal of the brand and product portfolio. Fast-forward to today and you have more than 17,000 Starbucks coffeehouses in the United States alone, serving hundreds of coffee drink permutations. Knowing they'll eventually hit a ceiling on adding new locations, Rachel and her team pour their energies into ways to further leverage the amazing asset those stores have become.

Through a commercial lens, one of the opportunity areas she homes in on is dead easy to spot. The typical Starbucks store is humming in the morning and afternoon, but calm as a church after 4 p.m. The root cause is the human body clock. The ritualistic functional pleasures of our morning joe and the reflexive, reflective 3 p.m. cup are deeply embedded. But by late afternoon, Starbucks faces a barrier of physiology. Even devout java junkies like me (Sumatra deserves its own credit in the back of this book) turn off the caffeine spigot by midafternoon, barring the occasional cup after dinner.

Starbucks' challenge in building late afternoon traffic is compounded when physiology meets social behavior. If a few friends are out and about together, and some want coffee but some don't, a single no vote is enough to steer the whole crew elsewhere. Rachel's conundrum is clear. As fundamental as coffee is to everything about the Starbucks juggernaut, coffee probably can't be the answer to late afternoon and evening traffic. Solving the post-coffee part of the day would require a new playbook.

Coming to this frank realization sets in motion a chain reaction of perspectives. If you just watch the ebb and flow of beverages through the day, where coffee tapers off alcohol steps forward. Watch human migratory patterns and it's obvious that as the coffeehouse thins out the bars and restaurants pick up steam. The basic dynamics are simple. The question is what to do about it. A clear commercial need without an unmet consumer need does not an opportunity make. There is a gap in customer traffic, but is there a gap in the market? Does Starbucks have any right to play and win in alcohol?

The insights Rachel and the team uncover will unlock the consumer side of a great two-sided innovation called Starbucks Evenings. The big conceptual leap is a realization that this isn't about competing with bars. In fact Starbucks' unique competitive advantage would be that it *isn't* a bar.

Rachel describes the opportunity that emerged this way: "Late in the day in any city or suburb, there's a woman who's spent her afternoon on the road for work, or dashing around for the family. Maybe she's just dropped one kid at soccer and another at piano lessons, or just checked into a hotel in a town she doesn't know. She's been taking care of everybody else and just wants a brief respite from it all, a chance to unwind with a nice glass of wine and a maybe a light bite to tide her over. It's too late for coffee, but a bar is a problematic answer. On her own or relaxing with a girlfriend, a busy bar is too amped up. A quiet one can feel awkward or even a bit predatory. And she's not going to pull out her laptop and catch up on her world in the middle of a bar. There's a big unmet need here, where Starbucks has a unique right to win. Close to home or far away, Starbucks is a friendly and familiar setting, just busy enough to be stimulating but not a pickup scene, and without waitstaff trying to turn tables or rush her along. There's no business out there offering such a safe, comfortable, and relaxed atmosphere for unwinding with a glass of really good wine and a tasty savory bite, with no pressure to socialize unless you want to. By focusing on these unmet needs of busy women, we realized we not only have a right to play, but a big right to win."

By adjusting the music and lighting, offering a list of fine wines (Rachel handpicked them herself), serving small, sophisticated savory plates, and maintaining the casual, laptop-friendly, stay-as-long-as-you-like vibe of the daytime scene, Starbucks Evenings goes live in select locations at 4 p.m. every day, filling a gap in Starbucks traffic by finding and filling an untapped gap in women's lives that no one had spotted before. Looking back on the journey that ultimately saw Howard give it the green light and consumers raise a glass in salute of the idea, two moments stand out to Rachel. "When we went live with the first prototype, I sat nervously at a table waiting to see if women would come and if our hypothesis about their needs would be borne out. The first customer in the door is a guy who steps up and orders a glass of wine. I'm thinking wow, were we that wrong? When he settles in, I come over and start chatting. He's a stay-at-home dad who'd just dropped his kids off at soccer! You can't make this stuff up. The other big moment was when I discussed the idea with some women and one of them broke down in tears. She said, 'I can't tell you how stretched I feel by that point in the day and what it would mean to have this option.'" As the program expands to select stores that fit a particular profile, there are a lot of happy women, and an occasional guy, too. Like Rachel and Howard Schultz.

Rachel sums up the journey this way. "It's an amazing feeling when you see a clear need of the business and a clear need of the customers you care about dovetail together so perfectly. It all just makes sense. In the end, it was an idea no one could say no to."

FUNNEL VISION

Now that we know what a two-sided solution looks like, let's look at why building innovations this way can transform the odds of success.

Think of all the innovations being cultivated in your company or industry. Whether you recognize it or not, innovation triage is happening all around you all the time, across your company, across the array of potential ventures a venture capitalist (or VC) may be looking at, or even in the eyes of a retailer debating whether to give shelf space to your team's cool new product or the one another company pitched ten minutes ago. You realize pretty quickly that while you may feel like you're working in a vacuum, in the cozy confines of a formally approved project or in the workshop of your garage while your dog nods approval, you're not.

In any healthy, forward-looking business, the fat end of the innovation funnel has a wide array of fledgling initiatives in various stages of exploration and development—far more than any company has the capacity and resources to successfully launch if they all were to come to fruition. VCs or angel investors are similarly looking at more potential bets than they could realistically engage. This teeming mass of early-stage opportunities needs food and shelter, in a landscape where there isn't enough of it to go around to support every ambition to realization. In the earliest stages, some of these initiatives may be founded in mission-critical strategic platforms identified by your company, but many others are set in motion with just an ambition, a fledgling hypothesis, a piece of raw technology, a hunch, or a gap in the innovation pipeline that needs filling with *something*.

Most of the initiatives are, theoretically at least, born with a decent shot at survival. But as they start moving into and through the company or investor funnel, they quickly lose the protective bubble wrap that comes with "hey, we're just getting started." You soon start to see some separation among these competing initiatives.

Whether your initiative is migrating along a company path, or is burning through your own exploratory funding, it will soon be competing for company or investor resources. The deeper you move down the funnel, the more Darwinist the competition gets.

By the midpoint of the funnel, any initiative that can't find a meaningful consumer need and a potential way to solve it is killed off, or squeezed out by the ones that can. The tapered shape of the funnel asserts itself. There isn't room for everything to keep moving forward. By this point, you can pretty safely assume that *every* initiative competing for those finite resources has a viable consumer solution in hand or in its sights. This is where the shortcomings of a pure user-centered design approach rise up. Having found and solved an unmet consumer need is just *table stakes* to enter the competition for resources in the funnel's back half. The consumer solution is necessary, but not at all sufficient to survive what's ahead.

Now let's jump ahead from the relatively plump middle of the funnel to the skinny bit at the end, where ideas flow out to market and scale up. What do we see and what's different? Beyond the numbers game, where so many went in and so few made it out, there's another fundamental difference. Those things coming *out* of the funnel, getting green-lit for launch into the world, have a very different profile from the stuff in the middle. The ideas that make it out separated themselves from the rest of the pack by being the most *attractive moves for the company* and the *best uses of capital* in pursuit of

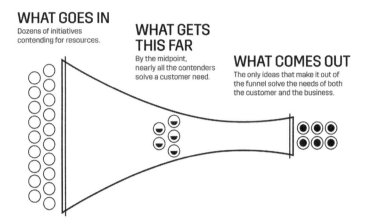

WHAT GOES IN
Dozens of initiatives
contending for resources.

WHAT GETS THIS FAR
By the midpoint,
nearly all the contenders
solve a customer need.

WHAT COMES OUT
The only ideas that make it out of
the funnel solve the needs of both
the customer and the business.

attractive returns. To flip the switch, the gatekeepers need to see that what's great for the consumer is great for the company, too. In essence, the ideas that get green-lit are what we call two-sided solutions. If you want to make it out of the funnel, this is what you're aiming for. Unfortunately, today's prevailing innovation methods aren't built to get you there.

RUNNING ON ONE LEG

Understanding the workings of this Darwinist competition for resources within a company or across investors' radar, you can start to see why we need a new playbook if we hope to transform innovation success rates, replacing hit-or-miss randomness with growth you can count on.

In a typical innovation model, you'll often observe a premature sense of euphoria take hold as a consumer solution is identified. Cries of "Consumers love my idea!" and "We've solved it!" ring down the halls. There's just one problem. The odds against getting to market remain severely stacked against you.

In the spirit of the elegant Bauhaus edict that form should follow function, there's a tough reality here. The function of modern innovation practice isn't actually to uncover consumer needs and conceive product ideas that align with them. That's just a means to an end. The true function of innovation practice is to *deliver impactful innovations to market* so they can improve lives and grow businesses. With the funnel working as it does, one-sided innovation doesn't actually fit this *function*. It's built around what it takes for an initiative to get *into* the funnel or at best to reach its midpoint. But not what it takes to emerge *out* of the funnel, which is the real goal.

Between that midpoint where just about everything in the funnel has a sight line to a valuable consumer benefit and the out spout where money gets made, the shape of the funnel is its own perfect analogy of what goes on.

What you have here are two slopes pointing in opposite directions—one trending downward, the other upward. What trends down as you move from the middle toward the end is the degree of tolerance for unsolved issues, like how an idea can make money or create competitive advantage. What trends upward is the amount of cost and risk involved in continuing to advance an idea as it migrates from words on a page and Styrofoam prototypes to real products, manufacturing, launch planning, investment in inventory, and retail slotting fees. All these things cost more and more money.

With that convergence of higher costs and risks with lower tolerance of unknowns, its easy to see how the odds of things conceived

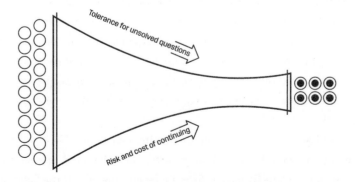

with limited concern for the needs of the business are going to get squeezed out by things that have solved both sides of the equation. An innovator's Achilles' heel here is a tendency to suspend critical commercial questions for far too long into the process. Raw optimism is an important and powerful thing in the right moments. But in the Darwinist competition for finite resources, whether those questions might *eventually* be solvable is purely academic. If they aren't *yet* solved at each point where you need more funding or renewed permission to forge ahead, your idea is vulnerable to getting left behind any competing idea that's already got those questions solved. Now, you could scramble at the back end of the process to retrofit a commercial solution to an idea built without one, but it's a bit like shopping for a caterer on the morning of your wedding day. You might get lucky and pull it off, but the odds are against you.

Using a method built for the first half of the funnel is what the business world has been doing far too often since the user-centered design movement caught fire. Little wonder that innovation hit rates remain painfully low in terms of getting successful products to market that generate revenue and growth.

Don't get me wrong. User-centered design thinking is a huge step forward from what came before. And it's actually doing *exactly* what it was designed to do—creating compelling consumer-relevant product ideas for companies or investors to consider. The disconnect is that somewhere along the line that was muddled with what *innovation models* need to do—which is not to generate interesting, even dazzling ideas to consider, but to deliver compelling marketable innovation ideas *out* of innovation funnels. User-centered models tend to deliver ideas that are way too easy for company gatekeepers to say no to. Too often, one-sided solutions get blindsided in the approval gauntlet.

So how do you create initiatives with a far better chance of surviving the gauntlet and coming to fruition? It's kind of common sense. Go back to Bauhaus—form following function. If the function we care about is not getting ideas into the funnel, but getting ideas out of it and into the world, where they can improve lives and businesses, design your process and your ideas toward that end. Run a two-track process, where the problems of the consumer and the business are interrogated with equal intensity from day one through to the finish line.

Here's a six-pack of suggestions on how to increase the hit rate and impact of two-sided innovation solutions on your team and in your company:

1. Two-sided thinking starts day one.

Form follows function. You won't get to two-sided solutions by running a program that's dominated by just one side of the equation, whether it's a consumer perspective or a commercial one. Design a two-sided program with the capabilities to match. Yes, a two-track model demands a broader and deeper skill set. The people you recruit for their ability to extract nuanced understanding of consumer behavior, interactions, emotions, and aspirations probably aren't the same people who can pick apart the P&L, uncover the hidden pain points of the business, and shape profitable outcomes. But outcomes are the point. The extra investment of time and talent it takes to work both sides of the equation will pay big dividends to those who do. Re-create the beginning of the process to fit the end you need. Explore the pain points of the consumer and the business with equal intensity before you start formulating and building ideas.

2. Pick big problems, not just interesting ones.

The value of an innovation is often proportional to the size of the problems it solves. As you scan across an array of consumer and company problems, pick out the biggest on each side and start there. Guessing right on driver risk profiles is a huge issue in the insurance business, not a peripheral one. Starting with small problems will tend to result in small solutions.

3. Connect across the dots.

The view that creativity is about connecting dots no one has connected before is common and right. But what's not yet common (and should be) is using the respective pain points of the consumer and the business as the two sets of dots you're working with, and trying to forge connections across them. Look for your equivalent of the way Korean Air found an intersection between consumer frustration and an operational nightmare. You'll be amazed at the ideas you'll ignite by looking for intersections like that.

4. Build win-win ideas at the crossroads.

Go in with the explicit intent of finding ideas that deliver big value to both sides of the equation. As you shape, filter, and hone ideas, recognize that anything that fails to solve both sides of the equation probably won't make it to market.

5. Sweat more at the front end, less at the back.

Taking a two-sided approach means more work at the front end than just putting the blinders on and working with tunnel vision on half of the equation. But it makes life much easier at the back end when smart decisions get made on what goes to market. I think you'll find, as we have, that the extra sweat on the front end saves you sleepless nights and nail biting on the back end.

6. Nail your two-sided elevator pitch.

A two-sided approach sows the seeds of the most concise and compelling elevator pitch you'll ever deliver. The consumer has a big problem with X. Our company has a big problem with Y. This idea solves their problem and ours.

When you serve up two-sided solutions, you can't help but win. In tennis terms, it's game, set, match.

Chapter 4

The Stretch Factor

In an age where any category you look at is saturated with almost crazy levels of consumer choice—how many different varieties of running shoes, credit cards, mobile handsets, gym bags, tortilla chips, air fresheners, cars, and socks does the world really need?— big innovations offer companies a way to transcend zero-sum share fights in the mature markets they've already conquered.

But in going beyond the close-in improvements to a company's time-tested products and business models to more dramatic moves that catalyze steeper growth curves, innovation leaders often find themselves caught in the middle of an awkward four-way tug-of-war, with aggressive growth goals, low risk tolerances, resource constraints, and short-term return-on-investment (or ROI) pressures all pulling in opposite directions.

The issue at the center of this tug-of-war is the relationship between scale of opportunity and degree of difficulty.

We call this *the stretch factor.*

On the question of scale versus difficulty, conventional wisdom will tell you there's a basic law of innovation that big ideas are by definition much harder, slower, riskier, and more expensive to execute than close-in incremental changes. While "big means hard" is sometimes true, accepting this assumption at face value without testing it dooms us to little more than incremental change. By being obsessed with raising both the scale and hit rate of innovation, we've tried to look for ways to circumvent this seemingly immovable law. What we've found is not a miracle panacea, but some powerful insights,

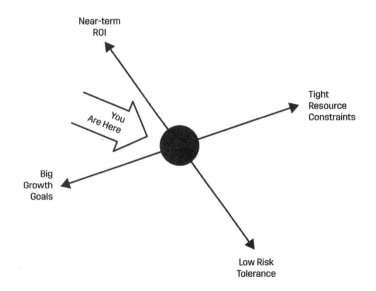

lessons, and frameworks that companies and teams can apply to the innovation challenges in front of them.

First, let's look at the roots of the problem. Is this ubiquitous assumption that *big = risky, slow, and expensive* actually true?

To test the premise, first flip it on its head. Ask your senior management how often they're asked to write *big checks* for *small ideas* that, despite their diminutive upside, are immensely hard to execute. Sounds crazy, right? Yet it happens far more often than common sense would suggest. In fact it happens so often that killing off this breed of idea has become a core executive competency. We've come to recognize that small doesn't mean quick, easy, and profitable. But is the inverse true—is big synonymous with hard and risky?

Our experience across categories and companies suggests that the connection between big and hard is not a rigid one. In fact it's often entirely a function of the choices we make as innovation leaders and practitioners.

The connection between big and difficult is one we can break, if we come at the challenge in the right way—from how we scope, resource, and staff innovation programs to how we think, invent, synthesize, and filter ideas at critical junctures in the journey. With the right orientation, we can create major, even transformative change in markets, coupled with vastly better odds of reaching market, lower risk, and higher ROI.

Solving this tension between scale and risk is a here-and-now commercial imperative. Companies' need for innovation to steepen growth curves has gone way up, but their appetite for risky bets has trended down. As we all face pressure to up the innovation hit rate, and to replace the shotgunlike proliferation of small innovation programs with "fewer and bigger," we need a way to reliably get high-impact innovations that don't break the company trying to execute them.

A SINGULARLY HUMAN ENDEAVOR

The way to break the "big means hard" trap spans both process factors and people factors. Let's start inside the heads of the eager, talented people that make innovation happen.

The human mind is an immense repository of images and associations waiting for the right switch to set them off. And the things innovation evokes are eclectic and electric, timeless and of the moment. The hybrid engine and coffee by the pod. The billion-dollar business born on a shoestring. The mating dance of art and science. The designer's soft clay. The glossy object. Old paradigms pushed aside and replaced. Better mousetraps, soaring share prices, and the relentless forward march of human endeavor.

Little wonder, then, that when an innovation team gathers for day one of a big new project and hears the project leader's rallying cry—*this is going to be big, guys, we're swinging for the fences*—imaginations are launched into motion.

The creative part of the human mind is propelled by a cocktail of instinct, adrenaline, pattern recognition, context, stimulus, and a contrarian desire to remake a flawed world. Rarely is all this creative firepower so primed for ignition as in that moment of kicking off a project with a blank page.

But without the right methodological tethers, the coalescing forces of imagination and ambition can easily send the team's explorations hurtling into deep orbit, past the realm of the doable, into the land of things we know will not be realized in this lifetime.

Spending time in those outer reaches of possibility is important, and can be worthwhile, particularly if you view them as vantage points to look back on present reality. Looking back on the present from the point of view of the future helps us see gaps in the here and now. But in pursuit of concrete market outcomes, being too fixated on far-off future states has risky side effects. In scuba diving, spend too much time in deep water and you get swept into a natural high called

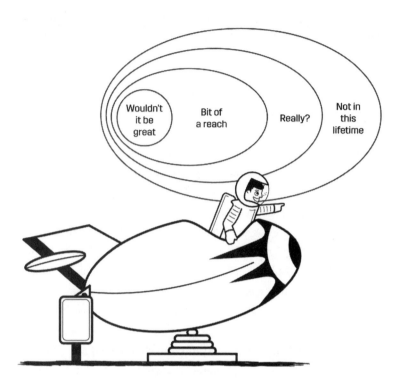

nitrogen narcosis, a euphoric state of distorted perception. During my years living in Asia, I got a firsthand taste of how good it feels, but how dangerous it quickly becomes. Diving over a World War II B1 bomber wreck in deep water off Papua New Guinea, my dive partner and I got so high on narcosis we almost overshot our safe dive time. People die that way. In innovation, we've found through experience that too much time in those outer reaches of possibility creates a similar narcosis—a distorted perceptual state capable of killing projects. You get detached from the imperatives, capabilities, and realities of the business you're trying to grow. With distorted perspective, you can find yourself equating *big* (scale of business opportunity) with extremely difficult. Ideas are on some level seen as big *because* they're nearly impossible to pull off. But back at sea level, where teams and companies have revenue to deliver and stakeholders to answer to, "big and impossible" just means impossible. It isn't big at all.

Equally detrimental is a mindset where some large-scale opportunities get scant attention *because* they're so doable. The psychology is that if it's easy to see how an idea could be executed, it must not be as big an idea as the impossible, futuristic stuff sketched on the opposite wall of the project room. What we're fighting here is the human imagination's natural drive to push the limits.

So is swinging for the fences a mistake? Don't we *want* our best innovators swinging for the fences? Yes, we do, but let's first think about what swinging for the fences really means. In baseball, that proverbial fence isn't proverbial. It's a known tangible boundary, three to four hundred feet from home plate. It sits at a distance over which a human being, with a weight shift from back foot to front and a well-timed whip of the hips and wrists, is known to be capable of propelling a baseball with a thirty-three-inch piece of tempered ash.

Home runs are big, loud, game changing—and relatively rare. The most prolific home run hitters in history homered in less than 10 percent of their trips to the plate. But home runs are doable within the existing capabilities of a baseball player. What swinging for the fences really means in baseball (and should mean in innovation) is let's go for the maximum impact possible with the capabilities we have or know how to get.

Unfortunately, when an innovation project leader says let's swing for the fences, we often hear something very different.

Let's swing for Mars.

Cool.

Now where's that atomic bat?

DISRUPTIVE INNOVATION—THEORY VS. PRACTICE

The human imagination's desire to want to push limits is natural. We don't want to rein that in. But what we can do is better equip innovators to deliver ideas that are capable of disrupting markets, without unduly disrupting the company we're out to grow.

Harvard Business School professor Clayton Christensen's work on disruptive technologies and disruptive innovation is an important contribution to the way the world thinks about innovation. Drawing a line between *sustaining innovation*—the close-in stuff that keeps the lights on within existing lines of business—and *disruptive innovation*—big leaps of technologies and the way they are applied to drive existing options into obsolescence—his framework helps categorize different magnitudes of innovation, their respective roles, and what each can do for a business. This is immensely useful for R&D leaders as a mandate to ensure their companies aren't left behind or missing big technology-led opportunities.

Valuable as that theory is, practitioners getting out of bed every morning to solve innovation problems need to step down from the academic theory of disruption to the daily reality of how project teams and companies develop and filter ideas. For innovation teams with boots on the ground, aiming to deliver real impact, disruption is a pivotal issue, but in very different ways I've found than Christensen's work lays out.

When an executive or investor bankrolls an innovation project, they usually aren't saying, "Gee, I hope the innovations that grow this business use disruptive technology." The mandate is typically simpler than that: deliver innovations capable of igniting meaningful sustainable growth. The project sponsor is probably losing a fair amount of sleep over whether their innovation pipelines are robust enough to deliver the growth they need. But they are often less stressed about which *type* of growth will get them there. Creating new categories through bona fide breakthroughs, entering established adjacent markets, or making big leaps in market share within current markets are all as sexy as the amount of growth they can deliver. At the end of the day, the goal is *disruptive growth*—hitting levels of growth beyond what's achievable by simple iterations and tweaks in current lines of business—rather than disruptive innovation per se. Those leaps to new technology curves are great when they happen, and important to a company's long-term vitality, but they're rare, risky, and often slow to unfold and scale. Waiting for their arrival to ignite the growth you need, or to make your idea work on an aggressive timeline, is somewhere between optimistic and dangerously naive. So what's the practical framework to help project teams deliver the growth they're commissioned to create?

What we've found immensely helpful is to look at the issue of disruption not from the theoretical standpoint, but instead through the lenses of the two-sided problem—namely, looking at disruption from the separate perspectives of the consumer we need to delight and the business we need to grow.

When you look at it this way, some big insights jump out that can help you make decisions about the kind of innovation ideas you want, the kind of ideas you have in hand, and which ideas you rally around to drive forward.

The premise is simple. Disruption of the *marketplace* and disruption of the *company* are the two disruption factors that really matter to a given project. (Technology can be a causal factor in either of these disruption fronts, but it's rarely the point.) Marketplace disruption and company disruption are surprisingly independent of each other, and they actually work in opposite directions in pursuit of a robust, growth-inducing innovation pipeline.

The ability of an innovation to *disrupt the marketplace* is a good thing. It speaks to the degree to which an idea creates shifts in demand by delivering new value in an appealing, well-differentiated way.

On the flip side, the degree to which implementation of a given idea requires *disruption of the company* is in nearly every case detrimental to the odds of that innovation making it to the street. This is not to say that requiring disruption of the company makes an idea a bad one, just that disrupting the company makes that idea far less likely to ever get *acted* upon, reach the marketplace, and deliver growth.

Disruption of the marketplace comes from many factors. Filling an unmet need with a big new value proposition. Relieving consumer tensions or fulfilling latent aspirations. Transforming the user experience. Disrupting the price/value equation. Leaping to a new form factor. Bundling things that were once separate. Or provocatively disrupting buying decisions through design, equipment, technology, a new route to market, or new channel strategies.

Disruption of the company also has multiple dimensions, spanning the degree to which an innovation fits with a company's

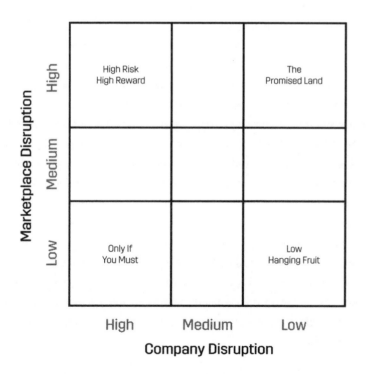

existing growth strategies, financial metrics, capabilities, technologies, operational assets, brand portfolio, distribution channels, and risk tolerances.

Plot these two axes of marketplace disruption and company disruption and you've got a potent framework to help your team shape and filter ideas, or to look at your company's innovation portfolio as a whole and make sure you've got a healthy balance.

LOCATION, LOCATION, LOCATION!

There are a host of insights about the pursuit of big, fast, doable innovation embedded in this framework. They start in the bottom left corner—which is best viewed as a no-fly zone, entered only when you have to. That corner is populated with ideas that require relatively big changes in the company to make them happen, but create a proportionally smaller shift in demand in the marketplace. There are a lot of important and valuable innovations that fall in that bottom left corner, but they're usually born of a need to future-proof the business—that is, protecting existing demand in years ahead, rather than creating sizable incremental demand in the near term. Seemingly small yet surprisingly tricky innovations like putting pull-tab tops on soup cans to spare consumers the minor inconvenience of using can openers would fall in this category. Soup companies had to make significant capital investments in changing production lines to get there, but did so out of a belief that it was necessary to stay in line with long-term convenience trends, with little expectation that the arrival of pull-tops would send consumers teeming to the soup aisle. Innovations that mitigate the risk of future erosion can create a vital foundation for long-term growth. But anytime you're delivering more disruption to the company than to existing demand, expect a lot of tough questions by company gatekeepers in trying to get the green light.

Disruption of the company isn't just limited to technology, man-ufacturing methods, and operations. Anything that requires a shift in the strategies that leadership has sold to the organization and in-vestors is a very big and painful form of company disruption. So too are things like needing to create a new brand to fill the new demand, needing to set up a whole new business unit to pursue the opportu-nity in hand or to sell into a channel where the company isn't already strong, or needing to build know-how and IP the company doesn't have. Again, none of these disruptions makes an idea a bad one; they just tip the odds against it reaching market.

Now move up the column to the top left corner and you have an innovation with high levels of company disruption, but high po-tential for marketplace disruption. More pain for the company, but more gain to justify it. Apple's successful leaps into retail—both brick-and-mortar in device sales and e-commerce in content and app sales—would have fallen in this top left corner. At the time these moves were considered, there was little in-house expertise to draw down on to ensure success. But the size of the opportunity justified the leap. E-commerce today delivers more than $16 billion a year of Apple's revenue. The brick-and-mortar shops have been visited by more than a billion people and delivered another $4 billion in the last quarter of 2013 alone. For your business, you want a healthy number of these top left innovation opportunities in gestation across your company's innovation portfolio. They keep your eyes on the hori-zon. Getting them to realization isn't easy, of course. As for how to do that, our experience says that while most innovators instinctively try to sell top left opportunities to company leaders by touting their upside, success in getting this breed of high-risk, high-reward in-novations through the company and into the market pivots heavily on the ability to dissect the risk side of the ledger. Perhaps fittingly, Steve Jobs said that the only time he ever felt compelled to seek out-side advice about an Apple initiative was when he was considering brick-and-mortar retail. The struggles of Gateway made the risks evident, so he wanted to understand those risks completely, and find ways to mitigate them.

Jump to the bottom right corner and you find the low-hanging fruit. Lower levels of market disruption are absolutely fine when paired up with minimal disruption of the business. This includes close-in line extensions, or what many companies refer to as "renovation."

If that lower left corner is a place to go only when a company must, and the bottom right and top left promise comparable levels of marketplace and company disruption, the upper right is the Promised Land. This upper right corner is where you want to land as often as you possibly can. This box gets you promoted.

In this coveted piece of real estate, you create maximum disruption of demand in the marketplace (that is, opening up demand that is highly incremental to your business relative to what you do and sell today) with minimum disruption of the company. The odds of these innovations making it through the company gauntlet and delivering sizable profitable growth are higher than any other part of the plot. For an example of what this can look like, circle back to Chapter 1. Samsung knew everything there was to know about making LCD panels and was strategically committed to innovating in translucent applications. Aiming those existing capabilities at a new market for the company in commercial refrigeration, and aiming the applications at companies already in the commercial refrigeration business rather than asking Samsung to jump with both feet and compete with incumbents, we found a way to create significant disruption of the marketplace while posing relatively little disruption for the company.

CONSTRAINTS TO CANVAS

Equipping the teams who develop ideas with this kind of practical framework for understanding the dynamics of disruption, in an individual innovation idea or across a portfolio of them, has proved immensely helpful to our drive to break this entrenched belief that big means hard to pull off. But a framework is only as helpful as the mindset you bring to it. You've got to come into it with a healthy way of looking at a company's capabilities, not just understanding them, but being excited by their hidden potential.

When you obsess over a company's capabilities at the front of a project rather than the back, you start to see a company's equipment, factories, technologies, and know-how not as a set of shackles to avoid or transcend, which they can appear to be when left to the back end of the process, but as canvas, limited only by the imagination we aim at them.

Chris Trimble, professor at Dartmouth's Tuck School of Business and, with his partner Vijay Govindarajan, author of several great innovation books, including *Beyond the Idea*, describes the pitfalls inherent in innovators steering their focus away from company capabilities. "In pursuit of innovation ideas and getting them executed, there's a tendency to fear the workings of the business performance engine and to see its strengths as limiting rather than empowering. With this comes a temptation to separate from it. But when innovators isolate themselves they forfeit the one and only advantage they have over startup organizations—the ability to leverage what already exists. I'm consistently amazed how often innovation programs fall into this trap, and die because of it."

WIRED FOR GROWTH

As Time Warner Cable's executive vice president and chief strategy, people and corporate development officer, Peter Stern sports a job title as eclectic as his background. He majored in music and English at Harvard. Picked up a law degree at Yale. Then went to McKinsey, where he helped lead the technology and media practices before joining Time Warner Inc., which spun off the cable company in 2009.

From a strategic standpoint, Peter and his team at TWC are laser focused on defining and igniting a portfolio of innovations that fit that top right corner of our disruption framework. Among the opportunities is one called SCMA (shorthand for security, control, monitoring, and automation). Another is in cloud computing.

Sitting outside TWC's core business of television, phone, and internet services, each of these opportunities holds the potential for significant new-to-company demand. In other words, each could be a gold mine. To make them viable growth opportunities for the business, two things need to happen quickly. First, each needs the injection of some form of X-factor—a unique way that TWC can compete and win against incumbents in those respective spaces. That's where Fahrenheit comes in. Second, those innovation platforms need to be strategically framed and brought to life, with a compelling rationale and business case so they can be appropriately represented to the company's leadership and board. Then, and only then, will those initiatives have a shot at getting the people and funding they'll need to come to fruition.

While they are new growth spaces for Time Warner Cable, SCMA and cloud computing are not new-to-the-world businesses. Each has established incumbents. As Peter put it in the kickoff meeting, "We have a great base of assets, capabilities, and infrastructure, but, to compete here, we need to define our own unique strategic twist that will set us up to win." Thinking about it relative to the disruption grid, that unique twist can put the play in the upper row.

While the strategic X-factor Peter describes is necessary to disrupt the market, the opportunities have to be defined and framed internally in a way that makes them relatively nondisruptive within

Time Warner Cable. No company wants to back strategies that cannot effectively balance risk with reward. TWC will carefully scrutinize the risk profiles of any new opportunities that push beyond the company's core business.

An interesting dynamic here is how disruption is viewed at different levels of an organization. The more revolutionary aspects of an idea tend to be the most inspiring parts of it to the project team—those that are closest to the opportunity. But that perspective may not be shared by company leaders charged with long-term stewardship of the business. The breakthrough thing that's never been done before gets the project team excited *because* it's never been done before, but it needs to go through rigorous scrutiny for that very same reason. Peter understands these dynamics well, so he makes the call to engage the management team and the board around these fledgling opportunities before getting the broader organization too far down the path. If the board can justify and support TWC's approach to winning in these markets without unduly disrupting the company to do it, the rest of the organization will come aboard.

In our experience at Fahrenheit 212, there are two ways to strive for that upper right corner of our graph where we create significant disruption of demand with minimal disruption to the company. The harder of the two is the "outside-in" approach of starting with a radical marketplace-based idea and working back in to see if and how you can connect it to the things your company is well equipped to do. Startups don't have that problem, as there isn't much to connect back into. But mature, scaled businesses have more history and a more defined base of assets and capabilities. The outside-in approach, which is pretty much what a user-centered innovation approach is, will have solid odds of getting you into that upper row of high marketplace disruption. However, in a mature company, you need to make sure you land on something that aligns well with what your company is capable of pulling off. As we look to open new growth for mature businesses, we often find that the easier way to get to that tasty upper right corner is to instead work "inside out"—hunting for new ways to apply known capabilities, then working out how to break through beyond the competition's offerings. That was the path Peter took to defining these new opportunities.

"Building out our innovation game board, we really used just two filters to get to the opportunities—size of the opportunity, and fit with our assets and capabilities."

Knowing the capability fit was there from the get-go, we set about sharpening the focus on where and how to enter each of these businesses and looking for that twist we'd need to succeed. In the SCMA territory, the first key question was which consumer needs should be our epicenter—home security (alarms and support services), home controls (climate, lighting), home monitoring (energy consumption and remote monitoring of aging parents, for example), or home automation (controlling functions of doors, locks, windows, and content distribution around the home). They were all interesting to consumers and potentially attractive business opportunities for the years ahead, with varying degrees of proven demand. No cable or telecommunications company had meaningfully exploited any of them up to the point when the project began. And rapid changes in enabling technologies were sure to alter the landscape in the years ahead. We had to define our play based on the known, while positioning TWC to benefit as expected changes in technology and consumer behavior took hold in years ahead.

On security, controls, monitoring, and automation, the elephant in the room (or perhaps the unicorn) was the visionary "home of the future." It's easy to imagine a future in which everything we want to see or do in our homes emanates from a single hublike device and interface. Turn on a light, play Miles Davis; open the window, call the kids to dinner; turn on the heat under the teakettle, say hi to grandma in Tampa while you wait for the water to boil; turn down the air-conditioning—all from a single hub. It's sexy to think about, but there were looming questions. The home of the future has a checkered past. These visions have been served up to consumers and in technology industry exhibitions going all the way back to the 1960s, *The Jetsons*, and world fairs. Twenty years ago, I shared an apartment with a tech wizard who devoted several years to a project for Novell (then a heavy hitter in software, at the top of its game) working on how to automate the kitchen. But for all the struggles to solve the technologies, the technology people were missing one key thing. Consumers didn't really want that hub. Or, more to the point, they liked what it promised but wouldn't promise to pay for it. In poring over this patchy history of the future, this factor of willingness to pay jumps out as the key thing we need to obsess over. It's a key theme in the failure of many attempts at the tech-forward home, just as it's now asserting itself as a critical barrier in the migration of music and printed content from physical to digital forms. We weren't out to change home life for change's sake. We were out to build a business. So we had to convince ourselves that our transformation delivered real value in the eyes of consumers. The strategy we ultimately landed on took aim at the epicenter where perceived value was high (home security), where the broadest array of existing company assets and capabilities could be leveraged (customer relationships and monthly billing models; field staff to do household assessments and installations; a well-known brand; data lines into neighborhoods and homes; 24/7 call centers; ability to integrate devices, software, and data flow), and where incumbents had an Achilles' heel.

Leading security companies were clinging to reliance on landline phone connections, making snipping the phone line a burglar's first move. This constraint also left security companies with little ability to support always-on video monitoring and playback. It wouldn't be economically viable for them to fill this gap by installing data lines. Mobile companies like AT&T were expected to try to compete in this space (in the end they did), but while they could solve the landline problem, they lacked the people on the ground to properly assess the needs of a given home or deliver turnkey installation. We believed there was a unique role and right to win for TWC. By leveraging existing TWC assets and advantages, and potentially bundling onto existing TWC products and services, the company could offer a big step forward for consumers. Due to the limitations of existing security systems, including complex installation, household penetration in home security was not as high as it could be—meaning we believed that TWC could not only win share from existing players but also build category penetration through the more effective and turnkey approach that a company owning the data line could deliver, and that rapidly improving wireless technologies could empower.

In saying yes to a security-centered innovation, TWC was not saying no to the broader opportunities in controls, monitoring, and automation that the company expected to become meaningful over time. (Nest, for instance, the highly successful entrant in the controls market that Google bought for $3 billion, didn't exist yet, but the writing was on the wall.) The strategy would be to use home security as an opportunity to deepen TWC's customer relationships by offering even more choice in services, building a broader set of touch points across the home, including a hub device that would initially drive security applications but, at the same time, could accommodate much more. This would open the door to step into the broader set of opportunities as technologies allowed. As a result, TWC believed it would be well positioned to play in the "home hub" opportunity if these visions of the future ever became an actual market. But until then, we could move step-by-step from one offering to another, building the business over time.

With this vision taking shape, we set our sights on the task of bringing the opportunity to life for the TWC board. We understood the orientation we needed to win their support. We had to bridge that disruption dichotomy—showing we had a vision for a well-differentiated approach that could bring enough disruption to these categories to open new demand, yet be relatively nondisruptive to the company, given that the approach was well within the wheelhouse of TWC's assets and capabilities. Presented with this vision of how TWC could deepen the customer relationship, the associated economics, the competitive advantages, and the strong alignment with existing assets and capabilities, the TWC board enthusiastically supported the move. Execution of the idea would ultimately require clearing a number of significant hurdles, including the need to manage a longer sales cycle and a more diagnostic in-home installation process than cable boxes or modems currently required. But these were things that could be overlaid on existing capabilities, without the need to build new ones from scratch.

Launched as Time Warner Cable IntelligentHome, the security-centered SCMA business was initially launched regionally, then offered nationally throughout the United States in late 2013. With a steadily expanding pipeline of additional services, sensors, monitors, and controls, IntelligentHome is moving in step with consumers' growing appetite for home technology and ease. And because it started in security, it's solidly anchored in a sweet spot—one in which you don't have to be a tech early adopter to be willing to write a check or add another line item to your cable statement.

HEY YOU, GET OFF OF MY CLOUD

The second opportunity on TWC's radar was the entry into cloud computing. Over the years, TWC had built a solid foundation in providing connectivity and communications to small businesses. At the same time, they had kept pace with the explosion in on-demand video and other core services that required development of massive infrastructure for data storage and delivery. In connecting the dots between these two things, the company saw a clear opportunity to leverage a significant, existing asset with the emerging marketplace need for cloud computing. In this case, a key part of the opportunity was leveraging the TWC brand name and its existing base of customer relationships to make cloud-based computing a more comprehensible and accessible offering for small businesses with big ambitions but limited expertise in IT. The trust factor was a big part of the X-factor. By controlling not only the servers at the back end, as a company like Amazon would, but also the data pipe through which sensitive, vital information flows, TWC had the ability to deliver a totally distinctive value proposition: giving businesses the equivalent of their own *private* cloud. Again, this was a top right corner innovation, as the company already had the customer relationships, an established role as a provider of connectivity and telecommunications services, and an asset base that could be leveraged.

The Time Warner Cable board's endorsement paved the way for this additional opportunity. To accelerate its realization, the board sanctioned the acquisition of cloud services provider NaviSite, which Time Warner Cable acquired in April 2011 for approximately $300 million.

Peter sums up the outcome this way: "Cloud computing is the future. Flexing our existing capabilities into that opportunity opened a big whitespace we weren't playing in. We've got a big, rapidly growing base of small business customers who are hearing about the benefits of moving to the cloud but need a more turnkey approach. And they've got security concerns, where our role in managing the data pipe becomes a big competitive advantage. In my view, we had a competitive right to win here with our capabilities; we just had to flex that capability in the right way. This opened a big growth business for us."

Chapter 5

The Wow and the How

If you log enough hours on the bar stool listening to war stories of promising innovation ideas going off track before they made it to market, you start to notice a similar arc: A spark of curiosity. An intellectual tug on a few loose threads as an unsolved problem first appears. The arrival of the idea. The visceral rush of certainty that your team has cracked the kind of idea capable of changing lives and creating a great business. The playful dabbling in early prototypes. Then seeing the assumptions behind the idea unravel before it ever gets off the ground, leaving its creators' passion, energy, and inspiration come to naught.

We've looked over the years not just at what goes right when all the pieces come together in a sucessful innovation but also at the undoing of many high-potential ideas. And one pattern we see repeated over and over again is *pouring a lot of time into worrying about "the wow" and not enough into "the how."* The connection between the stretch factor and the "how" is fundamental.

At Fahrenheit 212, what we mean by "the wow" is the truly big, differentiated idea that opens valuable new benefits and possibilities for people, and for the companies that create and market them. It excites you as an innovator and delights your intended consumers. In a crowded world, it is an idea that feels genuinely new and valuable. It fills a gap in the market. Maybe it opens a whole new category of products or services, topples an existing paradigm, or fixes something in life that just seems wrong.

Wow, wow, and wow. It all looks great. Until "the how" comes along and bites you in the ass.

What do we mean by the how? It's shorthand for a whole host of vital how questions.

How will this product or service actually do what we say it does?

How can we make it?

How much will it cost to do that?

How will we get it to market?

How will it meet regulatory and retailer requirements?

How will it make money?

How will it strengthen the company's competitive position?

How will we convince management or investors to bankroll it?

Staying fixated on the wow while ignoring the how is like planning a fantastic menu for a dinner party around dishes you have no idea how to make. Fantasizing about it is awesome. Talking about it with people you're inviting excites both of you. But chances are the meal will be a train wreck.

One of our firm's founders, Geoff Vuleta, sums up what we've learned about this phenomenon this way: *"It's far easier to excite consumers with a new possibility than it is to get a company to do something it has never done before. Yet we see 'the how' get glossed over or outright ignored time and time again, with a very high price tag, measured in wasted talent, imagination, time, and money."*

If you're pursuing innovation on your own in your garage or dorm room, worrying about the wow without the how can be good fun, can spark some wild and innovative new ideas—however unfeasible—and can do little harm, as it puts only your own time at risk. But if you're doing it in a commercial context on behalf of your employer, your investors, or, in our case, paying clients, it's irresponsible. The number of innovation projects that achieve a *wow* but get fatally lanced on the *how* is pretty staggering.

The answer, we found, like so many better ways of doing things, seems obvious in hindsight, but it's a pretty radical departure from today's conventional wisdom.

What we often do is this. When we spot a situation where the how is likely to be particularly daunting, which is usually a function of an ambition that's beyond the ways a given business makes its products or makes its money, or that represents a technology leap beyond what's proven, we find it's massively helpful to essentially turn the typical innovation process upside down: we *start* with the tough questions of how . . . then work out toward the wow that will excite the marketplace and create new demand.

This means moving a lot of the tough stuff from the back end of the development process to the front—starting the journey by surfacing the hardest operational and financial realities of the business. It means teeing up the issues that will kill a project now, rather than discovering them later.

If you're a Hobbit embarking on an epic adventure on a movie screen, it's okay to begin the journey with bare feet, a loaf of bread, and a pocketknife and not worry about how you'll slay the dragon until you're staring it in the face. But innovation doesn't work that way. You can't create real impact by ignoring issues that will upend a project. The odds of landing on a solution to those issues without you consciously and deliberately shaping it are astronomically low. On the other hand, if you stare down the toughest questions early on, and consciously construct the ideas you come up with to overcome them, you're a lot less likely to end up with your eyebrows singed, lamenting the death of your big idea as the credits roll.

A lot of user-centered innovation purists will cringe at this. They argue that worrying about the question of how from day one inhibits creativity. Our experience and dramatically improved hit rate have shown that's a misconception, and a shortsighted view. Creativity loves a problem to solve. The trick is to make the problem of how a part of the goal and the process rather than a distraction or a buzzkill at the back end. There's an implicit assumption by many innovators that you can't simultaneously chase hugely ambitious answers to an unmet consumer need *and* obsess about how you'll actually get those ambitious ideas to those consumers. To us, that is a false choice.

For a taste of it, let's look more closely at the way we shaped and built the Mosaic banking system I described in Chapter 2.

Long before we conceived the value proposition that would unlock the ultimate solution—the radical idea that signing up for your next financial product from the bank would better the terms you got on products you'd already had for years—we were deep into thinking about a whole host of how questions.

The first critical how question was *How can we weave an array of very different business models together into a single entity?* Different bank products make money in very different ways. Some are interest based. Some are service fee based. Some earn money not from consumers, but off their balances. Others, like mobile services, make money for the bank by taking costs *out* of the service equation. We realized that behind the scenes we would need to create some form of a common currency, allowing each bank division to objectively understand the economic value of each customer action the innovation would ignite. Only by getting to that common currency could a compelling commercial case be put forward to all the divisions.

Before we had synthesized the consumer idea, we were already thinking about key requirements of successfully getting all the divisions enrolled in the commercial case. Consumers might never see this common currency, but it would have to be invented anyway. Working out how to do this would take a few months of work. Had we deferred this question to the back end of the project, the project would have likely run out of time and money before it got solved, and our client would have been left feeling like we'd sold them a unicorn—a beautiful but impossible fantasy.

Another big how question was *How can we share costs and benefits across divisions?* This is a common deal breaker in any cross-divisional innovation effort. We've come across its pitfalls in everything from food to financial services to fashion. Walking in with a wow of an idea in absence of an answer to this key question has stopped many innovations in their tracks. This too would take a great deal of hard work, which progressed in parallel with the hunt for the wow of a winning consumer proposition.

In the end the consumer wow and the behind the scenes how would seamlessly merge, each feeding the other.

Mosaic is powered by an algorithm we conceived to fit the task. The algorithm works back from the incremental average profit that the addition of an extra banking product could deliver to the bank based on a given customer profile. It then uses a formula to spread a portion of that incremental profit back to the customer in the form of improved terms, benefits, or rewards on the products they already have. The benefit it delivered was revolutionary—instantly improving the terms on the existing products a customer already had.

The algorithm governed the back office management of how much the bank would be willing to invest to get a customer into their next product. But it was also the backbone of the tablet-based visualization tool. This algorithm allowed financial terms on any product in the bank portfolio to in effect be "renegotiated" by nonexecutive bank staff in real time on the branch floor, with no bureaucracy or approvals needed, because the algorithm prescribed acceptable adjustments of terms based on the overall profitability of the customer's mix of products and assets.

The fact that the bank dramatically overshot its most optimistic revenue expectations speaks to the wow of the value proposition and the way it was brought to life, but equally to the amount of lateral thinking and sweat poured into the how. None of it would have happened if we hadn't been thinking about the how from the earliest days of the journey.

We find that a fixation on the wow over the how is a widespread problem in innovation, and a root cause of a lot of heartbreak, wasted money, and missed opportunity. Leading with the how is not a new idea. But it seems to have been forgotten as a go-to source of ignition. Remember, the iPod was not sparked by some great epiphany about consumers' relationship with mobile music, but by a new how—Toshiba created a new ultra-small disk drive with no obvious ways to apply it. Thinking about what possibilities that new capability could open up got the digital entertainment revolution under way.

INCUBATING AN INCUBATOR

I'm always on the lookout for inspiring examples of innovators using the how as a springboard to innovation. One of the most enlightening stories I've come across comes out of a cause-based firm called

Design That Matters, from Boston. Increasing the availability of incubators to care for premature infants in developing markets can prevent thousands of infant deaths each year. Every so often, a well-meaning, well-endowed foundation steps in to address this by donating state-of-the-art incubators to poor villages in various parts of the world. For a few months, the lives of premature infants are saved, until the machine needs maintenance. But the villagers have neither the expertise to repair such sensitive equipment nor the replacement parts to do the job. So the machines go idle, becoming expensive, neglected monuments to good intentions gone wrong. Through its fieldwork researching the challenge, the team at Design That Matters noticed that resourceful villagers in these small communities have a remarkable ability (and supply of parts) to keep old cars and trucks on the road for hundreds of thousands of miles. So Design That Matters conceived a truly brilliant design solution: a new kind of incubator built entirely out of readily available car parts, serviceable by anyone who knows how to fix a car. The idea was featured in *Time* magazine in testament to the power of design to change the world. It seemed that from now on, benefactors who donate incubators could make a far bigger, more enduring difference. All thanks to some smart innovators giving equal time to what the how can open up.

This ingenious piece of thinking about the how sounds like an amazing success story. And it almost was. But in the end, the auto parts incubator became a parable not only about how vital these how questions are, but also how many of these how questions need solving for a visionary idea to come to fruition. The auto parts design approach was a truly inspired answer to the question of how an incubator can be aligned with local capabilities to keep it working in the field in the long run. But a battery of other critical how questions had been overlooked in staying so focused on the product. Like how to get medical equipment manufacturers interested in commercializing this machine, how to get it made, how to get it distributed, how to get it in front of the right people in the health care ecosystems who make procurement decisions or who allocate donor contributions to the field. The lessons of this inspired Design That Matters to think more broadly, and to openly question the adequacy of a user-centered approach. CEO Timothy Prestero reflected in a TEDx talk on the failure of the auto parts incubator to warm a single infant other than the baby placed in the prototype for the photograph in *Time*. He described the realization that the initiative failed to save a single baby's life because the team had solved the issues of the user and the product, but not those of the business system that had to be navigated to actually warm at-risk infants. This led not just to new wisdom, but to a change in methodology that he described as a shift from "designing for users" to "designing for outcomes." His vernacular is different, but the lessons have much in common with ours. They reinforce our belief that the how is often the harder part to solve, particularly the critical how questions on the commercial side.

Does the wow—that leap to big new transformational benefits for the end user and the business that serves him or her—really matter? Absolutely. The philosophy we drive home to our teams is that the wow and the how are each useless without the other. An idea that nails the how, but doesn't open big new benefits and opportunities for consumers and your business, won't get noticed or add much value. But a breakthrough idea that doesn't work in the marketplace or isn't viable as a business isn't actually a great idea—it's just a diversion, one that can waste valuable time and drain limited resources, when real impact is what you're after.

A big part of success is bringing the right level of how to a given point in the process. The distinction we draw is that in the early stages, we just need a sight line to how an idea *could* be done, could deliver on its promises, could be manufactured at scale, and could hit the profitability requirements attached to the endeavor. You can't have all the answers, but even pinning down the questions is meaningful and can inform the solutions you shape. As you move further down the track into the deeper phases of development and commercialization, the emphasis shifts from how something could be done to how it *will* be done. It's an important distinction. And the more breakthrough an idea is relative to what the company has done before, the more important and more difficult those how questions will be. The how questions are hard. Relegating them to the back end of the journey often makes them unsolvable.

BIG VS. HARD REVISITED

Putting all of these lessons together, there is no law that says big innovations are by definition hard, risky, slow, and expensive. Instead, another kind of physics comes into play. The meeting of a liquid and a solid. Human imagination is among the most fluid things in existence. When presented with a challenge, human imagination flows in amazing ways, creating new paths. But that fluid imagination sits alongside something more solid—the realities of the business, its strategies, its operations, and its economics.

Any solid can be reshaped, but it usually requires some form of physical force—the grating of a lathe, the pounding of a hammer, application of heat or pressure, like the ten-ton stamp that makes a car fender. The only two points in the history of a business where it's truly liquid are in its earliest days as a startup, when it's just forming, before the strategies, capabilities, and infrastructure have matured and calcified, or when it falls into such desperate financial straits that any path to survival is open to discussion. In thinking about innovation and trying to get ideas to market, we have to ask ourselves whether we want to reshape the solid to fit the liquid of human imagination, or equip the liquid to conform to the contours of the solid that is so much harder to change.

Working in an untethered way, guided only by the whims and desires of consumers, with barely a glance at the solid thing its inventions need to work with, the odds of imagination landing on

When the fluid arc of human imagination meets the solid realities of company strategies, operations, capabilities, and finances, it is naive to expect the arrival of a fluid idea to reshape those things that have grown solid over many years.

something that fits the edges and engines of a business are very slim. If you want to know why well over 90 percent of innovation projects fail to deliver any revenue at all, it's simple. Liquids can't reshape solids, at least not quickly. It took a few million years for water to reshape rock into the Grand Canyon. The person sponsoring your project can't wait that long. Even when we're pursuing disruption, ignoring rigid realities, rather than solving our way around them, leaves even the most brilliant vision as fragile as the premature newborns that inspired Tim Prestero.

DAY ONE 2.0

As a project leader, how do you up the odds of your team landing in that sweet spot of defining breakthrough ideas that don't break the company trying to pull them off? The fix isn't to put a governor on the engine of human imagination, but to do a better job of aiming it. And not through something bolted into the innovation process six months in, but six *minutes* in—right after pouring coffee and saying good morning.

For starters, frame the project mission with explicit clarity of purpose. Instead of just saying we're going big, and letting imagination and adrenaline race ahead, frame it more like this:

We're looking for big new intersections between emerging customer needs and the strategies, capabilities, and assets of our company.

Suddenly the orientation is very different. By definition, the only sane way to go about a task defined this way is to unleash a two-track interrogation of both the emerging needs of the customer and the latent potential embedded in the company's asset base, strategies, and capabilities. You build ideas at the crossroads. This doesn't take out of play ideas that require extending those capabilities, but it creates a helpful counterweight to ensure that as much passion is poured into the new and doable as into the merely new.

The second thing is to say yes, we're swinging for the fences, but show that clearing the fence is a doable thing, with no atomic bat required.

The third change is to view a company's current capabilities not as limitations, but as blank canvas, laced with possibilities, limited only by the imagination we apply to them. Some will cry foul here, saying that this way of thinking narrows the playing field. Okay, but imagine Leonardo, Picasso, Renoir, and de Kooning deciding that working with rectangles of stretched canvas was a buzz-killing constraint, unworthy of their imaginations. Or Mozart, Miles Davis, and Hendrix deciding a twelve-note scale was too limiting to make world-changing music. Yes, Miles and Jimi bent some notes for color, but you get the point.

This seems obvious, yet unless we consciously direct the inventive minds on our projects to think and work this way, they won't instinctively go there. They'll soar past existing capability and never look back.

And if they do, we'll forever be stuck with the myth that big means hard to execute, risky, and slow.

Start approaching challenges and filtering ideas through this two-sided framework of marketplace disruption versus company disruption, and you'll find something amazing emerges.

To tie it all together, here are a handful of ways to break the myth that big means hard, risky, expensive, and slow.

1. Embrace the real math of twenty-first-century innovation: big + undoable ≠ big.

2. Keep an eye out for the tendency to see ideas as big *because* they're hard to pull off. (Hard doesn't equal big, either.)

3. Being *exclusively* user centered can send your project hurtling toward implausible solutions and dead ends. Think "inside out and outside in"—look for ways to disrupt the marketplace without unduly disrupting the company.

4. Get away from thinking of current capabilities as constraints. Think of them as blank canvas waiting for inspired imagination to paint new visions.

5. Don't buy into the myth that creativity is most effective when it's unencumbered by practical imperatives. The

power of creativity to push boundaries needs to be properly focused, or it can fly off into implausibility.

6. Disrupting demand in the marketplace without disrupting your company isn't a function of what you do six months into a project—it starts with what you do in the first six minutes. Look for new intersections between the emerging needs of the marketplace and the capabilities and assets of your company.

Chapter 6

The Need for Speed

Reed Howlett is a man with a sense of urgency.

Part of that might be genetic. He's a CEO. Most CEOs you meet were born with the drive and talent to make big things happen fast. That's how they get the CEO gig. But Reed's sense of pace is also circumstantial. He's got two clocks ticking in his ear at once.

The first clock is external. His company, Nature's Variety, is the market leader in raw pet food, a $250 million category growing at more than 25 percent a year. More and more consumers are finding that trading up from conventional processed pet food to raw has a visible impact on their pets' health. Built primarily around a product form of frozen patties made of meat and veggies, raw pet food started as a cottage industry with small independent pet specialty shops, but has now extended into larger pet specialty chains. Newly installed raw pet food freezers are a hot new destination in the pet aisle. It's a landgrab moment. With multiple competitors vying for consumer and retailer preference, there will be winners and losers. The prize is to the swift and innovative.

Reed's passion for pet health is contagious, and his logic is elegantly simple. As he puts it, *"Nature meant dogs and cats to eat the way they do in the wild. When was the last time you saw a dog fire up a stove or grind fillers into his food? Turn him loose in a grocery store and where will he run . . . to canned foods, the cereal aisle, or the butcher counter?"*

Fittingly, Nature's Variety's lead brand is called Instinct.

Reed and his team are committed to not only setting the pace for category growth, but also defining the product standards by which raw food can become widely accepted as the gold standard for healthy pets. You can't lead by leaning back.

If the high-velocity competitive race weren't enough to stoke Reed's desire for getting innovations to market quickly, there's an internal clock, too. Nature's Variety is a majority-owned portfolio company of Catterton Partners, a highly regarded consumer-focused private equity firm with more than $4 billion under management. Catterton bought Nature's Variety a few years earlier as the raw market started to pop, giving the entrepreneurs at Nature's Variety the capital they needed to meet growing demand, bolster their product lines and processes, and educate the market on raw food's benefits. Like any PE firm, Catterton entered the business with a target time frame to realize a return on its investment.

Eager to ensure Nature's Variety would win the raw race, Catterton managing partner Scott Dahnke introduced Reed to Fahrenheit 212. Scott was aware of the unusually high hit rate our approach delivers, and of our willingness to take skin in the game with a vested interest in successful outcomes. But he was also attracted to a valuable side effect of the Money & Magic approach. By solving for the consumer and the business concurrently, rather than sequentially per typical innovation practice, our model significantly shortens the time it takes to get successful innovations to market.

Catterton's embrace of innovation separates it from its more staid private equity peers. Innovation has historically had little role in the private equity playbook. PE firms typically buy companies and hold them for four to five years before selling them at a healthy profit. To get there, they rely for the most part on just four moves: buy at the low end of valuation ranges, reengineer the finances, cut costs, and bring in better management. Where innovation did show up on the PE radar was as a cost center to potentially cut for savings. Through a PE lens, the slow pace of typical product development methodologies has meant innovation represented an uncertain prospect of long-term revenue, but with a guaranteed near-term cost attached to it. If the time horizon for innovation revenue hitting the P&L was likely to fall beyond intended hold periods, or if the opportunities in sight seemed like risky whims rather than strategically and financially robust chess moves, innovation was an easy target for cost cutting.

If speed to market was one key factor in private equity firms' reluctance to embrace innovation, the nature of the players and methods deployed to make innovation happen was another. PE firms had two imperfect options. The first, management consultancies, used extensively in pruning and tuning newly acquired PE portfolio companies, are comfortable defining strategic landscapes where innovation might be pursued, but lack the creative sparks it takes to turn strategies from mere theory into compelling products and real revenues. At the other end of the spectrum, the second option, design firms, have the creativity, but are seen by PE players as overly fixated on esoteric nuances of the product and user experience, relatively disinterested in the practical or profitable, and unable to put a concrete case on the table for why a potential innovation is a sound investment. Design firms' default answer of "consumers tell us they would like a product like this" does not an investment case make. The way their business model works, PE firms have no choice but to assess innovation opportunities as potential uses of capital in pursuit of an attractive return. Their needs are ignored in typical innovation methods. Little wonder the PE world has shied away from innovation. But change is coming.

The combination of increasingly efficient M&A markets and an abundance of committed but unspent PE money hunting for companies to buy has driven up the valuations PE firms pay for businesses they acquire. Financial reengineering is having less impact on company valuations than it once did. And fewer businesses seem to be carrying a lot of fat for an acquirer to quickly trim away. The combination of these factors is in some cases stretching PE hold times toward five to seven years. This is putting new pressure on PE firms to grow the businesses they buy, rather than merely tune and resell them.

Columbia University Business School professor R. A. Farrokhnia, a veteran of private equity and an architect of Columbia's "Private Equity 2.0" curriculum, senses that a tipping point is coming. "Private equity as an industry is only a few decades old, and it was born out of a small group of bankers and financiers. A few pioneers worked out a finance-based model, and it was successful, so a herd rushed in behind those early movers and used exactly the same playbook. The financial crisis and a new market environment have sowed seeds of change. In the new climate, there's a tension between hanging on to the old models that aren't working like they used to, and being ready to adopt a new playbook once the momentum and success stories spread. Once the early movers prove that innovation can be a reliable lever to create sustainable value growth and competitive advantage, beyond what financial engineering alone is capable of delivering, it's inevitable that innovation will matter more than it used to in PE, simply because growth will matter more than it did before."

Nature's Variety was clearly a business to be grown rather than honed, and Reed and Scott saw innovation as an accelerant. But to deliver impact with the speed that both Reed and Catterton wanted to see, innovation itself would have to be accelerated.

At Fahrenheit, Marcus Oliver was just the man to lead the project. A remarkably observant Oxford-schooled psychologist, devout pet parent to Bob the schnoodle (a feisty schnauzer-poodle mix who's often found patrolling our offices), and igniter of many of the best innovations Fahrenheit 212 has ever created, Marcus came at the challenge with a rare ability to change perspectives on a dime. He would zoom in close to the product experience, and then pull back to the rapidly evolving dynamics in pet food retail. He'd pepper conversations with insights imported from unrelated categories whose growth required new consumer behavior. He'd spot parallels between raw pet food and religion—noticing that many raw food devotees see the choice between raw and non-raw not as a matter of better versus less good, but of right versus wrong. He'd also obsess intensely over the operational realities of the factory floor, where the need for speed would likely meet its most severe tests.

After an inspiring kickoff session with Reed and his team, we get busy. Reed and Scott's urgency is now ours. But the rigor of our front-end explorations is nonnegotiable. Experience has taught us that speed to market is helped not by shortcutting the foundational work at the front end, but by building sharp strategies, making smart choices about where to play, and ensuring the solutions you take forward are purpose-built from the ground up for rapid execution—leaning wherever possible on existing company capabilities and assets.

Our two-track immersion process takes us deep into the worlds of pet parents on both sides of the raw/non-raw divide, and into the strategic, financial, and operational realities of Nature's Variety as a business. The brief is deceptively simple: deliver rapidly deployable innovations capable of accelerating raw food adoption. But the simplicity of the one-line goal belies the difficulty of making it happen. As always, we will need a potent strategy to guide the idea development process.

In a world that has come to equate innovation with creative leaps and shiny new objects, innovation strategy is a big deal that gets far less attention than it should. It's the critical filter between the infinite possibilities at project inception—the many things you *could* do—and the few very important things you *should* do. Filling rooms with interesting Post-it note scribbles is not hard; knowing which ones matter is. Innovation strategy draws lines around the playing field and the end zone based on where the most lucrative outcomes are likely to be found. And at Fahrenheit 212, it defines the areas of overlap between wins for the consumer and wins for the business.

Beyond ensuring that energy and talent are focused on the right things, powerful innovation strategies are instrumental to speed. Speed to impact is impossible if you're veering all over the map with no clear sense of true north. In absence of clear strategic focus, ideas are just whims and random shots in the dark, driven by what's interesting rather than what's valuable. You're running down dead ends while the clock keeps ticking and cash keeps burning. Great strategy avoids that, and gives you a richer set of consumer and commercial criteria to judge ideas against as they begin to take shape and you decide which to run at, allowing more robust and timely decisions through every stage of the process.

Innovation strategy's two pieces of flint are consumer and commercial insight. The front end of this project delivered insight in spades. And while we didn't see it when it first appeared, the insight that would ultimately make all the difference was tucked in a throwaway piece of consumer vernacular that kept popping up.

To understand the consumer side of the two-sided problem, our line of inquiry would span the functional, emotional, experiential, and economic dynamics of a pet parent's journey from one side of the raw/non-raw divide to the other. Pet care is one of the most emotionally charged businesses you'll ever encounter. My family dog Cody's battle with cancer was one of the most intense experiences our family ever lived through. His emergence from that to live fifteen amazing years was a source of immense joy. Every devoted pet family has stories like these. Perhaps this explains one of the striking statistics of the Great Recession. In 2009, when the economy imploded, U.S. household food spending plummeted, yet sales of pet treats grew by 10 percent. We were willing to scrimp on feeding the two-legged members of the family, but spent more on our pets. The rapid growth of raw food, at a hefty price premium to canned or dry food and with considerable degrees of inconvenience, was another data point in this phenomenon.

As we delve into the question of how and why families migrated from conventional processed pet food to raw, one consumer describes it this way: *"First my sister made the leap. Her dog had persistent allergies and someone suggested she try going raw. But the change she saw was much bigger than that. Spike's appearance, energy level, and demeanor seemed so much healthier that she stuck with it. I followed her lead and was amazed. I never looked back."*

This phrase she uses—*made the leap*—keeps popping up in consumers' stories. We don't think much of it at the time, but it gradually creeps into our jargon as we discuss our growing body of insights. Eventually "the leap" becomes shorthand for a series of hurdles that a switch to raw food entails: a price point roughly *three* times ordinary pet food, the new behavior of shopping for pet food in the freezer, the need to plan ahead and thaw food by mealtime, and the potentially messy experience of handling raw meat. The leap is pretty big. You have to really want what raw can do to deal with all those changes. The intense conviction level we were seeing from raw users suddenly made sense. You wouldn't jump over all those hurdles if you were on the fence about raw. Fortunately, the change in pets' well-being was so noticeable that most families who made the leap never went back.

As the immersion process goes on, we begin to filter these consumer perspectives, marry them up with key insights about the business and the rapidly changing retail landscape, and shape our innovation strategy. We realize we're looking at a basic seesaw situation. All the benefits of raw sit on one side, and all the things that make it such a leap sit on the other. Clearly what we'll need to do to accelerate raw adoption is to somehow amplify those benefits to the point that the positives outweigh the disruptions. That was, after all, what had tipped current users into raw.

As we're hovering toward consensus around some sort of "benefit elevation" strategy, Marcus drops one of those transformational questions that changes the air in the room: *"Aren't we missing something obvious, guys? Just because everyone talks so casually about the leap, why are we taking that as an immovable given? Isn't the real problem here the leap itself?"*

It's a simple question with big implications.

Innovation is often thought of as a quest for differentiation. In our line of work, we get up every morning, inhale caffeine, and march into the day with a mission of cracking the idea that no one has ever thought of, let alone done. In competitively crowded categories, we obsess over finding those new points of uniqueness that can separate our hot new thing from everything around it. The reality embedded in Marcus's question was big and obvious only in hindsight— that the raw pet food experience was *over*differentiated. It was as if consumers contemplating putting a toe in to test the raw food waters had to go over Niagara Falls in a barrel. The task of educating the public in the coming years about the health benefits of raw food would remain a critical part of success, but for now we would look at that as the role of marketing more than innovation. The strategic focus for the upcoming wave of innovation would be on the other side of the seesaw, reducing the amount of behavioral and experiential disruption consumers would face in making the transition to raw. Great innovation strategies are always elegantly simple. In this case, it could be summed up in just six letters: *de-leap*.

Riffing on this line of thinking with Reed and his team, the vision sharpens and the invention process starts to surge ahead. We set about defining what kinds of products could get us to that "de-leaped" outcome with the speed to market we needed. Melissa Tischler, driving the project from the Money side with a unique ability to marry the possible and the pragmatic, goes to the whiteboard and analytically distills the challenge down to three simple parts. "Here's the equation, guys."

Success = existing consumer behavior + existing operational capability + big new ideas.

We start hunting for existing consumer behaviors we can use to piggyback our way into more pet homes. One behavior that jumps out is supplementation. Some pet parents are content to give their pet a "one-note" meal—like an unadulterated bowl of kibble or canned food. But a sizeable portion of pet parents like to supplement their base food with something extra. Some throw on a little people food to make dinner more craveable. Others add nutrition supplements, making pet supplements a billion-dollar business.

When we look at raw through a supplement lens, opportunities for transformation spring into view. "De-leaping" could mean doing away with the either/or choice of "raw or not." We could let families retain more of their current mealtime products and behaviors, at least at the outset of their journey into raw. We'd open a new supporting "top off" role for raw as the thing to be added. This would also soften the economic hit of an outright conversion to raw. Depending on the brand of food a dog is eating today, a full switch to raw can dramatically increase the cost per meal. Melissa does some quick math that says as a supplement we could probably shrink the increase in meal cost to about 15 percent. It's looking like a great way to de-leap both the behavior and the economics. But there are two other key questions we have to solve with the Nature's Variety team.

From a nutrition science perspective, would using an ounce or two of raw as a supplement make a difference to pet health? We turned to the experts at Nature's Variety, who confirmed that, yes, it would. Next we have to ask whether or not Nature's Variety has the capability to manufacture a product like this on our aggressive timelines. The operations team steers us toward the all-natural freeze-drying process they recently brought on board to make raw treats. Using that existing process has big implications. We could avoid the capital cost, risk, and time lags we'd face if we needed new manufacturing equipment. And a freeze-dried product wouldn't have to be shipped or sold frozen. This would knock down yet another leap— the need for new category users to make the trip to the freezer to experience the benefits of raw.

The first idea in the portfolio of innovations we'd take forward was now taking shape: Raw Daily Boost—a way for non-raw house-holds to find out what all the fuss was about without turning their routines or budgets upside down. It was raw Nature's Variety food, freeze-dried and ground into a powdered form that could be sprin-kled onto whatever meal a pet was eating in its current routine. Dogs went nuts for the taste and cleaned their bowls with gusto. Pet own-ers noticed a difference in their dogs' appearance and demeanor. And non-raw households had the gentler on-ramp we were looking for.

This was a promising start toward de-leaping, but a relatively small one. Pet supplements are growing fast, but are still tiny com-pared to pet food. De-leaping meant easing the transition into raw, but we didn't want to just play at the fringes of pet meals. The cen-ter of the bowl was where we needed to be. But the path was still blocked by formidable barriers.

We circle back again to the strategic premise that raw food is an overdifferentiated experience that needs to shift closer to current consumer behavior. With supplements as our first piece of behavioral piggybacking, we continue to deconstruct existing mealtime rituals. It's easy in innovation to get overly fixated on products, when the star of the show is the consumer who uses them. Even our most de-vout raw fans readily admitted that handling raw meat could be a little gross. From the inception of the project we'd been troubled by the reality that something as seemingly silly as squeamishness was keeping so many pets from reaping the health benefits raw could bring. The stumbling block is the frozen burgerlike patties that need thawing, and become a bit wet and messy as they're defrosted and served.

We pose a challenge for ourselves: how can we deliver a raw meal a pet parent never has to touch? In an intense afternoon, we churn through dozens of potential solutions for getting raw patties from point A—the freezer—to point B—the bowl. We look at novel packaging, scoops, and even selling the food packed in its own dis-posable bowls. They're all interesting, but none is right.

Then Marcus chimes in with *"Well, I guess there's always gravity."*

What he means is that we should find a way to make raw food *pourable*—so a tip of the wrist could replace the messy handling. This would mean replacing the ubiquitous patty with little pieces sized and shaped in a way that would let them pour into a bowl. We workshop it with Nature's Variety's manufacturing team and a few months later a product called Raw Bites is in the pipeline and racing to market. Manufacturing-wise, all it takes is minor adjustments to the natural process currently used to make bite-sized treats. Using kibble-sized pieces would ensure a smooth flow in the pour. It would bring the whole experience closer to the way kibble is served today and bridge the behavioral leap. As a big side benefit, the small pieces mean the inconvenience of thawing could go away, too. The small pieces would have the kibble-like crunch dogs love, right from the freezer.

One by one, our collaborations with the Nature's Variety team picked off dimensions and degrees of leap consumers faced to step into raw, delivered to market with the impact and speed that Scott and Reed needed.

The impact on the business has been tremendous. Nature's Variety had been growing at a very healthy 30 percent annual rate. Where most high-growth businesses see growth rates taper off as they scale up, Nature's Variety's growth rate steepened to 35 percent when these innovations hit the market. Reed said about half the growth was directly attributable to the innovations we'd built together. Nature's Variety won pet industry innovation awards and was suddenly getting the lion's share of attention from major pet retailers, who saw it as the most forward thinking player in the business.

Reflecting on the need for speed, which we see across every company we meet these days, a client at a big packaged goods company once told us that his all-in cost of running a multifunctional innovation project, staffed with specialists from Strategic Planning, R&D, Consumer Insights, Design, Manufacturing, Finance, Marketing, and Sales, along with costs for external partners and research, comes in at about $7 million a year. Other companies run leaner programs, but at any run rate time is money. Compressing the journey to a successful outcome has a huge impact on increasing the return on investment. That's true in any business—all the more so if you're staring at the kind of vertical growth curve raw pet food was experiencing. Every month wasted has a high opportunity cost.

As for why we're able to deliver so much faster, it's not that our model is some stroke of genius that lops off time to market; it's that conventional methods in wide use today seem in hindsight like they were purpose-built to maximize wheel spinning and rework. Today's typical approaches in essence say spend your time unilaterally working on the consumer side of the equation, and don't pollute the purity of that by looking into the business proposition until a consumer solution is defined. There are two problems with this in terms of time to market. It's not just that the commercial requirements don't get addressed until the consumer work is half-done. Worse, the initial commercial interrogation often surfaces a need to go back and overhaul fundamental parts of the consumer solution. The commercial side of the innovation program often ends up dragging the consumer work kicking and screaming back toward the starting line to fix it. Maybe one time in ten you get lucky and the rework is minor, leaving you with the core idea intact but a few key changes to make it commercially workable. But the other nine results are ugly. You realize the very thing that was so enticing to consumers makes the idea commercially stillborn. So you have to tear it up and start over.

There's an irony in this. One of the important contributions of the design thinking movement is the mantra of "fail quickly and cheaply." That is absolutely right. Perfection is great in a piece of sashimi, but often detrimental to the pursuit of innovation. You learn more by road testing than theorizing. But there's an important point not to be missed. By deferring concern for the critical needs of the business until late in the innovation process, you may be letting the product fail quickly, but you are making the failure of the *business proposition* happen as slowly, painfully, and expensively as possible. Going through multiple iterations of the product, burning cash and talent all the way, without having a comparable level of definition and iteration in the business assumptions, is at odds with failing cheaply and quickly.

We all talk about how much faster life seems to be moving these days. To me, innovation practice is still unacceptably slow. Yet there is a commonsense way to get to great outcomes more quickly. Run on two legs not one. Our collaborations with Reed and his team put Raw Boost on the shelf in about twelve months, and Raw Bites inside of eighteen. In the pet food business, that's rocket fast. Yet no corners were cut. It was all a function of working both sides of the problem from day one.

Chapter 7

Seeing the Obvious
for the First Time

Groundbreaking innovations are far more likely to spring from the proverbial garages of startups than from the incumbent leaders of any industry. It's not surprising then that midsized and big companies, knowing we work with a lot of high-growth emerging businesses, often ask us to help them innovate more like a startup. They want to be nimbler, leaner, braver, more radical in their thinking—the very qualities they envy in emerging companies.

Those can be useful traits to cultivate. But they belie a key dynamic in many upstarts' breakout successes. Yes, successful upstarts are nimble due to their lack of scale, and action oriented because if they're not they'll die. But there's a fascinating thing you find when you dissect how some of these emerging businesses break away from established ways of doing things, and how they feel while they're doing it. The truth is, many of these upstarts don't see what they're doing as particularly radical while it's unfolding. In fact they often think the complete opposite. The ideas that seem so radical to industry veterans feel like almost obvious answers to the business problems and consumer problems the startups are staring at. While case by case you'll see in the origin of these disruptive approaches an alchemy of sweat, vision, focus, and doses of serendipity, to a large extent it's the problem and its challenges that shape the innovations.

Swap the inventor's garage for a converted granary and you've got

a breakout emerging business called Tuthilltown Spirits. Founded by
a rock climber named Ralph Erenzo and an engineer named Brian
Lee, neither with a day's prior experience in the spirits business, Tuthilltown came out of nowhere to become one of the most innovative
and successful players in America's booming craft spirits category.
Set in upstate New York's pristine Hudson Valley, in the tiny hamlet
of Gardiner, the Tuthilltown distillery is just ninety minutes from
Fahrenheit's Manhattan office, but feels a world away. Tucked amid
apple orchards, a sparkling creek, and a historic seventeenth-century
gristmill, there's a simple old-school pragmatism to the place and
the team of innovators that work there.

Despite the lack of pretense in its founders and facilities, Tuthilltown has rapidly become a revered player in craft spirits. In the nine
years since they opened their doors, they've created coveted products
and brands, pioneered new production methods, earned a shelf full of
industry awards, garnered enviable press coverage, and been courted
into a mutually beneficial partnership with the venerable Scottish
spirits house William Grant & Sons. They were named *Whisky* magazine's Craft Distillery of the Year in 2011, but barring the addition
of extra stills and improvements to the facility, the founders have
stayed true to their bootstrap roots the best way they know how: by
continuing to rewrite industry rules.

In their earliest days, the rewriting of rules was literal rather
than figurative. Ralph spent months working the corridors of the
state legislature securing permission to make the first legally distilled whiskey in New York State since Prohibition. He succeeded, and
he and his team have marched from rule to rule ever since. The list
of paradigm-busting innovations Tuthilltown has since unleashed
would be admirable for a business many times its size. By using tiny
barrels that big spirit houses would consider impractical, and exper-
imenting with barrel makers on a technique called *woodpeckering*—
boring strategically placed honeycomb-patterned holes into barrel
staves to alter the ratio of surface area to liquid—they dramatically

accelerated the aging process that turns whiskey from the rough clear liquid called white dog into smooth liquid gold. This made possible something the whiskey establishment considered unthinkable— delivering a briefly aged American whiskey so good it could command a higher price per ounce than most eighteen-year-old scotch.

The innovations didn't stop there. Rather than hide their product's relative youth from age-obsessed whiskey aficionados, they unapologetically embraced it in their branding, naming one of their variants Baby Bourbon, and pricing this precocious youngster at $45 for a 375 ml bottle—equivalent to $90 for the standard 750 ml bottles in which most whiskey is sold.

Those small bottles were an innovation in their own right, accelerating Hudson's trajectory to notoriety. As the brand began to win a fan base, the bottles' small size and high price became tempting to any would-be shoplifter with coat pockets and a taste for good whiskey, prompting retailers to shelve Hudson where they could keep an eye on it, in the high-visibility real estate at the cash register. This gave the brand exposure beyond the well-heeled ultrapremium whiskey drinkers who shop in the whiskey section. The merely curious began handling Hudson's stout little wax-sealed, hand-numbered industrial apothecary bottles, reading the Hudson story on the label and getting seduced. Partygoers started grabbing bottles as impulse gifts for their hosts. Hudson became practically viral in a way that ultrapremium products rarely can. And as the trade and consumer press began to devote more ink to the craft spirits dynamic, another benefit of the short bottles became apparent. In dozens of press pieces on the burgeoning craft spirits movement, from the *New York Times* to *Time* magazine to *Maxim*, there would be a beauty shot of six or seven bottles, but always with the short Hudson bottle stealing the show in the front row. Every photographer knows that when you're snapping the class photo, you put the short kid in front.

There was one more rule to break. Nearly every famous whiskey brand has spent its first few decades, or in some cases its first century, selling just one recipe, making the brand synonymous with one type of whiskey and flavor profile. Expansion of the line would only come much later, typically by launching premium-priced older stocks of a similar recipe. Industry veterans advised Tuthilltown to follow the usual model and take Hudson to market with just one recipe. Ralph and Brian ignored that counsel. Hudson launched a varietal line of five whiskeys—Baby Bourbon, Four Grain Bourbon, Manhattan Rye, Single Malt, and a clear, unaged Corn Whiskey. Each had its own grain bill, character, manufacturing methods, and story. This strategy gave the brand more visual prominence on the shelf as each variant got a facing, gave the blogosphere more to write about, and gave the craft spirit explorer a compelling set of experiences to try over time.

Asking Tuthilltown's founders how this array of departures from industry conventions came about provides interesting insight, wrapped in a mix of humble pride and forthrightness.

Brian, an engineer by background who helped build ESPN's production studios before a serendipitous meeting with Ralph drew him into the spirits business, describes the origins of accelerated aging. "It wasn't a case of us saying, 'Gee, wouldn't it be cool if we could age whiskey faster.' We wanted to make a great whiskey, but needed faster maturation because we didn't have the cash flow to wait years to sell it. Starting a business in a category where even the new products are old forces you to look at things differently. A big whiskey house sitting on vast warehouses full of ancient inventory wouldn't ever need to think about how to make great whiskey with faster maturation. But we had no choice."

Ralph, who is the marketing yin to Brian's engineering yang, has an innate instinct for knowing what will capture the public imagination. He describes the same urgency, but from an outward-looking perspective. "I knew that as soon as we finished the heavy lifting on getting the New York State distillery laws loosened up, the floodgates would open. New distilleries would be popping up all over the state, and that has happened as expected. We were excited about the opportunity we were opening up for other entrepreneurs like ourselves, but we didn't want to miss our moment in the process. I saw it as a once-in-a-lifetime opportunity to stake our permanent claim as the first legally distilled whiskey in New York State since Prohibition. I had no idea how we'd age whiskey faster, but we had to. Otherwise we'd be wasting a rare opportunity."

The small bottle strategy too had roots in pure practicality. Brian describes the thought process. "To be totally honest, we used small bottles initially because we just weren't making enough whiskey to fill a lot of big ones and get into broad distribution. When a retail customer wants a case, they want a dozen bottles. If we put a dozen big bottles in every case, we'd be in fewer stores. So we said okay, little bottles for now. Then we saw the value of that approach as a way to gate-crash a cluttered retail environment, get noticed a lot more quickly, and get more people to try our whiskey. So we stuck with it."

As for the varietal strategy, Ralph describes how it came about: "A few things converged here. Part of it was the way we see our role in the world. The whole point of craft spirits is exploration. The problem we were trying to solve was what exploration should mean in the very conservative world of whiskey. Historically, whiskey's been all about age and different points of origin. Our whiskeys weren't going to be old and were all coming from one place, so we had no choice but to think differently about variety, and were inspired by visits to grappa and cognac houses in Europe. They all had dozens of variants, yet no whiskey makers had gone there. The other spark was our commitment to local sourcing. From day one we wanted to help local farmers. So instead of picking a recipe and shopping all over the country for the cheapest place to buy the grains it called for, we started with a place—the farms in our area—and looked at what they had that we could work with. There were all these different types of grains and that sparked broader thinking. At some point those two themes converged. The best way to fulfill our exploratory mission and emphasize local sourcing was to look at a range of new combinations and permutations of locally available grains."

So what's the recipe for igniting innovations like this on the challenges you face? There are some themes here innovators everywhere can draw down on.

Beyond being an inspired, imaginative group with little industry knowledge and no vested interest in the way things had been done before, Ralph and Brian got to these innovations above all because they were, as a function of circumstances (tight cash flow, limited inventory, and lack of vintage stock) and their choices (embracing exploration, committing to local sourcing), working to solve a very different set of problems than everyone else in the whiskey business.

The answers were different because the set of problems was different.

As these innovations came into view one by one, there was excitement about the possibilities, but a general sense of a head nod that these were merely intelligent practical solutions to the problems at hand, rather than mind-blowing epiphanies.

Brian is emphatic on this. "Look, this isn't about lightning strikes. There's a problem in front of you. You're trying to figure out how to get from point A to point B in the fewest steps. The answer may be circuitous, but it's still A to B. With accelerated aging, we had a hunch early on that increasing the surface area of the barrel was the key. Okay, then what are the ways to do that? You could float extra staves in the barrel, or drill holes. Okay, drilling holes is more interesting because the different layers of the wood have different sugars in them from the charring process, so let's go that way. Okay, how can you drill as many holes as possible in a barrel stave without compromising the structural strength of the barrel? Well, ask the bees—a honeycomb structure optimizes surface area and strength. Okay, how to you make honeycomb-shaped holes in a barrel stave? Okay, the furniture industry in our barrel maker's region had collapsed, so we found computerized boring machines on the cheap. It's all nothing more than what I call farmer's logic. Each answer seemed obvious as it came along. Step by step, day by day you just keep moving forward."

That sensation of seeing the obvious for the first time would play out again in Tuthilltown's next foray.

Crunching through fresh snow on a bright February morning in 2012, Ralph and I wander the distillery grounds rounding up the crew—Brian, Ralph's son Gabe, Gabe's wife Cathy, and master distiller Joel Elder. We make our way to the living room of the old farmhouse next door, which doubles as a conference room. As they fire up the woodstove, our coats stay on as we start to talk in frosty breath about Tuthilltown's next innovation challenge.

With the Hudson Whiskey brand's success unfolding in market, the point of the February gathering isn't just a desire to do something new for its own sake, but once again to respond to a very pragmatic need. Brian frames the challenge: "Aged spirits like our whiskeys are beautiful to look at, beautiful to drink, and a beautiful business, but they guzzle cash. Even with our accelerated aging process, we have to feed success by laying down more and more inventory trying to anticipate the shape of the growth curve a year or two out. White spirits have their own fans, their own charms, and also a more charming cash flow picture. Since they're not aged, you can sell them the day you make them. If demand spikes, you can address it in real time. We have a vodka in the pipeline, but it's time to look at gin."

Every innovation challenge starts with some form of anchor. It may just be a number at the top of a blank page representing a growth target, or a piece of technology, or a brand with a well-defined equity, or maybe a category you want to enter, like gin. Whatever that anchor point may be, we ask ourselves a question at the outset: *is this a business in search of an idea, or an idea in search of a business?* A business in search of an idea is a case where there's a tangible, established pot of money you want to draw from and a pretty well-defined model for how the business can unlock it—but no clear path for how to create the demand you need to make that business happen. An idea in search of a business is just the opposite. Maybe there's a novel product taking shape, but no obvious product category, value proposition, operating model, or source of business from which that product will get its revenue.

Adding gin to Tuthilltown's portfolio was clearly a case of a business in search of an idea. They had the operational capability, route to market, and a clear source of revenue, as seen by the scores of gins that were out there already in the market. The missing piece was an idea capable of igniting demand.

With a bias toward action, within days of deciding they want to create and sell a gin, the Tuthilltown team begins researching and prototyping various botanical blends, and sketching out preliminary ideas for packaging and branding. Inspired by living in the Hudson Valley, they are again drawn to the history of explorer Henry Hudson, landing on "Half Moon," the name of the ship Hudson sailed up the river that now bears his name, as a working name for the gin. The clear liquid prototypes Joel serves up do not disappoint.

But as we talk about the opportunity ahead of us, we realize we're missing something important. We're working on exactly the same problems gin's incumbents have worked on—namely, what blend of botanicals to use, what to call it, and what the package should look like. Tuthilltown's successes in whiskey came about because they'd taken on different problems from the rest of the industry. We'll have to find and solve for a different set of problems around gin. We agree to cap the meeting there, and go off to think about what problems we should set out to solve.

We meet again the next week, this time at Fahrenheit, in our open-plan boardroom, a massive steel table parked in a wide-open part of the office, so the energy of project teams throughout the office animates the conversations in the conference space. The Tuthilltown guys and our strategists, idea developers, and designers share observations and insights that have bubbled up since we last met. We're looking to find a fresh set of problems to work against to inspire and guide the gin effort.

As we start riffing, a few different problems jump into view.

We start with consumer problems. For openers, gin is a pretty tough, angry drink, high in proof and dominated by a biting and often polarizing hit of juniper. A lot of consumers aspire to gin's sophistication, but find it's just too hard to drink. We pin down the functional problem the liquid will have to solve: we're out to make gin more accessible and pleasant on the palate.

Next, we shift our attention to the selling channels—the environments of the liquor store and the bar. Our designers, Faun Chapin and Meg Paradise, observe that if we look narrowly within the world of gin, we don't see any obvious problems to fix, other than the category feeling dated. But when we widen the aperture to look at gin relative to other categories, a big issue jumps into view. Gin fails what we call the ten-foot test. In the store or behind the bar, the other liquor categories have differentiation you can see from a distance. There's a clear color difference of liquids like dark rums and *añejo* tequilas versus their lighter rum and tequila cousins, a semiotic difference in the branding aesthetics of bourbon versus scotch, and clear differentiation across the flavor ranges of big vodka brands, which telegraph their taste cues. How to create a gin with differentiation you can spot from a distance was an important and valuable problem to take on. Gin fails the ten-foot test pretty miserably. Some bottles are prettier than others, but there is no way to tell what's different about one versus the next without tasting it. This problem has an expensive side effect bearing on the business plan: if people can't tell from ten feet away that our gin is clearly different, we'll be reliant on expensive sampling programs to create tasting trials. And that wasn't something we could afford on any meaningful scale.

The next problem we come onto is perhaps the most interesting: how to create a gin worthy of Tuthilltown's mission, values, and reputation. Tuthilltown's ambition to serve the exploratory needs of the craft spirit fan, its commitment to local sourcing, and its reputation for using spirit traditions not as shackles, but as springboards to new possibilities, give us additional problems to solve that, by their nature, will almost inevitably lead us to disruptive thinking.

The last problem we come to is about money. From a manufacturing standpoint, gin's cash flow demands are far less burdensome than aged whiskey's. But we don't have millions to invest in marketing. To be successful, we would again want to ignite the blogosphere and craft spirit press to spread the word for us. That kind of coverage has to be earned. Our gin would need a story worth writing about. The arrival of one more gin would not be news in its own right.

The array of problems is taking shape. In aggregate, there is a very Money & Magic mix of consumer issues and commercial issues to be solved:

Consumer Issues
- Gin is a tough, inaccessible drink.
- For the craft spirit explorer, botanical variations are all that the gin category offers—there is far less terrain to cover than other spirit categories present.

Business Issues
- A need to create concrete differentiation you can spot ten feet away in a store or bar
- How to give our commitment to local ingredients a meaningful role in a category that's just about botanicals
- How to make the innovation big enough for bloggers to write about
- How to deliver a gin innovation worthy of Tuthilltown's mission and reputation
- How to use gin's traditions not as a shackle, but as a springboard

Since the innovation ultimately has to solve all these problems, we bounce freely among them in an electric conversation that runs for hours, but feels like minutes. We're trying to build our gin idea at the intersection of consumer and business problems. The provocation posed by each problem causes a chain reaction in our thinking that spills into the other problems. Commercial considerations like how to create long-distance differentiation at the selling moment dovetail into discussions about the user experience and accessible drinkability. Talking about the different classifications of other spirits, like tequila's smoother *reposados* and *añejos*, leads us to ask whether we're out to create a new *classification* of gin rather than just a new product.

Ralph shares a little history. "You know, when we introduced Baby Bourbon, a lot of people immediately thought of Baby not as a new product, but as a new category of bourbon. Other microdistillers tried to use the term on products of their own. Let's aim high and create an idea that feels like a new category."

Marrying this up with drinkability, which any bartender will tell you is often synonymous with sweetness, Gabe throws out a big provocation—what if we create a new category called Sweet Gin? The energy in the room keeps building.

Ralph says that in sourcing locally, and being set in the heart of New York's biggest apple-growing region, we might end up using apples to create the neutral spirit base.

I often liken innovation to a weaving process: first finding the threads, then looping them around one another, then aligning them properly into durable, patterned fabric. The weaving has now begun. I ask Ralph whether he's aware of anyone having ever used apples to make gin's spirit base before. He says he's not sure, but that traditional gin-making methodology is to just use grain to make a tasteless neutral spirit base, then add the botanicals like juniper to give it flavor.

"There's something cool happening here. We've been talking for an hour about how to make a better gin, and botanicals have hardly come up. That's a sign that we're onto something. In trying to solve for a more drinkable experience, for our supply chain, and for what is worthy of Tuthilltown, we're talking about bringing innovation to the base spirit rather than just the botanicals you add to it. Gin's been around for four hundred years, but nobody's talking about it this way. By shifting the innovation spotlight to the base spirit, we're not just opening a new gin, we're opening a new door. It feels very Tuthilltown to do that."

We realize this is not just a product idea, but a platform idea—a construct capable of igniting multiple innovations over time. We give the strategic platform a name, *Open-Base Gin*, and start tossing out possibilities of what other things this might include beyond Sweet Gin (an idea we'd ultimately set aside after consumer research showed it to be a bit too feminine). Thinking about the local farmers in the supply chain inspires an array of ideas. Orchard Gin. Harvest Gin. Even an Autumn Gin, bringing in earthier flavor notes. We're not worried about what these things mean yet, but simply testing the platform to see if it has legs. And it does.

We then circle into the question of rules. For the platform to be coherent, strategically focused, and meaningful to consumers, bartenders, and retailers, we would need to define what the anchors would be that would govern both the lead product and those that might follow, and that would respect traditions enough to be authentic and in line with gin's standard of identity. We come up with a construct that the base spirit in anything we create will be distilled from a combination of a single identified grain plus a single fruit. We would experiment with various grains, but would use apples as the initial fruit, given their abundance in the region and their importance to the local farm economy. We would strive for the base to have very subtle back notes of grain and fruit, serving to create a smoother and mellower drinking gin.

Ralph throws out a hypothesis that would ultimately be borne out—that having a bit more nuance and complexity in the base spirit might allow a lighter use of botanicals, avoiding the overwhelming hit of juniper that makes many gins so polarizing. The inspiration of local grains and the local preponderance of apples might just be the springboard to the easier drinkability we're after in the product.

The last rule we land on consolidates the transformation. The dominant branding component in describing our gins would be the components in the base spirit, rather than the botanicals.

We feel like we're seeing the obvious for the first time. Here was a four-hundred-year-old category that had used one playbook—a tasteless grain-spirit base made interesting through botanicals. Opening up experimentation in the base spirit felt like something totally obvious that should have been done ages before. It was a brave new way to think about the category, yet once it was in sight, it just seemed like a head nod. That's the feeling you want every time.

Storytelling is a big part of turning strategy into demand. Over the next few days, the Fahrenheit team translates the series of leaps we made that afternoon into a strategic concept to guide the work ahead. It reads like this:

For all of gin's revered heritage, its greatest possibilities are untapped. Because it's been made one way for 400 years—taking a tasteless neutral grain spirit, and adding flavor through botanicals. Named for the ship Henry Hudson used to explore the river that now bears his name, Half Moon Gin has arrived to explore the other half of gin's creative potential—innovating not just in the time-tested way of varying the botanical infusions, but pushing further to explore the boundaries of the base spirit itself, letting the interplay of the base and the botanicals take the palate to delicious new destinations.

The result is not the gin world's usual pompous proclamation of the arrival of the definitive gin, but a varietal collection to be savored, explored, and extended over time. The journey begins with Half Moon Orchard Gin—with a base spirit made from

Hudson Valley wheat and apples, imparting subtle flavor notes and complexities that play beautifully off the botanicals for exceptionally smooth drinkability.

In parallel with the distillery team's experimentation with various bases and botanical infusions to get to our lead spirit, Faun and Meg get to work on turning the Half Moon concept into differentiated packaging to celebrate the "open base" approach, giving the ingredients in the base spirit a starring role. Trading in the category's vivid greens, reds, and blues for a distinctively earthy painted copper metallic color, it presents a modern take on the age-old ship in a bottle, playing on gin's nautical traditions and the explorer's ship from which Half Moon takes its name. And does this in a way that allows future concepts that take the base spirit in new directions to get the attention they deserve.

Half Moon went live just six months from that cold February morning. The market response has been amazing. Fascinated with the idea of innovating on the base spirit, bloggers started writing about it before the product even reached the shelves. Expectations were high. The idea is obvious. It's just four hundred years overdue.

Reflecting back on it, like Tuthilltown's other innovations, the making of Half Moon is a case of what happens when entrepreneurs come at a market powered by a different set of business and consumer problems than the incumbents have set out to solve.

The idea we created may seem disruptive to the incumbents, but it came about as a series of logical leaps from that unique set of problems that in aggregate defined both the task and the point of view we had to bring to solving it.

On whatever innovation challenge you're trying to crack, look for that distinctive set of problems that your competitors aren't working on. If you find and solve them, you'll be well on the way to differentiated innovation. Unique problem sets can't help but spawn unique answers. The odds are good that you, too, will soon experience the sort of calm excitement that comes with seeing the obvious for the first time. Know, too, that as you look for that unique set of problems to solve, thinking in a two-sided way will be immensely helpful to getting there. The problems your consumer faces are important, but they will tend to be known to all your competitors, so those alone won't get you to a unique problem set. But as you open that second aperture, combining a consumer perspective with the business lens and the unique constraints and challenges faced by your company, a more unique problem set emerges.

In many cases, you may find that the problems of your business are more unique than the problems of the consumer that you and your competitors are courting. Or, to push it a step further, the *combination* of the needs of the business and the needs of the consumer is more likely to result in a unique set of problems to be solved than the needs of the consumer can on their own. And that can lead to genuinely breakthrough ideas.

The experience of Fahrenheit 212 itself offers another illustration of how chasing a unique problem can be the genesis of disruptive ideas.

When we were founding our firm, every innovation practitioner we knew of was working on a common problem: *how to more effectively uncover consumer needs and use them to spark innovation ideas.*

We tasked ourselves with a very different problem: *how to transform the success rate of breakthrough innovations making it to market.*

The realization that ideas built unilaterally around consumer needs have a very high propensity to fail to make it to market came soon after.

The concept of Money & Magic—blending commercial and creative capabilities to solve for the needs of the business and the consumer—felt like a very obvious answer as it came into view.

As Brian would say, it's just farmer's logic. It just happened that this pretty obvious thing hadn't been done yet.

Chapter 8

The Question of Transformation

As Tuthilltown's experience shows, emerging companies often get to big innovations as a function of facing a different set of consumer and business problems than the incumbent players are facing. Ideas that seem so fresh and new through the eyes of established market leaders can seem like almost obvious answers to those emerging businesses, largely as a function of the hand they're playing.

Leaders of established businesses face a very different challenge.

They've earned leadership positions by mastering valuable aspects of their industry and serving up scaled answers to marketplace needs. They've got deeper pockets. And a deeper bench of talent and capabilities. They know a lot more about the ins and outs of the businesses they're in—sometimes too much. The hard thing for them is to see past what they know and do today to find new vectors of innovation to push their businesses further. Internally, they're fighting the gravitational pull of the proven models that got them where they are today, and externally, the tendency of competitive offerings to cluster together over time.

So how can established market leaders get to transformational answers that create competitive advantage?

They have to first come up with transformational questions.

Here's a case in point.

We get a call from one of the world's leading hotel companies, a multibillion-dollar business with a stable of world-class hotel brands and a strong innovation track record. They present us with an exciting though somewhat daunting challenge. They're out to reset the bar on what a loyalty program should be and do for their cream-of-the-crop customers.

Since the advent of the world's first frequent flyer program in the late seventies, loyalty programs have proliferated over the past four decades across everything from travel to banking to soft drinks to your neighborhood hardware store. And with good reason. The economics of getting the proverbial "one more purchase" from an existing customer are a lot sexier than the costly acquisition of new customers.

The hotel company's award-winning loyalty program acts as the commercial backbone uniting all their brands and properties in a single guest relationship. Spotting and solving guest pain points faster than rival programs, they have taken bold bets over the years on highly differentiated services and program features that put their program ahead of the competitive pack. But past successes do not a bright future make. The company's leaders have one eye on the road ahead, and one on the competitors chasing hard in the rearview mirror. The competitive gap has narrowed over time as other programs have copied their moves. The goal of the project ahead of us is to once again widen that competitive gap. In essence, the question we're out to answer is this: *What's the next unique perk we can offer our most valued guests?*

As we discuss the past, present, and future of loyalty programs, looking at it in a Money & Magic way from the perspectives of the consumer and the business, the head of the project team uses analogies to describe the situation. "From a business perspective, this is your classic arms race. Every move one player makes to sweeten the treatment of valued customers raises the cost of doing business for everyone else who wants to keep up. You want to put caviar on ice in every top-tier guest's room? You can, but it costs a lot to do that, both financially and operationally. And if guests like it, competitors follow, so at best you get a short-term win. From a consumer perspective, though, it's kind of like a government entitlement program. Once expectations of a certain benefit take hold, it's hard to ever take that benefit away. Our program is great for our guests and for our business, too. But if you don't change the game, at some point every arms race gets to a point of diminishing returns. You end up adding more cost without creating much new value for anyone involved. We need a new angle that's really meaningful for our guests, and that makes more sense for the business than a never-ending game of one-upmanship."

Obsessed with guest satisfaction and backed by very sophisticated data systems, the client team comes into the challenge armed with every data point you'd ever want to know about the ins and outs of the category's loyalty programs. They have ranking studies on potential new features guests might want in the future, segmentation studies providing insights into the behavioral economics of various types of guests, and payout analyses that show how investments that move loyalty metrics will lift company profits.

The bull's-eye target for the project would be the elite top 2 percent of their membership. These top-tier customers aren't a unique pocket of our client's customer base, but the universally coveted apple of the hospitality industry's eye. These are the hard-core road warriors with jobs and lifestyles that keep them in perpetual motion around the world. Spending more nights on the road than at home, they're relatively insensitive to price in deciding where to stay. They deliver big for their companies and have come to see perks from hospitality companies as a hard-earned part of their lifestyle, often as a reward for the families they spend so much time away from. Every travel and hospitality company has a piece of this audience's business and wants more.

As a natural side effect of a life of midnight room service and knowing desk staff by name, these travelers are rewards program black belts, knowing the ins and outs of each reward system, often using spreadsheets to track their points and miles across multiple programs. They plan their annual vacations entirely around when their status will peak and their rewards will have accrued. They choose flights and rooms with an eye on their status in each program, trying to optimize their way to maximum status in as many programs as possible. They know they're worth a lot to the hospitality companies, so they expect seamless service. They're quick to share any dissatisfaction with a staffer or property manager if there's a misfire, and to let all their friends know about it. Keeping these men and women happy is a delicate game of carefully managing expectations, aiming to perpetually overdeliver by just enough.

Out of the gate, that question governing the project seems pretty straightforward: *What's the next great perk to separate us from the pack?* There's just one problem. Every player in the hospitality business is chasing answers to that same question. That question is in fact the basis of the entire arms race. You put one chocolate on the pillow? Okay, we'll put three. And in the end, this isn't great for the guest, either. At a certain point, perks you don't actually want can feel wasteful or annoying, or make you feel the property doesn't understand what's important to you. There had to be a better way for everyone involved.

As our two-track discovery process unfolds, we see in the analytics a granular picture of why this market segment is so sought after. The top 2 percent of customers represent more than 20 percent of company profits, more than justifying additional investment in keeping them happy. There are surprises in the data as well, like an unexpectedly high turnover rate in the top tier. A big portion of this group disappears each year, not just backing off in frequency of visitation, but not returning at all. Given that our client's properties and their rewards program were both top-notch, this was a mystery to be further explored.

Equipped with these analytics showing us *what* consumers were doing and the economic impact of that behavior, we start talking to these road warriors to uncover *why*, and ultimately to find a transformational question to ignite big innovations.

A QUESTION OF COMPETITIVE ADVANTAGE

Why are we doing all this work to get to a question? Because we've found over time that the likelihood of an innovation project resulting in *transformational answers* pivots almost entirely on whether it uncovers *transformational questions.*

The real alchemy of transformational innovation isn't about the answers at all. The answers are the relatively easy part. The tough bit is what comes before: finding transformational questions.

A staggering amount of competitive advantage lies in the

definition of fundamentally new questions around which to engage the marketplace and mobilize your team's pursuit of breakthrough innovation.

I'm not talking about the familiar "what if . . ." questions—which are, in truth, just potential answers with question marks at the end. What we look for at Fahrenheit 212 is much more fundamental and strategic.

It's about framing high-altitude questions that pack a healthy disrespect for present reality, that dare to challenge the fundamental nature of the categories, businesses, behaviors, experiences, and companies around which we're asked to innovate.

In our experience, transformational questions have superhero-like powers. They materially change the conversation, both inside a company and with the customers it's out to serve. They challenge underlying assumptions that have come to be mistaken over time for immutable truths. And above all, these transformational questions spawn transformational answers—breakthrough innovations and the new competitive advantage that comes with them.

A QUESTION OF PERSPECTIVE

Assume you and your competitors are chasing the same consumers. Sensibly enough, at the outset of an innovation project, you round up a bunch of customers and observe what they like and love, dislike, and barely tolerate about their current experience. You tease out their pain points and unfulfilled aspirations and conjure sparkling new offerings that do away with the bad and usher in the good. Perhaps it works for a while. But eventually the thrill wears off.

Everyone in that space is rallying around the same questions and chasing ever more marginal improvements. You're left relying on fleeting advantages in technology or execution rather than sustainable, highly differentiated, and scalable strategic and conceptual market-making platforms. In the long run, the commonality of questions becomes strategic gravity, begetting narrowly clustered innovations across the competitive landscape.

Of course, finding new answers to age-old questions isn't a bad thing. You'll occasionally pluck low-hanging fruit that way, and that kind of innovation has an important role to play in a balanced innovation portfolio. But, as a general rule, a same-questions approach will tend to make future growth elusive, leading to margin erosion and sleepless nights for the company's leaders.

THE PROBLEM BEHIND THE PROBLEM

The way a transformational question changes the odds of getting to a big answer is that it shines a klieg light on something we call the problem behind the problem—not the surface-level challenge the project was initially chartered to solve but a big hairy thing lurking behind it in the shadows. More often than not, the surface problem is just a symptom of the bigger one.

For instance, a beverage company once engaged us around the question of how to reignite the interest of twenty-one-year-old guys in a once-hot category on the wane. The problem behind the problem was that the powerful underlying technology platform had been leveraged against only a narrow and fickle segment of society. Solving that bigger issue in the background by broadening the market, aiming new uses for the technology against other consumer segments, would open bigger growth opportunities and ensure that a similar problem wouldn't resurface in a few years when twenty-one-year-old tastes took their next inevitable U-turn.

Finding the problem behind the problem takes some practice, but solving it does two big things. Since the foreground issue is usually just a symptom, solving the problem behind it makes the smaller problem go away. And since the problem behind the problem is usually far bigger, its resolution opens bigger opportunities.

On the hotel loyalty project, our consumer explorations are

aimed at unearthing one of these transformational questions. As we try to do on most projects, we begin our explorations not by starting close in to the category in question, but further out, in something bigger, deeper, and more fundamental. Having recruited heavy travelers from that most loyal top tier of the client's customer base, we open a line of inquiry not about loyalty programs but about loyalty itself. The kind that ties people together not across transactions but across decades or lifetimes, good times and bad. Keeping the discussion open-ended, we let consumers guide us to pockets of life where loyalty manifests itself, probing how it comes about, what implicit rules govern the way it builds, and how it gets tested and strengthened over time. The discussion is rich and emotional. There's talk of loyalty to spouses and dear friends, the unconditional love we get from pets, even loyalty to a local dry cleaner or shoe repair guy.

Laying out loyalty's implicit rules, consumers describe a long-term, two-way, reciprocal relationship of give-and-take, where each party over time makes deposits in the relationship that deepen the ties. Loyalty, they say, is by definition unconditional. And it is about continually moving forward, rather than wavering. Some speak with a sense of loss about loyalty having meant more in the past than it does today, with companies and employees no longer showing the mutual loyalty they did generations ago.

After this foundational work, we gradually migrate into an area with which these consumers are intimately familiar—loyalty *programs*. They start pulling out their wallets and tossing down their program cards as if they're pocket aces in a poker game. There's obvious badge value in slapping down the gold and platinum. The guys with high status from multiple hotel programs make sure everyone notices. There's a bit of friendly gamesmanship, too. One multiplatinum guy pokes fun at another guy: "Oh, I didn't know they still came in gold."

After this bit of fun, the road warriors begin to showcase their ninja-like mastery of the ins and outs of travel industry loyalty programs. We notice a pronounced shift in body language between the discussions around human loyalty and loyalty programs. From a behavioral and financial standpoint, these are some of the most loyal members of travel company programs, yet there's a slightly edgy vibe in this line of discussion. After a while, we pin it down. It's something we hadn't expected at all: an undercurrent of disdain.

One forty-something sales exec goes on a tirade about airlines: "Look, at the end of the day, airlines use me and I use them. I steer my company's travel money their way. They give me miles so I can take my family somewhere nice. They want to get everything they can from me and I want to get everything I can get from them. That's just how the game works."

As the discussion gains steam, the fuzzy warmth of the way they talked about human loyalty is long gone. Another traveler chimes in. "Last year I got a pretty big promotion to regional manager. It was a big deal. So now I have staff making sales calls I used to make myself and I'm traveling less. The congratulations I got from the airlines and hotels for getting promoted was getting bounced out of platinum. It's all kind of *what have you done for me lately.*"

This "us versus them" picture is getting clearer. And with it comes a realization. We could potentially succeed at finding that new experiential perk that would reopen the competitive gap, yet fail to fix this somewhat adversarial current that seems so at odds with what loyalty means. Becoming just a better version of something these customers actively dislike is an uninspiring goal. It's time to aim higher.

But before we hunt for solutions, we need to figure out one more thing. Why are we seeing such high attrition at the top levels of the program? Why are top-tier members of the program suddenly dropping completely off the radar? Job changes like the scenario described by the sales manager may explain part of it, but we suspect there's more to it. We circle back to that de facto poker game at the outset, where they were proudly slapping down their upper-tier cards. We get them talking about their journey up through the levels, how it feels and what changes as they step up. These changes in status represent inflection points, and inflection points are always ripe with insight and opportunity for innovation.

Many of our road warriors have similar stories, where the climb didn't go in a straight line. It was almost always a few steps up and a few steps back. A flurry of travel earned them a taste of higher status one year, only to have them slip back down a level the following year. Only as they got deeper into their careers did they stay put in those higher tiers.

When we ask how they feel when they step up, everyone is excited. "I feel like I've won." How about the step down? Here, while some shrug it off as just part of the game, others describe feelings ranging from mild frustration to abandonment. "When you're moving up, you feel like a valued customer. But when you're moving down, it feels like you're being punished for bad behavior. Whether it was your fault or not."

The insights are starting to pile up like program points. But we still haven't explained the mysterious phenomenon of attrition at the top—why does a portion of the platinum-tier group disappear from the program each year? How, we ask, does it feel the first time you reach platinum? "Amazing, of course. It's the ultimate travel achievement," says one guy. "It's total victory." "It's like after all those years of stepping up and falling back, I've finally made it to the top of Everest." So what do you do next? While some people say what we hoped to hear—that they stay active in the program and be sure they keep that status—other answers are less expected. "Look, once I've made platinum, there's nowhere else to go. So I steer my travel people to book me with other airlines and hotels, so I can keep climbing in those programs."

The implication is huge. This mountain-climbing psychology had taken hold so thoroughly that what a lot of newly anointed platinum members were doing was akin to Sir Edmund Hillary's reaction upon reaching the top of Mount Everest. Moments after planting the New Zealand flag on the summit, he looked at the horizon, saw the unclimbed peak of K2 in the distance, and began pondering angles of ascent for that next challenge. For a slice of that top-tier group, reaching platinum status on one travel program had become a trigger to shift attention to other programs that were at lower levels. This explained why they were falling off the cliff.

As we regroup with the project team, we realize that, as is often the case, the noisiest finding in all the research lies not in what was said but in what wasn't. Here we were deep in research on loyalty programs with consumers who at least in financial terms are our most loyal customers, yet nothing in their descriptions of their feelings, decisions, and behavior had anything to do with real loyalty. What consumers were describing sounded more like a competition, based on a transactional arrangement of voluntary mutual exploitation.

Project lead Nithya George grabs the marker and heads to the whiteboard. She draws a big line down the middle of it and labels one side Human Loyalty and the other Loyalty Programs. We start listing the respective characteristics of each and suddenly realize how little either has to do with the other.

Human loyalty is unconditional. Loyalty programs are entirely conditional.

Human loyalty moves steadily forward. Loyalty programs kick you back to start over.

Human loyalty is a two-way give-and-take. Loyalty programs actually aren't reciprocal, they're sequential—they never give you anything until they've already received your business.

Human loyalty is measured over long terms and lifetimes. Loyalty programs are all calibrated around twelve-month time periods.

This time factor is especially interesting. We're always looking for that one degree of change that makes all the difference. I lob in an observation that if we changed nothing other than the time frame in which loyalty programs measure the worthiness of a guest for various tiers of membership, we would be well on the way to closing that gap between human loyalty and loyalty programs. Many companies in the customer relationship business focus on lifetime customer value, rather than annual value. The loyalty program paradigm had somewhat artbitrarily been set at twelve months by the pioneers of these programs, and everyone else had essentially followed suit.

Suddenly, the transformational question we've been after leaps into view. It's this:

How can our loyalty program work and feel more like human loyalty?

The juices are pumping now. As we migrate from our strategy phase into developing ideas and solutions, we won't be out to find the next great perk in the rewards arms race. We'll be aiming much higher, at solving the structural issues that had turned loyalty programs into a game of "you use me, so I use you back." Real loyalty would be about cultivating a reciprocal willingness to invest in each other over time.

As we start tossing ideas around that can answer this transformational question, we latch on to the tale of Sisyphus, the deceitful king in Greek mythology condemned to an eternity of pushing a boulder up a hill, only to have it roll back down. In trying to incentivize transactional loyalty by making annual nights the key metric for determining a member's status level, travel programs had institutionalized a punitive policy of knocking people back to the base of the mountain every year, effectively making them start pushing the boulder all over again. In doing so, they weren't necessarily punishing disloyalty but punishing infrequency. And over time, the fact that it was a climb and there was the risk of backsliding had subsumed any ability of these programs to embody or engender loyalty as people would define it.

Inspired by that simple transformational question of *how to make loyalty programs resemble the workings of human loyalty*, a transformational answer quickly came into view—a new program model for top-tier travelers built around a more human definition of loyalty. Launched in 2012 and tailored to those top-tier customers who have spent many years at gold or platinum, it throws out the "what have you done for me lately" dynamic that had over time become a defining and antagonistic characteristic of hospitality loyalty programs, and a source of the resentment we heard from the programs' best customers. It's the first hotel rewards program based around lifetime customer value. Throwing out the old twelve-month algorithms that determine status, this new approach works more like the way an old friend does, who will never forget that you showed up to help him move during that blizzard in '98. Unlike other hospitality programs, this new approach places high value on things you did years ago. The six nights you spent in one of our client's properties in Seoul in 2007 still count, and the hiatus you took when the baby came doesn't fling you back down to the bottom of the mountain. Hitting a certain number of lifetime nights earns you perpetual lifetime status in the top tier of the program. If a change of job or lifestyle means you aren't on the road as much as you used to be, the hotel company remains loyal to *you*, protecting your status and the privileges that come with it. Your privileges can still move forward—new benefits continue to open up over time as your lifetime visitation grows—but they never go backward. The significant emotional shift this represents was brilliantly brought to life by the client team in the way they communicated the launch of the new program to these valued guests. One collateral piece delivering the new card to a longtime Platinum member showed a map of the world with dots marking of the company's properties that specific member had checked into since joining the program. It brings to mind what loyal friends do when they get together. They don't just look at what's next, they look back over the good times they've shared. Loyalty suddenly didn't mean chasing the next transaction, it meant celebrating past, present, and future, a lifetime together.

It's a compelling answer, born of the power of transformational questions to raise the ante.

TO SAVE SAVING, QUESTION SPENDING

We got a call from a bank looking to frame an innovative new way to teach people to save more. Racking up savings deposits is a big win both for the bank on the receiving end and for consumers' hopes of a comfortable retirement. Based on prior research, the client team had concluded that the enemy was ignorance—consumers weren't saving enough because they didn't fully understand the consequences of not saving: namely, an inability to retire comfortably and retain their homes.

A quick glance around the bank category revealed no shortage of attempts at this same sort of thing—stacks of brochures, interactive tools, seminars, and even games. Clearly everyone in the category was having similar conversations with their customers, resulting in similar questions, and similar answers. The unthrilling truth was that better execution of the same type of answer was the best this project could hope for.

Enter the transformational question.

We kick-started our thought process by questioning the question—was *"How do we make financial education more palatable and effective"* the right thing to ask? Rather than begin in the narrow space of financial education and views on retirement, we started at a much higher altitude.

We asked everyone we knew—from the mailman to the pizza delivery boy to the stockbroker to the soccer mom—something far more fundamental: did they think they were saving as much as they should?

A funny thing happened. No matter whom we asked, whatever their social stratum or level of financial acumen, we couldn't find a single person who said yes. What this meant was that whether they were financial black belts or white belts, they all knew enough to want to save more. They just weren't getting there.

Then we asked them why they weren't saving more. Here the answers were vague, varied, delivered with little conviction, and tending toward post rationalization. In fact the loudest thing in the conversation was what wasn't being said at all. No one ever described having made a conscious decision *not* to save.

The big picture, and the transformational question, suddenly snapped into view.

In the go-go consumerism of the past few decades, saving had gradually been transformed from a conscious thing, to little more than a derivative consequence of dozens of decisions to spend. The problem behind the problem was that *saving competes with spending.* And it loses almost every time they go head-to-head.

As simple and obvious as this sounds, it's actually a profound statement that completely reframed the challenge and approach to this initiative. The shift from "how can we make financial education palatable?" to "how can we give saving a fighting chance against spending?" would change everything about our approach.

If you begin to look at spending as your archrival, you see the world differently. Do a classic Strengths/Weaknesses/Opportunities/Threats (or SWOT) analysis on saving versus spending and you see that saving is brutally disadvantaged. Spending is impulsive, hedonistic, emotional, instantly gratifying, fun, rewarding to the senses, and irrationally layered with feelings of freedom, power, and self-reward. Saving, on the other hand, is premeditated, rational, moralistic, and synonymous with saying no.

Rituals are fundamental to any battle between conflicting behaviors, and they're a big deal in this one. One thing that has helped shift the competitive balance in spending's favor is that saving has lost its anchoring ritual. In the days before automatic paycheck deposits, there was a moment every two weeks when you walked into the branch, handed over your check, and told the teller how much to put in savings and how much in checking to cover your expenses. You took the cash you needed for the week and parked the rest. That ritual has evaporated. We no longer have that pivotal moment where the question of how much should I save is thrust upon us in real time. Spending, meanwhile, has acquired new rituals. Years ago, when the stores were closed or you didn't feel like going out, you couldn't spend much from the comfort of your couch. Online shopping is a new ritual. Along with the late-night ATM stop. Advantage: spending.

The transformational question, "How can we make saving compete more effectively with spending?" can only be answered through transformation. Not a me-too attempt to educate, but a disruptive new model for capturing savings deposits. The innovations in development here set out imbue saving with the new dimensions of hedonism, impulsiveness, and immediate gratification, things it needs to make meaningful inroads in day-to-day life in a pleasure-seeking society.

THE WRITING ON THE WALL

One more example of the power of transformational questions comes from another of our many successful Samsung projects. We'd been working on ways that Samsung might more deeply penetrate two multibillion-dollar markets: the trade shows & exhibitions market, and the market for the design of retail environments. Companies big and small spend a fortune each year trying to present themselves and their products in an impressive way at massive conventions and industrial shows all over the world. Similarly, retailers spend billions each year upgrading their store environments, trying to make them dynamic, fresh, and vibrant. In both of these markets, large-scale multi-screen video walls were an attractive option. This can be a great opportunity if you're the world's leading maker of the screen components those video walls rely on, as Samsung is. The question on the table is how to innovate to make those video walls more common in trade shows and retail spaces.

We start work by asking ourselves how we could make retail and exhibit designers more excited about the benefits that high-impact video displays could deliver to their clients. This wasn't wrong, but it was reasonable to assume that all of Samsung's competitors were asking the same question, trying to sell the benefits of video walls, and trying to compete on price. To open a new high-margin business, we would need a unique approach.

One day as a few of us are heading out to grab lunch, we ponder New York's skyscrapers and begin thinking about the structural properties of glass. Around us are all these big glass towers. The glass isn't holding them up, of course, but many of them look that way. We get to thinking not about the benefits of video walls, but about construction methods and the structural properties of glass. In a fish tank, glass and a simple frame provide enough structural strength to make a wall. We start thinking about how the process of creating a video wall works today. First an architect or designer has to determine the size and placement of the wall. That takes time and money. Then carpenters are hired to frame it, incurring cost for labor and materials. Electricians and video technicians have to run cabling inside the frame, with yet another set of time constraints and costs. After the wiring is run through the wall studs, the carpenters come back to apply wallboard. Next come the painters to tape, spackle, and paint the wall. Only after all this time and cost is incurred does this wall even begin to become a video wall. The video technicians hang the screens in position, connect them all to power supplies and data input cables and the content source. This process takes days if the various contractors are all in sync and on site, or weeks if they're not. Specialists come and go in a sequence of steps, requiring considerable oversight, and costing thousands of dollars.

Once it's up and running it's great for as long as it's needed. In a retail store, that wall might be used for a year or more. But in the case of a trade show, that structural wall is only used for a few days, then it's dismantled and trashed.

Which brought us to a transformational question:

If glass has structural properties, and creating a supporting wall is such a time-consuming, expensive hassle, why does a video wall need a wall at all?

This question inspired a transformational answer called Samsung ID. Short for Interlocking Displays, Samsung ID is a Lego-like system of screens that allows two people to snap together a fully operable, structurally self-sufficient, large-scale multi-screen video wall in about thirty minutes. An ingenious 3-in-1 connection point that links the screens provides structural integrity, power, and content connections. The design allows the screens to pivot into different configurations, even creating freestanding multisided rounded video towers. By removing the need for the wall to be designed, framed, wired, taped, and painted, it cuts weeks of time and thousands of dollars in costs out of video wall applications. Bundled with a piece of content management software that automatically detects the position of each screen, it makes it easy to plan and deliver a content matrix across the wall, and reduces the need for expert video support.

And since the wall can be taken apart as quickly and easily as it's put together, it can be removed for storage and reuse, or, in the case of retail applications, shifted to a new application in a different part of the store, in just a matter of minutes. This also means all the timber, wallboard, nails, paint, and wiring that a typical video wall would have included don't get dumped into landfills.

By deciding to compete with the cost, time, hassle, and inflexibility of the construction process, rather than with component price or screen specifications, Samsung ID created a whole new innovation vector and a new high-margin business that the competition couldn't match. That's what transformational questions can do. Samsung ID made it to market in less than eighteen months, bringing new nimbleness, creative possibilities, affordability, and efficiency to the way video walls are designed and implemented.

One of Fahrenheit's teams went up to Cambridge, Massachusetts, recently to meet with some folks from the MIT Media Lab to talk about a project. They asked us to present a few case studies of our work just to get the flow of ideas started. When our team asked where we could plug in, the MIT team led the way down the hall and pointed at their Samsung ID system. Fahrenheit 212's team leader said, "Well, we won't have to show you that case study." It turned out that the ID system was one of the MIT team's favorite things in the lab, and that they use it all the time. When we came up with the idea, we hadn't thought about how bringing new nimbleness to video walls would create value in additional markets like academia. But that is the power of transformational thinking—it can open opportunities far beyond the things you have in your sights.

HOW TO GET TO TRANSFORMATIONAL QUESTIONS, AND THE BIGGER ANSWERS THEY OPEN UP

While the transformational questions that unlock transformational answers on your innovation initiatives will be specific to the category and task at hand, here are some principles that can guide you in finding them.

1. Assume transformation is necessary.
The only way to get to transformational questions is to purposefully chase them, and this starts with assuming that transformation is necessary, rather than an option. Assuming transformation is necessary changes the conversation in the team from "should we transform something?" to "what will we transform?"

2. Cultivate a healthy disrespect for present reality.

Consciously try to identify things in your category, consumer experience, products, and business that just are the way they are, without needing to really be that way. In most businesses, you'll find a long list of them, with transformational questions hidden inside. In an age of personalization, when there is such tremendous breadth in consumers' financial means and trajectories, why do most fixed mortgages come in only fifteen- and thirty-year increments? When just a small segment of the population finds full-strength spirits palatable, why is 98 percent of the category sold in a way that's stronger than consumers can handle?

3. Temporarily forget what you know.

Knowledge is a potent form of competitive advantage. But there is often a razor-thin line between a knowledge base and the entrenched paradigms that have been attached to it over time and permeated innovation in your category. Knowledge is power in certain moments in the journey, but kryptonite in others if not properly harnessed.

4. Ask yourself how likely it is that your competitors aren't working on the same questions you are.

Picture yourself right now sitting in the room with a project team at your key competitor's office. Would they be working around similar questions? If so, you probably haven't cracked the transformational questions you'll need to get to transformational answers. The point is not to second-guess what your rivals are up to, but simply to gauge your own conviction that you've uncovered transformational questions. Big thinkers find big questions exciting. So if you don't viscerally feel that you've broken new ground, you probably haven't.

5. Move the camera around the room.

Finding big transformational questions usually happens by distancing ourselves from the prevailing category context we live in every day and approaching it from a fresh angle. This doesn't just work metaphorically; it works literally, too. Looking at your ice cream business not through the eyes of the consumer, but from the perspective of the ice cream behind the frosted freezer glass watching consumers go by (like an orphan hoping for adoption), may open a powerful new set of questions to ignite transformational innovation. If that doesn't work, deconstruct the life cycle of an ice crystal born in the churn at the factory, or ask what the spoon would say as it's bent in the act of scooping.

6. Learn to hear the thundering sound of the thing that isn't being said.

Paradigm-creep isn't just a company phenomenon. It happens to consumers, too. They often become so accustomed to embedded characteristics and compromises that they don't even think or talk about them. (When was the last time you got to work and said "Boy, how about that gravity today?") A great innovator needs to ask at every touch point—what *didn't* we hear that was interesting? We didn't hear a single person say they had consciously decided *not* to save. We didn't hear a single hint of loyalty in a conversation about loyalty programs. In the pursuit of transformational questions, the unsaid is often the most telling.

Chapter 9

Lessons from the Spatula

The power of a great transformational question is that it sets you in motion down a road less traveled by your competitive set, upping the odds of landing on truly transformational answers. Sometimes those transformational answers take a particular form that in our practice we call a strategic *inversion*. But they more often go by a more casual nickname: a spatula job.

Avis shelling out a cool $500 million to buy Zipcar isn't just the latest example of a big company getting a wake-up call from visionary upstarts, then writing big checks to buy the innovation they need. ZipCar's success is also an illustrative case study in this particular innovation approach that's worth pursuing in whatever business you're trying to grow.

What we call an inversion is an innovation that takes the most glaring flaw or weakness in a company or category's established paradigm and flips it on its head, creating a breakthrough new competitive advantage, business model, or innovation platform. Coming at it through the Money & Magic two-sided framework, an inversion can be a flip on a key aspect of your category's consumer value proposition, or its business model, or even both in one bold move.

In Zipcar's case, the inversion went like this. Barring the occasional dirty ashtray, the defining negative characteristic in the consumer's age-old rental car experience had nothing to do with the car or the trip you needed it for. It was the trip to get the car. For the urban consumer, renting a car was the trip before the trip. It required premeditation, a potentially expensive cab ride, and either lugging your luggage to the rental office or looping back home and dodging the meter patrol long enough to load and go.

And embedded in that consumer pain point of the trip to the rental office was a big commercial pain point of the rental car business—the capital- and labor-intensive model of having big rental car lots, often in pricey real estate in prime neighborhoods, staffed with sizable teams that spent all day shuttling cars around as customers picked them up and dropped them off.

Insert spatula, roll wrist, and flip.

The inversion Zipcar pulled off is beautiful. Where incumbents in the category have focused on iterative improvements to make the trip to the rental office slightly less painful, Zipcar did away with the pre-trip trip altogether. Wrap it in a membership fee business model and fractional pricing where you can rent for a few hours rather than an arbitrary full day, and you've got a superior new paradigm that makes you wonder how we ever put up with the old one for so long.

This move not only created differentiation, it also allowed new category-building consumer behavior to come into play. Instead of a purely premeditated behavior (popping by the rental office without calling to check availability was always a risky bet), grabbing a car could now happen on impulse. Fractional pricing meant that those quick-dash occasions that never seemed worth a full-day rental suddenly came into play to grow the category. And the prospect of paying membership fees for the privilege of accessing a rental instantly went from inconceivable to downright attractive.

The flip also extended to that commercial pain point—the cost of real estate and significant staff at each location. Replacing those costs with a bit of technology was a big economic win, and arguably the only way a new entrant could step into the mature car rental category against incumbents who had already locked up the most desirable urban locations.

Consumer and commercial pain points, inverted in one smooth move.

O_5H (WATER INVERTED)

While health trends have poured healthy growth rates into the water business for some time, water long had an Achilles' heel relative to the other beverage categories with which it competes: it was a deadly boring one-trick pony.

Water had but two tangible levers of differentiation—proprietary source and packaging.

The inversion Vitamin Water pulled off was nothing short of spectacular. It's as if they said, "Okay, water's weakness as a beverage experience is that it's so basic. So let's *use it as a base*."

Turning this weakness into a strength, parent company Glacéau recast water as a carrier for a dynamic, delightful, ever-expanding array of tasty, colorful, functional modern beverage experiences. Along the way, they were able to implicitly say provenance doesn't matter. No one knows or cares where Vitamin Water comes from, so they can theoretically make it anywhere, which sure beats the business model—and the brutal carbon footprint—of shipping water in from Fiji. Fortifying water broke open new price points. And left room to react to flavor and health trends in a way no brand in any other beverage category can. When an ingredient like coconut water pops, Vitamin Water can pounce on it, and move on from it when the consumer decides it's time.

In the end, what came of it was not just a more dynamic and interesting water, but arguably the single most dynamic and interesting brand in the entire beverage business today. Which is why Coke bought the franchise and made it part of their beverage portfolio.

PUTTING THE SHOE ON THE OTHER FOOT

Through the early years of online shopping, there was a prevalent belief that some categories would face tough sledding in trying to lure consumers from brick-and-mortar shopping to digital. Apparel was seen as one of the tricky ones, as it didn't fit the "look don't touch" nature of online buying.

Worse yet, the ill-fitting shoe is apparel's ultimate torture test—enough in the conventional wisdom to frustrate consumers and investors alike, with return costs putting an uncomfortable pinch on the P&L.

Online shoe company Zappos is another company that pulled off an immaculate inversion. Zappos turned returns from a pain point to the whole point. Something not to mitigate, but to embrace, invite, and celebrate. And a funny thing happened. A lot of consumers came to realize that choosing from an amazingly broad selection online, getting a good price, trying them on at home, and returning a pair or two was in many ways a less painful experience than the prevailing retail paradigm—driving to the mall, wading through a crowd, standing in a shop, waiting for surly help, hoping they have your size, waiting to find out, and being disappointed when they don't.

In the end, the question of fit didn't give anyone fits—barring of course the brick-and-mortar folks.

Here are a few other examples of strategic inversions.

In Europe, we helped Pringles get a nice growth spike out of an initiative that turned a weakness into a strength. Pringles chips had long been maligned by their competitors for being made from extruded potato dough rather than sliced potatoes. Armed with a new technology that leveraged rice's unique ability to absorb lip-smacking flavors that sliced potatoes can't, Pringles unleashed an innovation called Rice Infusions, which made its cooked-in-flavor in the dough a point of superiority. It made powder-based potato chip flavors a lot less appealing by comparison. Do you want flavor that's cooked in, or just dust that's sprinkled on?

Last, we can't help but give a nod to the inversion Apple pulled off. Forgotten in the parade of stunning successes that commenced with Steve Jobs's second coming at Apple is the string of failures and near bankruptcy of the prior decade, both of which were largely attributable to Apple's greatest weakness as a computer company—a staunch insistence that they maintain 100 percent control over every aspect of both the hardware and software.

In the computer business, that was looking like a near-fatal flaw, as it gave them an untenable cost structure, sluggishness in responding to leaps in technology, and troubled relationships with retailers and developers.

The inversion came about when they set their sights on markets beyond computers through their digital hub strategy, where the integration they had long obsessed over could create a great deal of new value. Where controlling both the hardware and software was in many ways a flaw for a computer company, it was a killer app when igniting seamless, category-defining, new-to-the-world user experiences in new markets like music players, smartphones, and tablets, and integrating those experiences around the hub a computer could be.

The lesson here is that if you look at them in the right way, the experience gaps and competitive *disadvantages* you seem to be facing can be as fertile ground for breakthrough innovation as playing off your strengths.

So grab the spatula, roll that wrist, and flip, and watch big new possibilities come into view.

Here are some ways to help bring the power of inversions to your innovation efforts:

1. Aim beyond small improvements in your strengths. The best you can hope for from that breed of innovations is a marginally happier customer. That's not a bad thing, but if you pull off an inversion, you'll create a bigger leap in differentiation and market power.

2. Be willing to have your future compete with your present. There's no reason why a breakthrough in online shoe retail couldn't have come from a big incumbent selling shoes in brick and mortar. Unless, of course, they were so fearful of cannibalization that inertia set in, letting disruption come at them, instead of from them. It's smart to think about cannibalization, of course, but not to be paralyzed by it.

3. Hunt for late-mover advantage, even if you're the incumbent. Ask yourself and your innovation team that classic question—if we were starting this business today, would it look anything like the way it looks now? The answer, particularly in this amazingly dynamic age where possibilities

and experiences are being rapidly transformed by emerging technologies, is probably no.

4. Remember that the big flip never happens by accident . . . you have to actively look for it. As I mentioned earlier, one of the most important ingredients in creating transformation is an ongoing belief that transformation is necessary.

5. With all due respect to the importance of core competencies, don't neglect the potency of core incompetencies. Any scaled business will instinctively steer the lion's share of its innovation resources and energies toward its areas of strength. But if you don't occasionally let the things you're awful at ignite fresh ways of thinking, you're missing a trick.

6. Remember that the opportunities you're after are probably hidden in plain sight. The hassles of brick-and-mortar shoe shopping, the blandness of water, and the pain points of the trip to the urban rental car office had been there all along. Your business probably has an equally obvious set of these things that are ripe for the spatula. While many innovations are born of digging deeper and deeper beneath the surface, we often find that great inversions come about by deciding not to dig at all—just taking on things that have been right there on the surface all along. Water's basic nature wasn't an epiphany. It was so fundamental and ubiquitously known that incumbent water companies hadn't paused to think of it as a source of possibility.

Chapter 10

Bend, Don't Break

Charles and Ray Eames's molded plywood chairs aren't just iconic designs. They're four-legged parables. Inspiring studies in pliability and persistence. Lessons in how hard it can be to build new manufacturing capabilities to drive an idea to fruition. And proof of the value of looking at the capabilities you already have in fresh new ways.

Between the Eameses' brilliant design concept and its realization lay a big manufacturing challenge: how to take plywood—long synonymous with hard lines, straight cuts, and boxy figures—and bend it into 3-D organic shapes that cradle the contours of the human body.

The lines of the plywood collection are so graceful that your eye curls into them as comfortably as the rest of your body. But behind those fluid shapes was a jagged journey. Six years of fits and starts, highs and lows, trials and tribulations.

The design required bending plywood in pretty extreme ways that neither the Eameses nor anyone else really knew how to do. Figuring it out required bending a law or two. Not just laws about the tensile nature of wood fibers, but also the statutory variety, climbing power poles to tap into additional electricity as their initial wood-warping machines blew fuse after fuse. The Eameses endured the literal snap of repeated setbacks. The early versions were so prone to breakage that they had to be upholstered to cover up the cracks that quickly appeared. The partnership behind the project broke, too; architect Eero Saarinen, a partner in the collection's conception and development, quit the project out of frustration as the production problems dragged on. The chairs that *Time* magazine would five decades later dub "The Design of the Century" came perilously close to not happening at all.

Serendipity intervened. What allowed the bending of plywood to become a robust, scalable manufacturing process was not the tireless pursuit of a visionary furniture concept, but the mounting toll of World War II. Aware of the Eameses' experiments at shaping plywood, the U.S. military placed a big order for molded plywood splints for injured troops. It was the War Department's urgency, cash, and facilities that accelerated the development of scalable methods for bending plywood. The chair project that limped along for years would ultimately owe its fruition not to its triumphant aesthetic, but to the intervention of wartime necessity and lucky timing.

As the capability became a real thing, with evident limitations, the Eameses abandoned their initial vision of making a contoured chair from a single piece of bent plywood, resorting instead to multipiece designs with less acute curves, and rubber-ringed fasteners to add flex to the sitting experience that they couldn't get from the plywood alone. In essence, they were bending their product designs and manufacturing methods to fit one another. Only by doing that could they make the chairs that would make history.

If the questions Charles and Ray Eames faced seven decades ago were how to bend plywood, and how to sustain momentum in the slow and painful process of creating a capability that doesn't exist, what's the here-and-now moral equivalent for today's innovators? We'd frame it this way: it's how to bend the capabilities of your company without breaking them.

In the chapter "The Stretch Factor," we took a high-level view of how to disrupt demand in the marketplace without unduly disrupting the strategies, operations, finances, and assets of a business. Finding the point where capabilities and assets bend but don't break is a key subset of this. But it's easier said than done, so it merits a closer look.

Beyond their elegant products, the Eameses also left a legacy of elegant thinking that's helpful here. The Zen-like line *"The details aren't the details, they make the design"* has inspired generations of designers to go deep into the most granular aspects of a product or experience. But through an innovation lens, there's a powerful double meaning here. On one level, of course, *the details make the design* means they make the product compelling. It's not just the devil that's in the details; the angels are there, too. But there's a second meaning not to be missed. Seemingly insignificant details of the inner workings of manufacturing methods, company capabilities, and assets have the ability to make all the difference to whether your big idea gets made and launched, or relegated to innovation purgatory—that domain of interesting ideas, fantasies, and unicorns destined to never see the light of day.

THE I'S HAVE IT

Before diving deep into the fine art of bending capabilities without breaking them, it's important to grasp *why* leveraging existing capabilities is fundamentally important.

At the core it's pretty simple. Whether you're a one-woman startup, an innovation leader in a huge company, or a VC angel, any attempt at innovation is a form of investment. You're pouring in something highly valuable—your inspiration, your sweat, your passion, your time, your tenacity, and somebody's money (your company's, your own, or your investors'). Presumably you're doing all this in pursuit of some form of meaningful outcome; you want a worthwhile return on your investment. ROI can mean different things to different people. Economic yield relative to other things you might have done with the resources you sank in. Or if your motivation is more about the emotional gratification of seeing your idea come to fruition and make a difference, we might call it Return on Imagination. But you want impact.

In pursuit of whatever ROI means to you, scribble this on your innovation wall: *a capability in hand is worth ten in the bush.*

What this means is that the odds of obtaining impact for effort are vastly greater if you set out to bend and cleverly reapply *existing* operational capabilities—yours, your company's, or your suppliers'—than if you operate far outside of them.

The world undoubtedly needs more Eameses with that tireless persistence to spend years toiling away to solve a production challenge. And to be sure, many of Apple's successes lay in the way they pushed the limits of what their suppliers knew how to do, developing new production methods, ever-smaller components, and new standards of fit and finish. But conceiving an innovation that's predicated on the arrival of a capability that's not readily accessible dramatically ups the odds that it won't see the light of day. Not, at least, without some form of serendipity or a uniquely deep-pocketed and patient project sponsor who isn't counting on your project to keep the company afloat (aka Google).

If, like most innovation teams, you have finite resources and pressing timelines, experience says that a capability in hand is everything.

Finding valuable ways to bend existing assets and capabilities requires both intent and intensity. Fahrenheit partner Marcus Oliver has made it something of a personal mission to unlock the potential in this way of thinking as we try to build big ideas that work and deliver great ROI. A natural-born spotter of patterns, he traces his fascination with flexing capabilities back to a very accidental discovery on visits to the factory floor. It would prove to be another of those insights hidden in plain sight. He describes how these insights surfaced:

"To understand what we have to work with, we always try to make a factory tour part of the onboarding process on a new project, as anyone in innovation would or should. We found ourselves doing that one morning, looking sharp in white coats, yellow hard hats, steel-toed boots, and protective goggles, going machine by machine along a food company's production line. I've loved machinery since I was a kid and still get a thrill every time I see a production line. We're learning how the systems work and having fun doing it, and I'm asking goofy questions like 'Hey, that machine over there that looks like a pregnant aluminum octopus ... what does it do?' Our host laughs and has an answer at the ready, something like 'Oh, that's a re-thermalizer that gets our cold-stored fresh ingredients to the same temperature as the ambient ones, so everything cooks at the same speed and comes out crisp and tasty.

"The interesting bit is what happens next. I innocently ask her, 'What else *could* that machine do?' She seems surprised and sort of blushes. She thinks for a bit and says, 'You know, I've been showing people around this factory for years, company execs, new marketing people, suppliers, even innovation teams like yours, but no one ever asked me that. Let me ask Bob, maybe he knows.'"

Marcus goes on: "I don't think much of it at the time, but on our next factory tour, this time for a technology company, there's a similar thread—asking what various pieces of equipment do, getting solid answers, then asking what else they *could* do, and again hearing 'Wow, no one ever asked me that.' On the flight home that night it struck me that these innocent Q&As might be deeply meaningful. Maybe it's just that those of us in innovation are suckers for hearing 'no one has ever' at the beginning of a sentence. But I had a feeling that we'd stumbled onto an underutilized lever capable of meaningfully lifting innovation project success rates."

Nudged along by curiosity, and wanting to figure out how to put this realization to work, what Marcus did next was ladder up these very specific moments on the factory floor to the broader constructs of the innovation process.

Part of the realization was that across companies and industries, there's a widespread tendency in current innovation processes that holds success rates down: innovation teams paying too little attention to, or even outright ignoring, the latent flexibility of their asset base.

How does it hold hit rates down? It increases the odds of innovations that require lengthy R&D explorations of new capability, new capital equipment, or new manufacturing methods to be executed, which increases the time and investment required to get innovations to market and puts downward pressure on ROI. If there is any certainty in this capricious pursuit we call innovation, it's that the lower the projected ROI, the higher the odds of the project dying off with no products reaching market.

What is important to keep in mind is that these innovations that require new capability aren't necessarily being put forward because they're bigger opportunities than things that could have been born of flexing existing capability; rather, they're put forward because they happen to be the ideas that surfaced from a conventional method. The opportunities that could be created by flexing existing capabilities have been given little attention. A healthy business moves forward, of course, leaping to new capabilities over time to deliver new value to the marketplace. Big ideas shouldn't be rejected because they require new capabilities. They need an objective assessment of their long-term ROI. But a gold miner doesn't dig a new hole every time he needs more gold. He mines the holes he's already put in the ground for all they're worth. Interestingly, making the case to management for why your company should add a new capability nearly always involves taking a long-term look at the flexibility that new capability will have. Ideally you should be able to say it's not just about delivering this idea we have in hand, but it will open up all kinds of follow-on opportunities over time. Yet that orientation is too rarely applied retroactively to existing capability.

Another interesting realization that surfaced here was the way the talents and imagination of R&D and operations people are often underleveraged. Innovation used to be synonymous with R&D, focused on technical product improvements. Marketing gradually stepped up to a bigger role in driving innovation to a more consumer-centric orientation. User-centered innovation models in turn taught us to obsess over the new value we're out to create for consumers, and worry later about the means of getting products made. An unexpected side effect of this is that in many organizations, we see talented, imaginative R&D and operations people too often asked just three questions: can you execute this idea consumers are excited about? if so, how quickly? and with how much capital required to pull it off? We find that R&D's greatest value in the pursuit of big, fast, doable innovations is at the front of the process, helping us do what the Eameses ultimately did to get their amazing innovation to market: bending the idea and the capabilities to fit one another. The earlier they're involved, the softer the clay is at the point when they're unleashed, and the more they come to the table understanding not just what existing capabilities do today, but other things those capabilities *could* do, the higher the odds of a project landing on something big/fast/doable. We often end up pursuing ideas that do require new capability, but consciously rather than randomly, out of conviction that these capability-pushing ideas are worth the trouble and worth more money than the ideas we found by bending capabilities in hand.

As Marcus pursued his curiosity about the role that flexing capabilities could play in driving up the odds of innovation projects landing on successful outcomes, he came to an important realization: "Applying creativity to existing capabilities is a capability in its own right. Perhaps ironically, to show companies how to flex their existing capabilities, we would have to build this new capability ourselves. We weren't aware of anyone having written about it, codified ways of going about it, or teaching it." To fill that gap, Marcus used every project Fahrenheit touched for the next few years to get to the principles and methods that would make this capability a piece of intellectual property and a killer app for Fahrenheit for years to come, and a big source of value to our clients.

He harvested learning and distilled it into a training program and insight bank called *The Factory Factor: The Art of Flexing Capabilities.*

Here are some of its key tenets.

1. Expose the raw competencies.

The first step in flexing capabilities is to go beneath the surface to tease out the deepest, simplest definition of a business's underlying strengths, know-how, equipment, technologies, or all of the above. Part of the thought process here is uncoupling capabilities from the lines of business they're applied to today.

In the Eames case, the pivotal moment in making the chair

possible was the military looking at the Eameses' emerging capability in a broader way—not as a way of making chairs, but for designing molded plywood products. They flexed that capability to make splints.

Similarly, in our work with a leading diet company, we unlocked a big new opportunity by realizing the value of a competency they had in sorting and boxing a complex array of items in their warehouse.

2. Look for the transformational points of impact in production.

It's helpful to think of every step of the innovation process as a hunt for that one degree of difference that makes all the difference. Dell's march to becoming a multibillion-dollar business can largely be traced back to one basic change in the business system: selling the computer before they made it. That one change allowed personalization, a better cost structure, better margins, and a level of nimbleness that took competitors fifteen years to replicate.

Marcus's advice to new Fahrenheit hires on how to scour capabilities for flexibility is this. "Ninety-five percent of the production line in most mature production facilities either can't realistically be changed, or is capable of causing very little variation in the finished products coming off the back end even if you did change it. But there's usually that golden, pliable five percent of the business system that's not only capable of being modified, but capable of unleashing big new things when you play with it. As you look under the hood of the business, understand what those catalytic flex points in the production line or in the service chain are, and aren't. Find the magic spot where changing the input in a tiny way can create a big difference in the outcome." Go into the front end of a project asking, where is there flexibility? Is the diameter of a product running down the line the fixed thing, or the height, or neither? What are the tolerances? What ingredients, components, materials, actions, and interactions can you add, substitute, or remove and what possibilities open up when you do? Go in assuming it will take digging to find these flex points, but know that there's treasure there when you do."

While we call this body of knowledge the Factory Factor, the same principles apply to service systems. Certain core functions need to be delivered that can be hard to transform. Changing a POS system, for instance, can be a scary undertaking for a mature retail business where that system is integrated all the way back to finance and procurement. But look at it hard, consciously hunting for that pliable 5 percent. It's probably there.

3. Don't just look at mechanical capability; look at the human and strategic assets, too.

A common mistake for teams tasked with creating ideas is to equate assets and capabilities with just plants, machines, and business systems. Mine the human capability, too. For starters, the knowledge base of the people behind the processes, within the plant, or across the company.

Veteran staffers in R&D or operations have vast experience they're rarely asked about. They know about stuff beyond what's in the building. They remember other methods of production, other machines, and other types of outputs that aren't in the mix today, but could be re-created if they align with a here-and-now market need. The number of times a big company builds a capability to serve a specific idea, finds that the idea doesn't work, then mothballs or divests that capability is pretty high. But often the knowledge of that experience hasn't left the building. You just need to dig for it.

Understand the backgrounds of the people in the factories and R&D as deeply as you understand the machines. They often have a wealth of information and experience that can help with the inevitable problem.

Have a coffee with the guy on the floor before you start creating ideas.

And don't just ask him what the facility in question could be doing that it doesn't do today; ask him what's under that tarp in the corner. You'd be amazed how often you find an idle machine capable of doing amazing things that's already paid for and sitting idle because it was attached to the wrong idea at the wrong time. If you want amazing ROI, find amazing uses for things that are already paid for but lying idle.

Marry up the possibilities under that tarp with big unmet consumer needs and you'll find yourself printing money.

4. Don't just think about innovating with new types of products; think about new target markets, occasions, and channels.

There is a natural bias among innovators to come at a challenge thinking the answer will be a novel type of product. Yes, novel products are an important subset of the playing field. But you should pour comparable energy into opening new consumer segments, consumption occasions, and channels.

The appeal of this route is that it typically demands zero flex on your manufacturing capabilities. The merits are obvious. An idea built on a product form that's similar to what your company makes now begins life with the "can we make it?" question already answered. Again, the goal is not to confine the exploration to these opportunities, but to not ignore them.

5. The key to the future may be hiding in the past.

In the classic film *Monty Python and the Holy Grail*, a man pulling a cart rolls through a plague-riddled medieval village, ringing a bell like a cheery guy in an ice cream truck, nonchalantly calling out, "Bring out your dead!" A hapless villager gets tossed onto the cart by a neighbor. He protests with understated chagrin: "I'm not dead yet."

"Bring out your dead" has become a mantra at Fahrenheit 212 in how we probe the flex points in a company's existing capabilities.

Understanding the history of production for the company, the things it made years ago or tried and failed to do, can bring to light things that can be done but aren't obvious in the here and now. Many times the right type of product was launched at the wrong time—but may align with today's market needs. Or the execution may have been botched. Asking R&D to open up their closets is a favorite exercise of ours. There is often huge passion and excitement for things that previous teams did not see value in. Depending on who's in the room, you sometimes hear things like "This was one of the best product ideas we ever had, but marketing couldn't figure out what to do with it!"

We once spent half a day in the lab of one of the world's leading beverage companies doing nothing but tasting beverage recipes they had developed for projects over the past ten years that never made it to market. Embedded in those products were capabilities that even their top R&D people hadn't thought about in years. Ninety percent of these things had died for good reason. But the other 10 percent gave us a new appreciation of things that could be made that we might be able to connect to emerging consumer needs. It wasn't the old products we were looking at, but the capabilities embedded in them.

6. Relationships are capabilities, too.

It's increasingly rare to find a business with a supply chain and manufacturing process that doesn't have a long list of partnerships embedded in it. The capabilities of those partners—be they suppliers or contract manufacturers—are every bit as rich with flex-worthy capabilities as the assets of your company. Take the time to explore what they *could* do that they aren't doing now, what they've done before that they don't do now, and to "bring out their dead." It can uncover new ways to bend capability without breaking it.

Procter & Gamble has done an amazing body of work pioneering this discipline they call Supply Chain Innovation. Other companies are trying to catch up, and there's gold out there for those who do. In our experience, we've found a dynamic not unlike what we described with the untapped potential of R&D and operations people: supply chain partners tend to get asked "can you do this, how fast, and what will it cost," rather than more helpful idea-sparking questions of what are you capable of doing that we're not taking advantage of today. Changing that orientation can open big opportunities.

7. Capability without capacity isn't worth much.
One of baseball's greatest hitters was a guy named Wee Willie Keeler. He was once asked to sum up his hitting philosophy. His famous answer: hit 'em where they ain't. He meant aim for the open space.

In trying to bend your company's capabilities, coming up with new uses for a manufacturing capability that's running at full capacity isn't actually leveraging anything. On the other hand, show me a division head with an expensive factory with idle manufacturing capacity and I'll show you someone eager to green-light an idea that gets that idle capital working. We've seen this play out so many times that we occasionally define a project brief around getting a semi-idle facility up to full utilization. Idle factories kill company profits and cost good people their jobs. If you want to talk about attractive ROI, both financially and emotionally, you'll find it there.

8. Create new pairings.
As you uncover current and past assets and capabilities, ask yourself what happens if you pair them up in new ways.

And remember, go beyond just plants, equipment, technologies, and people to all the existing assets within reach.

Here's an interesting example of that principle, found in a great innovation from the Coca-Cola Company. One of their breakthroughs that we were proud to have helped out with was the tremendously successful PlantBottle initiative. PlantBottle is a new PET plastic technology (and the bottle made from it) with more than a third of its raw materials coming from plant-based sources, rather than the petroleum most plastics are made from. With Coke's scale, that's a big deal. Working with their team, we debated different ways we might maximize the impact that PlantBottle innovation could have on the planet and communicate that to the marketplace. We realized it would not be by treating PlantBottle as just a renewable innovation, but also highlighting its recyclability and strategically linking it to Coke's world-leading recycling efforts. Since the 1960s, the company has actively promoted recycling. In the early nineties, they debuted the first ever PET bottles made with recycled material. And since the turn of the millennium, Coke has continued to ramp up a recycling effort of unprecedented scale, spanning big investments in public education, grassroots activities, incentives for local governments to increase their recycling collections, distribution of recycling bins, ensuring downstream demand for recycled materials, putting new sustainable practices into the way materials get recycled in their own production facilities all around the world, and partnering with other players in the recycling ecosystem to keep pushing the envelope. But the active ingredient that ultimately determines recycling's environmental impact is public cooperation: returning empty bottles to the recycling system. In the United States, for instance, only about one in four recyclable PET bottles are put back by consumers into the recycling stream. For a company so committed to recycling, that's a very frustrating thing.

What came out of our sessions with the PlantBottle team was a realization that the way to maximize the difference Coke could make in reducing packaging's environmental footprint would be through the double-pronged impact of the new PlantBottle initiative, which would put less petroleum-based material into new bottles, and, over time, driving up consumer participation in recycling. The logic was simple: more PlantBottles plus more bottles getting recycled can meaningfully drive down the amount of petroleum-based new plastic entering the ecosystem over time. Indelibly connecting Plant-Bottle to the recycling efforts in the way this new innovation was communicated to the public would help bring about the desired environmental impact. To bring that vision to life, one of our young designers, Julie Regina, came up with the initial design concept of a leaf inserted into the traditional recycling icon, which inspired the now ubiquitous PlantBottle icon that appears on beverage bottles all around the world.

To date, about 25 billion PlantBottles have been sold worldwide, saving roughly half a million barrels of oil. That's tremendous impact, and a great lesson in how connecting a new thing—in this case, the PlantBottle technology—to an existing asset—Coke's massive recycling program—can add up to a winning approach. And we've just seen the tip of the iceberg on how far this can go. Heinz ketchup now uses PlantBottles, with the Coca-Cola PlantBottle icon proudly on the bottle. And in November 2013, PlantBottle made the leap beyond packaging. The Coca-Cola Company and the Ford Motor Company announced a partnership to bring PlantBottle technology to automotive textiles, marking the next leap forward in the pursuit of greener cars with reduced reliance on petroleum.

9. Look at capabilities with informed naïveté.

There's a mindset called phenomenology—the art of seeing things as they are, divorced from the baggage of context and associative meaning that builds up over the years. This way of thinking is particularly potent as you look for new things that old capabilities might do. Ask yourself, if a person would look at this for the first time, what would they see?

10. Play on competitors' weaknesses.

It may not be imperative that you're great at something as long as you do it better than your competition. Don't just look at your capabilities in a vacuum; look at them relative to your competitors' and then look again at how your assets can be utilized to take advantage of the gap. Yes, look for the thing your company is best in the world at doing. But don't ignore the areas where good enough is good enough to win in the marketplace.

Chapter 11

Insights About Insights

The innovator's most valuable and most abused tool is overdue for an overhaul.

Insight is unquestionably an innovator's most vital tool. But its edge is dulled by confusion over what insight is, by entrenched myths about where it can be found, and by letting staleness creep into the ways we access it.

Let's undo some misconceptions around its definition and where it resides. Then we'll look at different types of insights and their unique value to innovation, and offer some fresh perspectives on how to raise your own personal game at unlocking the gold that insight represents.

QUEST FOR DEFINITION

In an age where nearly every human and commercial phenomenon is measured, benchmarked, and analyzed with incredible granularity, where businesses of immense scale are built on the premise of giving away things of value solely to acquire the sellable data beneath them, and where the relentless march of the digital algorithm threatens to neuter that precious human gift we call intuitive instinct, *insight* has been sliced, diced, diluted, and bastardized with liberal abandon.

Today, companies great and small face an unprecedented need

for the growth that transformational innovation can unlock, and insight is the hard-edged flint from which innovation's brightest sparks fly.

But you can't get sparks by banging marshmallows together.

Much of what is touted today as insight is merely information in plain sight.

So how do we remove the unhelpful haze around this and better define what we're after?

Look in the handy digital dictionary bundled into Microsoft Word and you'll find this: *Insight (noun): 1) perceptiveness, 2) clear perception, 3) self-awareness, or 4) perception that hallucinations are not real.* (Oh, my.)

Many researchers will tell you it's the "aha" of realization (defining it by the reaction it creates rather than what it is that we're reacting to).

Merriam-Webster calls it "the act or result of apprehending the inner nature of things or of seeing intuitively." (This captures insight more as a capability than a thing.)

IDEO's CEO, Tim Brown, says of it: *"That insight cannot yet be codified, quantified, or even defined—not yet, at any rate—makes it the most difficult but also the most exciting part of the design process."*

Wikipedia serves up a flailing aggregation of definitions, like:

- *Insight is a piece of information.* (It's never *just* that.)
- *An introspection.* (Sometimes)
- *The understanding of a specific cause and effect in a specific context.* (What?)
- *The act or result of understanding the inner nature of things.* (That's getting warmer, but it only describes the capability rather than what an insight is.)
- *An understanding of cause and effect based on identification of relationships and behaviors within a model, context, or scenario . . . see artificial intelligence.* (Yikes.)

Can we really say insight is all-important, but not really know what it is?

In essence, a lot of these stabs at definition just say, *You'll know it when you see it*—echoing the words of Supreme Court justice Potter Stewart in ducking the question of how to define pornography.

The innovation community owes the world a better answer.

A FREUDIAN BLIP

Fresh insights about insights come from Fahrenheit 212's head of consumer research, Dr. Barbara Nurenberg. A trained psychologist with an extraordinary gift for seeing through the layers of fog to what lies beneath, she comes at it this way: "You want to know who really gets insight? The psychoanalysts! It's their professional bread and butter. They define insight metaphorically as seeing with the eyes of the mind to make connections . . . a powerful integration and synthesis that, once put together, forms a new perspective. The result is an analyst being able to say 'Look!' to the patient, or the patient saying 'Eureka' to themselves. The 'aha,' however, is only half of the story. Yes, an insight is an endpoint—an intuitive leap, a synthesis of data—but more importantly, it's a starting point, valued so highly in therapy because it holds the potential for self-change."

This theme of *potential for change* is conspicuously absent from the litany of definitions in circulation. Yet I find it the defining characteristic of great insight—the kind capable of igniting transformational innovation.

Potential for change is *the reason* we get goose bumps from great insights—they hurl open the gates to new possibilities that weren't visible before.

Pivoting on this core idea of potential for change, we get to a definition of insight that's pinned to our wall at Fahrenheit 212, one that we teach our people to obsess about in our daily pursuit of transformational innovation for the world's great companies.

*In the pursuit of innovation, an insight is a fresh, potent, and en-
ergizing truth about the consumer or the business.*

This isn't perfect, of course, but it's massively more useful than
the other definitions we've seen. It defines what we're chasing, and
helps filter the wheat from the chaff.

Insight (noun): a fresh, potent, and energizing truth.

In pursuit of innovation, an insight can be a truth either about
a human experience, aspiration, unmet need, or tension, or about a
business, category, strategic ambition, or product that points the way
to a profitable opportunity.

It has to be a **fresh** truth because if we've heard it before, chances
are it's evident to all, rather than a bona fide insight. Insight is a form
of competitive advantage born of seeing things that our competitors
can't. Old truths aren't unhelpful, but they're table stakes, widely recognized, and therefore not a source of new competitive advantage.
Fresh answers require fresh perspective, be it from new depth of
understanding or sensing new connections between phenomena we
didn't realize were connected.

Why **potent**? Because there are many underlying truths about
life or a business that are merely interesting cul-de-sacs. (While it's
true that the human eye can perceive more than a million colors,
there isn't much innovation you can build off it; it's information, not
an insight.) To provide the sparks we need, our insights have to be
richly laden with opportunity for transformation and new possibility.
That potency we need usually comes from an unresolved tension.
Physicists, engineers, and architects obsess over tensile strength. In
innovation, great insights are springboards with tensile value. Throw
the weight of your imagination upon them and they will forcefully
propel you in new directions.

What do I mean by an **energizing** truth? Well, our reaction does matter. Insight needs to inspire and ignite ideas and action among the people it touches. Forget the images of the lonely inventor in the garage. Innovation is at its best a team sport. Great insights will electrify and galvanize teams around a sense of new possibility. We can't define insight solely by the reaction it creates, but it's a critical piece and source of its value.

ERASING THE INAUDIBLE PREFIX

Earlier I said the most powerful things innovators have to listen for are the things that *aren't* being said. The unsaid thing about insight is its inaudible prefix. When many of us hear *insight*, we think *consumer* insight.

That's not just a prefix; it's a psychological fence around the type of insight we hunt for. It's a fence that puts half of the playing field out of bounds. And the left-out half is mission critical, particularly to transformational innovation.

Transformational innovation is much harder to accomplish than a close-in line extension. It represents greater degrees of opportunity, change, and challenge for the business. Consumer insight is absolutely critical and instrumental, but it isn't enough to ensure an idea represents as big a step forward for the business as it does for the consumer.

Where consumer insights capture tensions in human experience, *commercial insights* capture underlying tensions in the current business paradigm, like hidden barriers impeding new levels of profitability, changing dynamics at retail, a gap in a brand portfolio, the impact of new technologies, or cracks in business models that once made sense but don't moving forward. The role of commercial insight is simple. As our cofounder Geoff Vuleta put it, where consumer insight points the way to consumer appeal, commercial insight points the way to how to shape and execute an idea, and above all, how to profit from it."

COMMERCIAL INSIGHT AT WORK

To unleash the full potential of insight—rather than just that rich subset we call consumer insight—the front end of any transformational innovation project should be designed to uncover equally big insights about the consumer *and* the business.

But what does a commercial insight look like and what role does it play? Here's an example of the power of commercial insight from a recent project we ran with the midsized consumer packaged goods (CPG) juggernaut Church & Dwight.

Church & Dwight is a highly dynamic company that has consistently outperformed its bigger CPG peers over the past two decades. Their stock price has posted annual gains of 14 percent or better in seven of the past ten years—with five of those years falling in the 24 to 33 percent range. That's quite a run. Most famous for transforming Arm & Hammer baking soda from a baker's commodity into a hero ingredient across a wide array of categories from toothpaste to deodorants, laundry detergent to air fresheners, the company's success has come about through a combination of strategically identifying relatively niche markets where it can win, running a lean business that doesn't overspend on exploratory R&D when strong science can be obtained externally, and building out its brand portfolio through smart acquisitions, marketing, and innovation.

While other Fahrenheit project teams down the hall are working on glitzy businesses like high-end jewelry for Gucci and the future of flash memory for a big technology company, our Church & Dwight team is working on one of the many businesses born of baking soda's unique ability to keep things fresh. Thanks to its baking soda equity and a host of other innovations, Church & Dwight has built a number three brand position in the $2 billion cat litter market. We are working together on how to define the next big leap in managing the litter box.

While the Magic half of our team explores the attitudes, behavior, and emotions of the 40 million cat-loving households in America, our commercial strategists dig into the business, hunting for insights hidden in the company's finances, operations, capabilities, technologies, distribution systems, or anything else that could hold the keys to profitable transformation.

On the consumer side, as we explore the functional, emotional, and ritual realities of cat care, we find that one of consumers' key emotional tensions has nothing to do with the practicalities. It's a social thing: an anxiety triggered by the sound of the doorbell, fearing an arriving guest might say "Oh, you have a cat," even though the cat's nowhere in sight. No one in the category has ever delivered what we're calling "whole home freshness." We feel instinctively that this has the makings of a breakthrough, but aren't yet sure how. And as always, we'll need to marry up our consumer insights with their commercial equivalents.

On many projects, the hunt for commercial insights surfaces a scatter of loosely connected insights about different dimensions of the business. Insights we find about operations, for instance, may be only tangentially linked to insights about pricing, distribution, technologies, or product performance thresholds. But as the Money team keeps digging, they find something atypical. Almost every dimension of the business is in some way or another a function of a particular raw material: the natural clay substrate that has, over the past ten years, become the predominant active ingredient for every big player in the category. That substrate delivers a great deal of value. Pebble-sized granules of it make today's products work. But there were trade-offs, too. As the material became ubiquitous across the category, differentiation had narrowed. The capabilities of the material and the category had become synonymous. And performance improvements had topped out across the board. As Church & Dwight's director of global new products, Bryan Harpine, put it, "Everybody's been working with this technology for a long time now and for all the great things it's done, we've hit a glass ceiling on product performance improvements. Consumer expectations have settled in, and claim fatigue has taken hold. Repeated proclamations of the arrival of the next big thing haven't lived up to the hype. Many consumers, over half in fact, have resigned themselves to accept that product performance can only go so far. They're using their own compensatory efforts to overcome products' shortcomings. And in a price-sensitive category, that glass ceiling on performance benefits means price points are locked in, too."

As we assimilate the pieces, the commercial insight emerges that will, in tandem with consumer insights, ignite the work ahead:

> *Leaps in differentiation, customer satisfaction, and pricing power are simply not attainable here without a step change in performance beyond the limits of what the clay substrate can do in its current form.*

In other words, even if we could conceptually articulate a way to deliver on this promising new strategic territory of "whole home freshness," we would need a leap of technology to break through the performance ceiling and unlock the next level of potential, for both the product and the business.

Delivering on this wouldn't be easy. While consumers were frustrated by the category's shortcomings, we couldn't just yank away the performance benefits consumers liked, which were tied directly to the magic "clumping" effect that this special clay delivered. Aiming high, we set out exploring ways to break through the glass ceiling. To kick-start the journey, our commercial strategy guys pulled out a map of the United States, flipped over a coffee cup, and traced a fifty-mile circle around each of the manufacturing plants Church & Dwight used around the country, hunting for potential alternate substrates in the vicinity. Over the months ahead, the hunt would go global. Working with task force intensity, Bryan and the Church & Dwight R&D and procurement teams tapped into specialists from all over the world in the hunt for the missing ingredient in the category's future—a way to replace or augment the capabilities of the clay. As the consumer-facing proposition was taking shape around "whole home freshness," over a hundred potential new technologies were reviewed, hunting for the silver bullet that could pass the neighbor-at-the-door test. As always, creativity is about connecting dots no one has connected before. In this case it was a job of matchmaking, finding a fit between a technology somewhere out there and the unfulfilled consumer aspiration we were out to fulfill.

Powered by this commercial insight that everything about growing the business—from boosting differentiation to creating new customer satisfaction to opening new price points—would pivot on our ability to break through the performance ceiling, the hunt struck gold. The big leap came in two parts. The first was a technology uncovered by the global search, a natural treatment never before used in the category that creates a seemingly magical sealing effect when it gets wet. The second was a new method the R&D team had to develop to refine the clay, making it work seamlessly as a sealant. Consumer response to an early product prototype was so overwhelmingly positive that company leadership urged the team to step on the accelerator, shifting more resources behind the effort. In quantitative research, it delivered the highest scores in ten years of testing. The combination of these technical performance leaps and the breakthrough consumer proposition of a seven-day home freshness guarantee have brought transformation to a category where innovation had seemed to be stagnating. Suddenly, for a whole lot of cat owners, the chime on the doorbell sounds a lot sweeter than it used to. So does the ring of the cash register for Church & Dwight and retailers. Launched in late 2013 as Arm & Hammer Clump & Seal, the innovation this work stream unleashed has brought a step change to the category. In a price-sensitive category where consumers had grown weary of big promises and had come to expect parity performance, the performance leap is so dramatic that it's commanding a 30 percent price premium over Arm & Hammer's base products, opening a whole new price tier in the category. Despite that steep premium, it's flying off the shelves. In just a few months, the product shot into the number three position of all items in the category in both revenue and velocity, and propelled the brand to the number two position, gaining six share points in under six months. That's what the collision of consumer insight and commercial insight can do for you. For Church & Dwight, it's playing a starring role in their next big success, keeping their juggernaut rolling.

FOURTEEN DELICIOUS FLAVORS

In addition to the immensely unhelpful ambiguity around what insight is, and the invisible prefix that has so many of those engaged in innovation thinking that insight only refers to *consumer* insight, there's one last area where insight is unnecessarily muted. It is in the desire to isolate one source or type of insight and say that's what insights should look like.

In our experience, we've come to realize that even within our strengthened definition of what an insight is—*a fresh, potent, energizing truth about the consumer or the business*—the insights that have ignited the best innovations we've created over the years have come in many different shapes and sizes. But most companies we've worked with have a strong cultural bias toward favoring one source or type of insight over another. Some companies believe that if a researcher didn't explicitly hear something stated in a piece of consumer research, then it's not an insight. (We would say that insight is the result of a human synapse revealing deeper, previously unseen truth—it is sometimes found or sparked by research, but often arises from the simple human act of contemplating a situation.) Some companies are only comfortable with insights that capture a functional problem or tension. Others say that if there's no emotion in it, it's not insight. None of these views are wrong, but they're unhelpfully limiting.

We've been involved in powerful innovations springing from so many different types of insights that we've bucketed them into a framework that innovation teams may find helpful, laying out fourteen different types of insights—seven on the consumer side, and seven on the commercial side. These are by no means the only types of insight out there. The goal here isn't to replace overly narrow definitions with a slightly wider fence. But these buckets may prove worthwhile in exploring whatever challenge you face.

It's important to go into any innovation challenge with a sense of due diligence—that if you haven't hunted for insight in all these areas, you may be missing something big. Many insights straddle these buckets, of course—a mother talking about how she wants to

INNOVATION INSIGHTS
FOURTEEN HOT HUNTING GROUNDS

CONSUMER INSIGHTS

 FUNCTIONAL
Insights about jobs that need doing

 EMOTIONAL
Insights about feelings

 CHOICE-BASED
Insights about trade-offs

 INTERPERSONAL
Insights about our interactions with others

 BEHAVIORAL
Insights about how we perform a given act

 CONTEXTUAL
Insights about time, place, surroundings

 EXPERIENTIAL
Insights about the user experience

COMMERCIAL INSIGHTS

 FINANCIAL
Insights about how the business makes mone

 OPERATIONAL
Insights about facilities, equipment supply cha

 COMPETITIVE
Insights about the competitive set

 CHANNEL-BASED
Insights about retailers, distribution, POS

 PORTFOLIO-BASED
Insights about the mix of company offerings

 TECHNOLOGICAL
Insights about the potential of our technologie

 ORGANIZATIONAL
Insights about org structures, sytems, etc.

equip her kids for a wonderful life is both interpersonal and intensely emotional, but the categories help you get there. Keep in mind that certain methodologies tend to deliver certain types of insights. Ethnographic observation, for instance, may reveal that young kids' smaller hands are best served by fatter toothbrush handles. But it won't give you insight about how to win over a retailer who thinks they shouldn't give you more shelf space.

WAYS TO UNCOVER TRANSFORMATIONAL INSIGHTS

Building your insight-generation muscle starts with figuring out what kind of insight generator you are.

Over the years, we've discovered that great insight generators tend to be one of three types: *detectives, empathizers,* or *introspectors.* All are equally capable of getting spectacular insights, but their means of getting there are very different.

The Detective

If you're a **detective,** your path to uncovering powerful insights is to aggressively hunt them down by observing and interviewing people in action, asking a hundred questions, then piecing together the clues. Detectives lean heavily on external research as a primary vehicle for discovery. Those who say "the answer is out there, not in your office" are probably detectives by nature, accurately describing what works best for them.

The Introspector

If you're an **introspector,** you instinctively look inward before you look outward, beginning your hunt for insight by exploring your own life experiences, and assessing your own actions, reactions, and inner motivations in situations relevant to whatever you're working on. Introspectors have an unusually high level of self-awareness that opens pathways to richer, more nuanced levels of emotional understanding

The Detective, the Introspector, and the Empathizer each have their own way of getting to great insights. There's no right or wrong, but the more you understand your natural wiring, the more effective you'll be.

than researchers readily get by interviewing others and chipping through their layers. Finding insight becomes a process of extrapolation, where they project outward from their personal experience and sift out things that ring true for the world around them from things that are idiosyncratic or purely personal. They look at external research as a way to validate gut hunches, or to spark new ones.

Researchers tend to be leery of using personal experiences and feelings as sparks, but a spark is just the start of something, so you should be open to any means of getting those sparks. I remember once when we were working on a challenging project in the ice cream business, I was lounging around at home after dinner and my son Jacob asked if he could have some ice cream. Without thinking about it, I found myself trying to steer him to a cookie instead, as it just seemed a little easier. I made a mental note and the next morning tried to work out why the cookie seemed so much easier to me as a parent in that moment. I mapped the ice cream experience and was pretty shocked by what I saw. Between thinking "I'd like some ice cream" and putting the last dish away, there are actually about thirty-five steps in the journey. Grabbing a cookie has about four. Changing the ice cream experience to remove some of those barriers became an important spark in the project. That personal tug in a very routine family moment opened a new line of inquiry that became fundamental to our subsequent round of consumer research.

The Empathizer

If you're an **empathizer,** you have an instinctive gift for putting yourself in other people's shoes and imagining how they feel. You're unusually adept at changing perspectives on a dime, and can put yourself into very different emotional frameworks with very little contextual priming. For empathizers, insight generation is less about interrogating the world, and more a mental process somewhat akin to Method acting—where you transcend your own personal circumstances. You look at external research as a source less of answers than of context—showing you the fabric of the laces on other people's shoes you're jumping into, which throws you further into that mental space to unlock the pearls that reside there. Empathy is rightly celebrated as one of the innovator's most valuable tools. We've simply found that it is every bit as valuable in the hunt for insight as it is in how you put those insights to work deeper in the innovation journey.

Ask transformational questions.

You know what the old questions are in your business. Tear them up and find new ones.

To find new questions, try on some new answers.
A technique we find incredibly powerful at uncovering big insights is using an array of hypothetical transformational answers to force us to think about the problem at hand in very new ways. For instance, we might say, *If the answer to this challenge lay in miniaturization . . . what tension would that resolve? Or, if the answer was about love, what tension would that resolve? If the answer was hedonistic . . . or exotic . . . or a power tool . . . what needs would these answers fulfill that the current products in the category ignore?* These hypothetical answers aren't answers we expect to be remotely right, but seeing new things is often a matter of looking from new vantage points.

Think two ways: Outside In and Inside Out.
Great insights themselves often consist of new connections, so forcing ourselves to make new connections can ignite surprising insights.

Try alternating between thinking Inside Out and Outside In. Outside In means looking inward at company assets from the standpoint of the consumer's tensions and emerging needs. Inside Out means looking out at the consumer from the perspective of the underleveraged assets and tensions embedded in the company.

You'll find that looking at each from the perspective of the other shines the spotlight on new connections you'll miss looking at either in isolation.

Learn the art of commercial ethnography.
Shockingly little is written about how to dissect a business to uncover hidden commercial pain points. That means project owners are on their own to dig out those commercial insights on which transformational innovation lives or dies.

The skill sets required to uncover big commercial insights have little in common with the ways we find consumer insights. You can't passively observe a business. You have to aggressively dissect it. This means poring through the financials, technologies, operations, capabilities, channels, institutional knowledge, and strategic imperatives to find the sparks—some in plain view, but some in darker corners—that will ignite new strategies and ideas that will deliver big for both the consumer and the business.

An ounce of provocation is worth a pound of justification.
Breakthrough insights begin life as fragile things. Sometimes they're snuffed out by worrying too much early on about how transformative they'll be, or whether they're as true for the population at large as they feel to you. But don't let these doubts slow you down. As Malcolm Gladwell puts it in *Blink,* Your subconscious is much smarter than you are. If something ignites a spark in you, there is a reason for it. Somewhere deep down you may know why, but the reason you're excited may not be obvious for hours or even weeks after the fact.

Let the fact that something excites you be enough impetus to yank hard on whatever's grabbing your attention. Pull on that loose thread. See what you uncover.

Chapter 12

Choice Advice About Innovation Strategy

Big innovation outcomes are elusive without clear strategic choices.

Spirits are high. Beer is flowing. Laughter is tumbling along the table. Half a dozen Fahrenheiters, all of us having been aboard from the earliest days, are in a modern-industrial bar in San Francisco's

Mission District. Celebrating the delivery a few hours earlier of the final presentation of an intensive five-month project, we're exhausted but ecstatic. The senior client's excitement is still ringing in our ears. We order another round of drinks, and raise a glass to raising the bar. We don't know it at the time, but this night will prove to be a key pivot point in our way of thinking about the discipline of innovation strategy. The lessons around that pivot may be as helpful to you as they were to us.

It's a warm night in the fall of 2008. After enduring the usual fits and starts any startup endures, our business is on a nice roll. We're a nose-to-the-grindstone crew, worried only about doing great work. But word about us is trickling out, spawning interest from the press. *BusinessWeek* has run a feature story labeling Fahrenheit 212 a "white hot idea factory." *Esquire* comes next, calling us "the epicenter of innovation." Projects keep rolling in. Awards, too. By this point, Procter & Gamble has named us their innovation partner of the year, complete with a shiny glass trophy for the bookshelf. Diageo, the world's leading spirits company, has named an idea of ours the company's Innovation Idea of the Year. Samsung and Coca-Cola have just used the global stage of the Beijing Olympics to unveil one of our inventions to the world, a new interactive vending platform.

Celebrating the day behind us, and the trajectory ahead of us, we go around the table making toasts. Jon Crawford-Phillips shares the client's parting comments, about how we'd given them the courage to aim higher and dream bigger. Rony Zibara speaks from the heart about striving to amaze one another daily, a mantra that's taken hold in our company's culture. Marcus Oliver talks about inspiration as the ultimate human condition. I share the news that *Fortune* magazine called and said they want to do a feature story on us (one that would eventually label us "the innovator's paradise"). Last to raise a glass is Pete Maulik. A big guy with a big smile and a shaved head, Pete isn't just the tallest and baldest guy at Fahrenheit; he's also the funniest. His toasts rarely disappoint. "Today was amazing. You guys are amazing. Our future is amazing. Too bad it's not working."

The line gets big laughs. Pete's laughing, too. But he's actually not kidding.

I come in behind him. "Pete's right. We were talking about it on the flight out. Kudos from clients, trophies on the shelf, and press attention are great things. But they're not the point of Fahrenheit 212. We got into this business to transform the odds of innovation projects delivering big concrete outcomes. Have we moved the needle? Yes, but nowhere near the degree we set out to. Over the next few months, we're going to figure out why a lot of great ideas are dying off, and start fixing it. Let's enjoy tonight. We have work to do."

What we're about to undertake has an analogue on the golf course. Back when Tiger Woods was more worried about his golf swing than his swinging, he was by all external measures doing really well. He was winning tournaments in droves, taking the Masters by a record twelve strokes in 1997. He then announced to the golf world that while his swing was good enough to win, it wasn't doing what he wanted it to do, so he was going to completely overhaul it. We weren't famous. And we certainly weren't making Tiger Woods's money. But we did something along those lines. It was something every startup should do—separating external signals of success from your own definition of it. Purpose counts. We hadn't set out to tweak innovation success rates. We set out to transform them. To do that, we would have to rebuild our swing. The recalibration that began that night would take unexpected twists and turns.

AUTOPSY 1.0, 2.0, 3.0 . . .

In the ensuing weeks, a few of us work as a task force on what will be the first of a series of attempts to decode the causes of death of seemingly great innovation ideas—ideas that had been met with excitement from our clients on arrival, but for some reason never made it to market. The body of projects behind us provides a healthy data set. We're not after a definitive academic study, just a way to inform the next iteration of our model. Hunting for clues, we retrace our steps across dozens of projects. We label any idea that didn't reach market an unsuccessful idea. Any residual learning it may have thrown off is great, but that wasn't the goal going into the project, so it can't be called a win coming out. We reach out to clients who have seen promising ideas come unraveled on the way to market. The clients aren't at all upset about these ideas that didn't make it; they think the ideas were great and derailments are common, normal, and natural. Some even wonder why we're so fixated on what didn't work when so many things did. But they help us out and serve up insights into the demise of once-promising ideas as they migrated through their organizations.

As we aggregate the feedback, we're gazing at a wide array of these "failure factors." Often an idea had more than one thing stop it. We put each cause of idea failure on a card. Trying to find patterns among them, we look at them every which way, bucketing and re-bucketing, shuffling and starting over. We stare at them, walk away, and drag in colleagues from the hall to join us, playing a game of "find the pattern." With the delivery date for the outputs of this fact-finding effort approaching fast, expectations take on a life of their own. We're an excitable bunch. It's as if the decoding of the Rosetta stone is imminent. Pattern recognition is one of an innovator's most frequently used tools. Surely there's a pattern here, and everybody wants to be the code cracker or be there for the unveiling. But the outcome is something none of us saw coming.

I stand up and say "Okay, drumroll, guys . . . the pattern is . . . there's no pattern."

It's a reluctant admission. The causes of death on promising ideas look like a random spray of very different causes, including things like:

"The CEO's pet project got priority over this one."

"Senior leadership just didn't really get the value of it."

"The CFO didn't like the risk profile."

"The project director left on maternity leave and was never replaced."

"Our distribution isn't very strong in the channel where the idea was aimed."

"The technology never quite got solved and R&D questioned whether it was worth the effort."

"The ROI wasn't certain enough."

"It was aimed at a business where the margins aren't as high as our baseline."

"The division changed its strategy and the idea didn't fit anymore."

"We had a re-org and the new regime did a 'not invented here' on us."

"The business units had their own agenda."

"The CEO wasn't sure it had legs . . . thought it might be a bit faddish."

"Funds were tight and other programs made the cut over that one."

"Actually the idea didn't die so much as it sort of faded away—everybody said it's really clever and interesting, but they never pushed the button."

For any group of serial innovators, a big problem is every bit as exciting as a big answer. Problem-solving sessions have a contagious buzz to them. But hearing that the causes of ideas dying off are random, everybody gets unusually quiet. Looking back, randomness was the worst possible answer.

The practical and psychological implications of accepting that innovation ideas fail for random reasons are profound. There's a model for it. It's called the lottery. In a lottery you have no way to know whether one number is better than another. The only way to up your odds of success is to buy more tickets. For us, the moral equivalent would be to just pump out more and more ideas and hope a few more stick. Approaching innovation by pumping out mountains of ideas is implicitly predicated on a tacit belief in randomness. Serendipity often has a role in the way innovation ideas are born, connecting previously disconnected things, but randomness as a determinant of what makes it to market is a very different thing.

In the wake of this first stab at figuring out why promising ideas die, the term *lottery tickets* actually creeps into our internal vernacular for a while. Filtering ideas, we find ourselves asking, "Is this a ticket worth buying?"—meaning a worthwhile foray to commit our time and energy against. A conflicted mindset comes with it. On some level, the possibility that upping the odds of success is about letting our imaginations go further and broader in search of more far-flung ideas is tantalizing. But in the end randomness is not empowering. It's quite the opposite. You feel like the idea you're working on is interesting, but you can't help but question its importance, or whether the sweat you pour into it will be rewarded. Ideas need love, care, and feeding. It's emotionally risky to get too attached to something that can disappear for totally random reasons, like a bus dropping on it from the sky. You feel powerless to make a difference. Instead of turning every stone to make something work, you can get fatalistic and perhaps hold back from the full-on commitment that bringing an idea to fruition demands. It's a natural defense mechanism.

Over the next few months, we begin to experiment with dialing up the number of ideas we develop on each project, to see what that does to hit rates. If hit rate ultimately does prove to be a function of quantity of ideas, we'll do what it takes. But deep down, we're feeling kind of hollow about it. If innovation success is driven by randomness, what's the difference between our team and a hundred monkeys with a hundred Sharpies and a hundred packs of Post-it notes?

While the real-time experiment commences to assess the impact of upping the quantity of ideas, Pete and I talk offline about not resting on that answer.

In the ensuing weeks, we keep circling back, trying different angles in search of that elusive pattern. What if we flip it, looking not at the causes of death of the ideas that didn't make it, but instead at the cause of life for the ideas that did make it? We dissect the successes looking for any consistent characteristics that separate the ideas that have made it to market from those that haven't. Are the ideas that make it better differentiated than the ones that don't? Are the insights more powerful? Are they performing better in research? Are the successful ideas consistently braver and bolder (or safer and lower risk)? Were their designs more compelling? Are they making leaps of form factor? Do they use existing business models or new ones? Again, there's no consistent pattern. The successful ideas, it seems, are just right for their respective situations. Interestingly, where failure could be ascribed to dozens of different causes, success seems to have surprisingly few, generally summed up as "This is what we think the business needs." Unfortunately, this is only marginally more helpful than randomness. It's too nonspecific to act on. Autopsy 2.0 delivers another non-answer.

THE FLIP

Vacillating between being disappointed and downright pissed at the prospect that innovation failure might be a random thing, solvable only by pumping out more and more ideas, we point some of the tools we typically use in idea development at this problem. What if we pull out the spatula and invert the way we look at this? What if instead of looking at the endpoint of projects—the point where ideas get green-lit or killed off—we look at the *beginning* of these projects? Are there discernible patterns about the conception, framing, and early stages of the projects, in what conditions existed *before* any ideas were created, that might hold the keys to how to take the hit rate to the next level?

Out come the note cards again. This time, instead of each card representing a reason a promising idea died, each represents a whole *project*, color-coded for how successful it was. Again, we cycle through a bucketing exercise in search of discernible patterns separating successes from dead ends. Is there a pattern of success rates by product category: technology versus packaged goods versus services, for instance? Consumer versus business-to-business? Size of the objective? High stretch versus low stretch? No, no, no, and no.

Getting close to giving up, we try out one last filter: how strategically specific was the ingoing assignment? Reviewing the initial parameters of scores of projects, we separate them into four buckets, on a spectrum from broadest to most specific, and slap labels on the buckets: Blue Sky, Fishing Trip, Jump Shot, and Layup.

The Blue Sky label means the project is strategically wide open, with the intent behind it summed up in two words: *grow me*. The impetus behind the project is simply to fill a gap between the growth the company needs and the ability of its current offerings and innovation pipeline to get them there. Going in, that growth could come from anything within reason. There's no clear definition of where to play or how. It's your classic fuzzy front-end job. There may be a few no-fly zones or thought starters, but it's essentially a blank page. We get a lot of assignments like this. Clients with this type of project want to see lateral thinking inform the question of where-to-play, so almost anything goes.

The next bucket, the Fishing Trip, is a bit more specific, but still quite loose. A Fishing Trip brief is in essence saying go poke around in that pond over there and see if you catch something. That pond may be a consumer trend like health and wellness, an emerging technology like 3-D printing, or a demographic group like Millennials that's of interest to the company but currently underdeveloped.

These projects are by nature exploratory missions to see what's possible and to see whether there's real value behind the topical curiosity. Unlike Blue Sky briefs, there's an indication of *where* to play, but relatively little clarity on why it's important, how to play, or what it's worth financially to win in that space. It's just an area worth exploring.

Further along the spectrum toward specificity is the bucket we call Jump Shots. In basketball terms, the goal, aka the basket, is set in concrete, well defined and not moving, but you're some distance away from it (maybe out near the three-point arc). There are formidable obstacles to get past (like seven-foot defenders). You know that getting the ball in the hoop has real value (it's worth at least two points). You also know it's necessary (no baskets, no points, no wins). In our practice, what we call a Jump Shot project is one where there is a clear, specific goal with recognized strategic and economic value to the business, great priority attached by the company to achieving it, but no clear way to get there. The obstacles standing between you and the goal may be competitive, technical, strategic, financial, brand equity based, conceptual, or all of the above. Jump Shot projects often arrive at our door after significant strategic decisions have been made about what needs to happen to grow or future-proof a business. It may be that a market adjacency or whitespace has been identified for entry and assessed at a high level, but there's a need to come up with the strategy, value proposition, product, and business proposition to unlock it.

We label the last bucket Layups. At the most strategically specific end of the spectrum, these are innovation briefs where the company has already aligned on the importance and value of a particular innovation play, and there is little doubt that *something* is going to market to serve an important need of the business. You just have to make the leap and convert the opportunity. These might be cases where there is already a preliminary product in hand, prior proof of consumer interest, and a commitment from the company to act on it, but it needs strategic elevation, the right product, and the best story, user experience, business model, branding, and vision to get it right. Being close to the goal doesn't make it a sure thing. In basketball, layups get blocked or missed more often than you'd think. The term *Layup* isn't meant to downplay the challenge in these assignments, only to reflect how clear the goal is, and how close you are to it, and how your eyes are only on the prize directly in front of you. In essence, the brief says this thing is probably going to happen; let's make sure it does, and that we get the biggest possible outcome out of it.

Having bucketed every project we've ever done as a Blue Sky, Fishing Trip, Jump Shot, or Layup, we again hunt for patterns. We take the Layups out of the data set, as their high odds of making it to market would skew the pattern. As we look across this array of projects, all the frustration of months of unsuccessful pattern hunting blows out the window in seconds. The pattern leaps out at us. While there's a healthy level of success within each bucket, the hit rate is highest by far in the Jump Shots. Blue Sky and Fishing Trip projects succeed at far lower rates. The conclusion is undeniable: the biggest driver of project success rates, it seems, is the clarity of strategic focus *before* any ideas are developed.

At face value this seems to imply that outcome-driven innovators should be leery of loosely defined project briefs, but there's another layer to it that says that's not true. Drilling deeper into the Blue Sky bucket, we isolate the most successful Blue Sky projects and find another pattern. The Blue Sky projects that delivered big successful outcomes were those where we had instinctively narrowed the playing field early on. We hadn't necessarily set out to do that. In fact, in our earliest days we thought narrowing the field of possibility would increase the risk of a project coming to nothing, since we feared we might unwittingly lop off an area where the biggest idea might be hiding in the weeds. This mindset of keeping things as open as possible was in line with the prevailing conventional wisdom, which emphasized going broad with your thinking and chasing a high quantity of disparate ideas. The pattern we were seeing here said that the conventional wisdom wasn't right, at least within the context of our practice.

The biggest determinant of project success was how specific we got in *aiming* the combined talent, know-how, and passion of our team and our clients at a well-defined, sufficiently narrow territory. The most successful Blue Sky projects actually weren't Blue Sky at all by the time we started developing ideas. Between the start of the project and the start of idea development a month or two into it, we had transformed the project into a Jump Shot. We had defined a clear area of strategic focus at an intersection of consumer needs, company needs, and an identifiable pot of money, and had aligned the key decision makers up and down the client organization behind that focal area before we conceived a single idea. On the projects that hadn't succeeded, that narrowing of focus hadn't happened to the same degree. We'd just chased whatever seemed relevant to consumers and interesting to us.

The same pattern appeared within the Fishing Trips. The successful Fishing Trips weren't still Fishing Trips by the time we started developing ideas. Big decisions based on data and strategic insights had created far tighter focus. We had essentially changed the orientation from "here's an area of broad curiosity" to "here's an area of clear strategic and economic value, and a way to unlock it."

The clincher was when we looked into that tightly defined set of Jump Shot projects. The pattern held there, too. Even when the strategic focus of the brief had been quite sharp on day one, the most successful projects were those where we had cranked it even tighter in the early stages of the engagement. Importantly, this wasn't at all about lowering the ambition or disruptive bravery we were bringing to the task, or picking off a small, simple problem. In fact we were often elevating the level of ambition from the ingoing goals, and more tightly attaching the direction of the project to the biggest strategic priorities of the company. That was a key part of what was compelling client organizations to mobilize behind the project outputs. Something broad and interesting was transformed into something specific, valuable, big, and strategically vital.

THE FOCUS FACTOR

For a company that was born believing in the power of a big idea to ignite consumer demand and to create its own momentum through an organization, this was a watershed moment. Transforming hit rates meant transforming not only the way we think about innovation ideas—coming at them from two sides, as we'd been doing for some time by that point—but about innovation strategy—forcing far more robust strategic choices to happen prior to generating ideas.

Seeing strategic focus emerge as such a key driver of successful project outcomes, we weren't surprised to see over time that the experiments in upping the quantity of ideas did nothing to elevate hit rates. In fact, zealously chasing quantity actually drove success rates down. We saw a bell curve. If you start from just a few ideas and work your way up, success rates initially improve, then flatten, then dip sharply as the number of ideas continues to escalate. It makes sense. Time, energy, and attention are finite. Going a mile wide and an inch deep, you inevitably struggle to solve the long list of questions that need solving to get an innovation to market before the clock and the money run out. Proliferation also makes decisions harder. Ideas remain so loose and vague that it's hard to say yes or no to them for extended periods of time. They limp along in half-pregnant gestation, burning resources. And in the end, you find yourself comparing apples, pineapples, and giraffes (or the occasional unicorn) trying to decide what's best. Sharp strategic focus solves these things.

INNOVATION STRATEGY DEFINED

Strategy, of course, comes in many shapes and sizes. While innovation strategy intersects and interacts with the widely studied domains of growth strategy and design strategy, it's not the same as either of them.

Growth strategy defines the hunt for revenue from any sources. Innovation may be one of them, but so can things that have nothing to do with innovation, like building distribution in China or buying into new categories. Design strategy, meanwhile, may apply to innovation, but it's at a different altitude. It makes choices about points of emphasis in the creation of a product, service, or user experience, but it implicitly assumes commercial decisions have already been made. Design strategy is as applicable to minor tweaks in existing products as it is to bona fide new-to-the-world innovations. It tends to make choices about desired *traits* of a given type of product rather than what *type of product* to create to ignite a business.

Innovation strategy is a different thing. In our practice, here's how it's defined. What it is: innovation strategy is the definition of a specific opportunity within a growth space in which new businesses, new categories, new products or services, new brands, new business models, or new routes to market will create new value. What it does: done properly, innovation strategy makes choices that narrow the playing field to define a *uniquely winnable battle* for the entity we're out to grow, how that battle can be won, and the commercial value of winning it.

If there is a well-defined growth strategy in hand, innovation strategy for a business or an individual project addresses how to fill the gap between the growth the business needs and the portion of it that can be generated by doing more with existing product lines (like rolling them into China). Innovation strategy speaks first to the kind of *business* that will be created, then in turn to the types of *products* that may be required to build that business. It often contains insights that will prove fundamental to design strategy months down the track, but the point of innovation strategy is to inform not the design of a *product* per se, but the direction, purpose, and value of a *business* ignited by one or many new products.

For an innovation strategy to be valuable, one of its key jobs is to ensure that what you're about to go create is well connected to fundamental imperatives of the business, rather than just peripherally interesting. You would think that most innovation projects would begin with a clear connection to the strategic priorities of a company, but it's true less often than you would think. Often a project begins with little more than an emerging consumer trend or a technology that popped out of the lab, with no obvious role in the future of the business. If you don't consciously look to connect the innovation back to the core issues and goals of the business, it won't happen automatically.

STRATEGIC AIR COVER

The importance of forging this alignment between the project and company imperatives cannot be overstated. General Electric's senior vice president, Chief Marketing Officer Beth Comstock, offers her valuable insights on how important this is.

Beth leads a massive community of innovators in a company with a big innovation legacy to live up to. When Thomas Edison is the founder your company, the bar is pretty high. Edison's definition of success was not just the invention of new things but the successful commercialization of them—an orientation that remains fundamental to the company's DNA today. This outcome-driven culture makes GE a company we love working with. Curiosity and imagination propel the culture, but the point of it all is not just to explore stuff. They want to make things real.

With thousands of innovation ideas in gestation at any time across a company of forty-five thousand engineers, scientists, sales teams, and marketers, Beth has a unique perspective on the role of strategy as the driver of what sees daylight and what doesn't. "Strategy is a point of view on the future. There are always unknowns to that. And there are always pressures to serve the near-term needs of the business that can make important innovations you'll need in years ahead vulnerable at any point in time. What our chairman and CEO, Jeff Immelt, and I have done is that we've isolated a protected set of innovation ideas that most closely reflect the long-term strategic needs of the business. There are about thirty of them at any time. They're protected from the triage everything else goes through every time budgets are set, or the economy softens. Jeff spends four hours a month rolling up his sleeves, checking progress and offering guidance on those protected ideas. Within that protected portfolio, there are some ideas you might call moon shots that will be slower in gestation—higher risk and higher reward, trying to get ahead of key emerging trends. Other ideas are closer in. But it's the proximity of these ideas to the company's strategic imperatives that earns them protection. Do we look at some things that are only tangentially connected to the strategy? Sure, every once in a while an idea is so powerful that you want to see what comes of it. But that's the exception. Strategy is air cover for fledgling ideas, and without strong connections to it, your permission to burn resources, and the patience the company will have waiting for tangible scaled outcomes, can be quite limited."

Connecting Beth's experience across a single massive innovation enterprise like GE with our small but diverse data set across dozens of different companies and industries, we see that it's the same pattern. Strategic alignment with big company goals is the insulator, the inoculator, the opener of doors, the procurer of resources, and the greaser of the tracks. Most important, it's not about playing it safe with the ideas. As Beth says, that protected class includes big leaps that may not work. But what keeps those leaps alive and moving forward is the strategic foundation they're built upon.

READY, AIM . . .

If innovation strategy's first job is defining this connection between the goals of the project and the strategic imperatives of the company, job two is to make clear choices about where the biggest opportunity lies. Within the addressable space defined by the project brief, the aim of strategy is to guide the exploration, homing in on the most promising parts of the playing field, saying no to things that might be interesting but appear to be less valuable. Those choices to narrow the field are based on where the intersection lies between big needs of the consumer; the needs, assets, and capabilities of the business; and the potential for revenue and profit in a given area.

BACK TO THE FUTURE

Running with this realization that hit rates and strategic focus are inextricably linked, we set about elevating the role of innovation strategy in everything we do. The good news for us was that we already had the capability; we just hadn't been using it in the most powerful way. Our Money team's initial mission had been to give us sparks of commercial insight at the front end of projects to ignite ideas, then to build out the commercial case at the back end behind the ideas we were advancing. The change here was that we would be unleashing a new level of strategic rigor to more accurately *aim* our inventiveness. To meaningfully, and often dramatically, narrow the playing field and understand its value, before a single idea took shape.

As we set out to codify what innovation strategy would mean at Fahrenheit 212, we use two inputs to shape the answer. One is the data set in hand—the extensive body of project work behind us where we transformed those Blue Sky and Fishing Trip projects into Jump Shots, transforming hit rates in the process. The other input is the experience base of our clients who lent their wisdom.

FIXING STRATEGY

Fully leveraging the value of innovation strategy wasn't simply a matter of applying it; first we would have to fix it. The picture our clients paint is that innovation strategies have their own set of problems and their own patchy success rates. When we ask them what goes right and wrong in innovation strategy, we get back a fire-hose blast of stories about innovation strategies failing to come to fruition. Whether these innovation strategies were created by in-house strategy functions, by management consultancies, or by design companies (who sometimes blur the lines between strategic design principles, which inform the creation of a product, and innovation strategy, which guides the creation of a business), three key themes jump out about where innovation strategies melt down on the way to creating revenue.

The first is the tension between the provable and the possible. As Edward de Bono eloquently put it, "The future can't be analyzed, it must be designed." Many people who find themselves working in traditional corporate strategy functions or management consultancies are world class at fact-based deductive reasoning, but less adept at the inductive (or abductive) reasoning required to traverse the known, the probable, the merely possible, and the emerging opportunity. By definition, anything that's a data point or a recent competitive move has already happened. Anything that hasn't yet happened is unproven. The balancing act in innovation strategy is to achieve a marriage of what is and what could be. A bold forward-looking strategic vision is easier to sell to company leaders or investors if it's backed by ample proof, but to shoehorn your vision to fit the limitations of a data set is to neuter its transformational potential.

Citi's chief innovation officer and chairman of Venture Capital Initiatives, Debby Hopkins, has a unique vantage point from which to see the shift in how companies have to approach innovation strategy. She and her Citi Ventures team set up shop a few years ago in

198 HOW TO KILL A UNICORN

a converted garage in the heart of Palo Alto, looking for opportunities to invest in and champion emerging technologies, while also leading the push to return Citi to its long-held position as a leader in financial services innovation. The projects we collaborate on straddle two worlds—one of a big established financial institution, and another of a highly dynamic financial services landscape undergoing rapid transformation as new technologies converge with changing customer service expectations and new economic realities. "What we're seeing," Debby says, "is that the traditional approach to strategy—one of competitive assessments and extrapolation of recent business trends—has really grown ineffectual as the marketplace has become so much more dynamic. We're no longer competing just with other big banks. We have to take a wider view, including banks, tech startups, retailers, and more. In this new environment, very few companies get strategy right anymore. Strategy has to be far more forward-looking than it used to, centered not just in what's happening now but in where the *opportunities* are, and in directing company resources to capitalize on them."

What Debby is describing is not unique to banking but something we're seeing take hold across category borders. Strategy demands a broader skill set than it used to. Debby's eclectic background, which spans CFO roles at engineering- and technology-driven giants like Boeing and Lucent, and life in the ventures frontier, leading Citi into investment positions in disruptive technology plays like Square's mobile payments platform, is exactly the kind of diversity of skills and perspectives that innovation strategy will require in the years ahead. So, too, is an eye for big ideas and disruption. Debby adds, "We're finding that strategy today should be joined at the hip with forces of disruption—in fact, we use disruptive forces as pillars of our strategy—viewing these marketplace shifts as things we either need to be a part of or counter, but can't ignore. We then take a portfolio approach, placing a range of bets along each disruption vector we believe is likely to be important."

For us at Fahrenheit, this emerging realization about the tension in innovation strategy between the provable and the possible, or as Debby puts it, between current business reality and new *opportunity*, was exciting for us. It meant that the blending of analytical and forward-looking creative perspectives is not only helpful to the future of innovation strategy but fundamental. With our Money & Magic philosophy and capabilities, we seemed to have the right tools and capabilities to raise the bar on how innovation strategy is approached, coming at it in a way that neither a management consultancy nor a design firm readily could.

Beyond this tension between the known and the possible, the second big pain point where companies saw innovation strategies coming up short was a tendency to be one-dimensional. Often companies would hold up an emerging consumer dynamic (like health and wellness, for instance) as a strategic innovation platform, without any embedded commercial perspective on what pockets of this broad consumer dynamic were likely to be addressable, winnable, and profitable for the business in question. Or the converse was true, where their strategies pointed to a pot of money, but with an inadequate sense of whether there was an unmet consumer need to solve in pursuit of that revenue, or an opportunity for transformation. To be effective, innovation strategies need to be more 360 degrees in nature. A two-sided orientation exploring the realities of the consumer and the business—from the financials to channel dynamics, competitive context, and operational perspectives—and creating a sight line to transformation, seemed as necessary in innovation strategy as it had shown itself to be in idea development.

The third pain point our clients described about innovation strategies was the fumbled handoff. Innovation strategies are rarely created by the same people responsible for translating them from PowerPoint slides into tangible, demand-creating innovations. As the strategy is being shaped and locked in, there's often no one in the room applying the filter of "what can we really create from this?"

Then, once the strategy is set, it's handed off to the idea developers. The separation between the authors of strategy and the creators of market-facing solutions essentially absolves anyone involved of accountability. If nothing succeeds, the strategist can blame the idea developer for misfiring on a brilliant strategy, and the idea developer can blame the strategist for pointing them down a dead end. All this points to the value of having the same entity accountable for innovation strategy and the solutions that come out of it. By luck or by design, we found ourselves equipped to help clients solve this.

HOW TO BUILD A GREAT INNOVATION STRATEGY

The sequence of events that began that night in San Francisco would transform the way we develop and unleash innovation strategies on our projects.

While great strategies are by definition situation-specific, and we could devote a whole book to what we've learned on this front, we've at least codified a methodology for how to go about building great ones that I'll share in hopes it helps you find greater success on the challenges in front of you.

Step 1: The Two-Track Immersion

As discussed elsewhere, it all starts with a two-track interrogation of the realities of both the consumer and the business. We often use that map of the fourteen types of insights to ensure we've done due diligence on both the consumer and commercial front. On the consumer side, this spans things like behavioral, experiential, emotional, functional, interpersonal, trend-based, contextual, and choice-based insights. On the commercial side, it includes insights about the company's goals, financials, assets, operations, channels, technologies, competition, and organizational structures. We typically devote the first six weeks of a project to this insight hunting.

Step 2: Distillation, Pattern Hunting, and Connections

With this battery of consumer and commercial data and insights, we start looking for themes, patterns, and potential connections between consumer and commercial insights. This is a distillation process, separating out what's merely interesting from what's important. We then pull four key insights out of this vast array that we think hold the keys to opportunity:

- Key Consumer Insight
- Key Company Insight
- Key Channel Insight
- Key Category Insight

The consumer insight points to unmet needs we're out to solve. The company insight points to the key unmet need(s) or strategic imperatives of the company or brand in question. The channel insight points to the key dynamic around retailers or a key aspect of the route to market that we'll need to address in order to successfully get the product into the world. The category insight points to the gap in the market, and the market we want to create in that gap.

Think of each of these insights as a lens on the problem. Overlaying a set of lenses and finding out where they overlap narrows the field of view to the most important and valuable piece of terrain. The strategy emerges at the intersection of these four key insights.

Step 3: Leaning Forward

To make the strategy a dynamic springboard to ideas rather than a static tautology, we shape three to five commercial hypotheses that grow out of the strategy. Like any good hypotheses, they are if/then statements that highlight how resolving a given tension we've identified will unlock a desired commercial outcome. For instance, if we extend the brand in question to solve an identified pain point for consumer segment X, we can be expected to deliver increased frequency of use and increased lifetime value for each customer. These hypotheses look very different from project to project, and within a given project, each hypothesis points to a different way of fulfilling the defined strategic intent. This helps force the subsequent exploration of ideas to go broad and limit the overlap among the ideas, while staying within the focal area the strategy is pointing to.

Most important, we've found that innovation strategies and the hypotheses within them are best viewed as living things, initially directing the exploration of innovation ideas, then in turn being informed by them. Again, Beth's experience and perspective have similarities to ours. She describes it this way: "There's a symbiotic relationship between innovation strategies and the ideas they spark. As I said before, a strategy is a perspective on what might play out in the future, and there are always unknowns. The progression of the

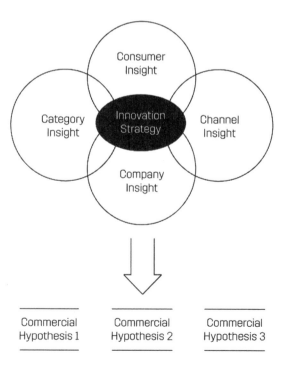

ideas pursued under a given strategy, and their successes or struggles, can validate, tighten, or reshape the definition of the strategy moving forward. Innovators have to be nimble, and this interplay between strategy and ideas is a big part of it."

While we treat strategy as a living thing, it's important that the dynamic relationship between innovation strategy and the hypotheses and ideas that spring from it not be held up as permission for lack of rigor in shaping strategy at the front end. We don't need to relearn the lesson that loose strategic intent sinks projects. The recipe that works for us is to go into idea development as strategically tight and focused as you can be, but to be open to the lessons the journey surfaces, rather than dogmatically clinging to something developed before your early-stage ideas and experiments made you wiser. At the end of a project journey, where we've gone through our strategy development process, into idea development, built ideas into solutions, and iterated them based on consumer and company guidance, we always circle back to reassess the definition of the innovation strategy. Sometimes it stands proud. Sometimes the lessons of the journey point to honing. Sometimes to more fundamental redefinition. But the right rigor at the front end makes that a rare thing.

In the end, project failure isn't a random thing. There are levers we can pull to hoist our hit rates, and innovation strategy is one of the most powerful. Think of it this way: we all have big ideas in us. Let's assume we could invent an idea to do anything on earth. Innovation strategy answers one question. Of the million things we could do, here's the one we should.

SHOTGUN TO LASER

With these realizations in hand, we had one more experiment to try. We had to see what would happen if we simultaneously raised our game on innovation strategy and actually developed fewer ideas on every project. In fact, we cut the number of ideas we developed on each engagement by half, and something amazing happened: success rates skyrocketed. In our early days we were succeeding in getting ideas embedded into company pipelines on about 25 percent of our projects—a rate far higher than the single-digit project success rates many companies experience year in and year out, but far less than we wanted to see. But as we made this pivot of bringing new rigor to innovation strategy, and building a few powerful, more deeply considered big ideas to answer a well-defined task of clear strategic and economic value, success rates took another quantum leap. Year on year, we were seeing project success rates ranging from 60 to 80 percent. This was a big deal.

One other really interesting and unexpected thing happened. The difference in success rates between the Blue Sky, Fishing Trip, and Jump Shot projects practically disappeared. Marrying the potency of approaching each idea as a two-sided solution with a better way to strategically aim that capability, the pieces had all come together. We had found a way, not the only way I'm sure, but the only way we'd ever seen, of transforming innovation from that hopeful rain dance in search of random lightning strikes into the reliable growth engine companies need it to be. Strategic focus was the final piece of the puzzle.

Circling back to that initial conclusion that promising ideas die for random reasons, we saw that we had been dead wrong. The real problem, obvious now in hindsight, was that the ideas themselves were too random.

Todd Rovak, our managing partner who has spent several years raising the bar on what innovation strategy means in our practice and teaching our teams how to do it, thinks that what was actually happening was that lack of clarity about the strategic importance of a given path was leaving ideas *vulnerable* to a seemingly random array of things derailing them.

As he puts it, "When you're trying to drive an innovation to realization, clarity of strategic intent works like a strong immune system. It doesn't fend off one potentially fatal malady; it fends off hundreds of them. Innovations that are strategically critical get the resources they need for troubleshooting killer issues. They get the top-down support they need to overcome organizational resistance. They survive changes of leadership. And they rise to the top of the pecking order in triage moments. And sharpening the focus of a team's talent and energies—ours and our clients'—creates what amounts to a great mismatch. Getting everyone focused on a very specific and lucrative piece of territory, where all that intellectual horsepower and passion is pointed in one clear direction, it actually becomes quite hard to lose."

THE ART OF THE MISMATCH

Embedded in Todd's comment is an interesting piece of philosophy about how you unleash your innovation team's formidable talents to best effect. We've come to believe that a big part of success in innovation lies in creating what sports coaches call a mismatch. In any sport you look at, game strategy is almost entirely predicated on trying to create favorable mismatches. The soccer coach wants to create situations where his fleet-footed wing faces a slow defender one-on-one. A baseball manager wants to throw off an opponent's fastball hitter by putting in his slow, junk-ball pitcher to face him. The basketball coach wants his big man getting the ball against a little guy.

In a way, what we try to do on innovation projects is create a mismatch where the combined horsepower of our team and our client represents a total mismatch against a very specific, narrowly defined problem.

Not a small problem, but a narrowly defined big one. That's a mismatch.

Instead of diluting all that firepower by going a mile wide and an inch deep, if we aim it tightly we figure there's almost no way we can lose. Maybe the right metaphor is cutting open a safe with a lot of money inside. Spread the heat around broadly and all you get is a slightly warmer, unopened safe. Concentrate the combined heat of your team—all that intellect, passion, knowledge, experience, instinct, and energy—in a single tight beam of a steel cutter, and you get the intense heat you need to cut through the thick walls of that safe and get the booty inside. The steel door that seemed impossibly thick is still impossibly thick. But instead of taking on the whole mass of it, you're pitting all your heat against one tiny piece of it at a time, working your way around until there's a hole you can reach through and grab the treasure. Aiming a team of amazing brains at a tightly defined, highly valuable, highly important strategic task makes success extremely likely. Does this make the opportunity smaller? Not at all. The level of specificity in the challenge you pin down has no correlation to its size. But our experience has shown that it has an immensely high correlation to the odds of success.

DE-LEAPING STRATEGY

Here's an example of how our innovation strategy framework plays out, in the case of Nature's Variety, using our "Four C's" framework of the four key insights, around the "de-leap" strategy we discussed in Chapter 6.

Key Consumer Insight
A lot of pet parents who believe raw food is the way pets were naturally meant to eat are staying away because the transition to raw is too big a leap, a big departure from the mealtime rituals and price points they're accustomed to.

Key Channel Insight

Until big numbers of consumers become acclimated to shopping for pet food in the freezer, our ability to grow household penetration of raw pet food will be constrained.

Key Company Insight

As the category leader, it's not just our job to carry the flag for how right raw food is, but to spearhead its march toward normalization, growing a lucrative niche market into more mainstream stature and scale.

Key Category Insight

While raw food is different on many levels, it's the form factor anchored in the messy realities of raw meat that's the biggest barrier limiting category expansion.

The innovation strategy, born at the crossroads of these key insights, brought a clear focus to the project: *Create penetration-building margin accretive innovations that reduce the leap consumers face in transitioning into the health benefits of raw food.*

Beneath this strategy, three hypotheses served as springboards to ideas, aiming the idea development explorations at three discrete aspects of the "leap" and ways to overcome it:

Hypothesis 1: De-leaping the Form

If we can replace the somewhat inconvenient and messy experience of thawing and handling raw meat with a simpler and more elegant raw experience, we'll open significant new penetration opportunities.

Hypothesis 2: De-leaping the Channel

If we can increase the retail footprint of raw pet food products beyond the freezer, we'll be discovered by more mainstream consumers who would never think to look in the freezer for their pet food.

Hypothesis 3: De-leaping the Math

If we can give consumers ways to experience what raw food can do for their pets with only a modest increase in cost per serving, they'll be able to see what they're missing and take the first step toward making the full transition over time.

The ideas that came out of this, including the move into a freeze-dried raw kibble, which allowed us to step out of the freezer and consumers to never touch the food, and the Raw Boost supplement that allowed pet parents to step into raw without jettisoning the food and cost-per-meal they were used to serving, successfully delivered against each of these hypotheses. In the long run, the hypotheses are just tools to ignite the process. Future work we've done against that overall strategy of de-leaping the transition to raw has used different sets of hypotheses to aim idea development, specific to the task at hand.

Chapter 13

2B or Not 2B

Trying to crack a thorny question on an idea in development, with the features of the product very much up in the air, the conversation in our back room can sound like a shrink teasing out feedback from a client on the couch.

"What about Phil?"

"Phil who?"

"The truck driver. Let's call him Phil."

"What about him?"

"What are his problems?"

"Traffic jams, a stiff back, gas prices, finding good parking?"

"But what are his problems with the vending machines he's paid to service every day?"

"He gets up on a cold morning, stops for gas and mediocre coffee, and starts his usual Wednesday loop. He sits in traffic with a stiff back and an idling engine. He finally gets to the first machine on his route, opens the door, sees how much inventory is gone, takes the money, restocks it, and moves on."

"Okay..."

"He hops back in his truck and heads eight blocks to the next machine. He loads his dolly with inventory and heads into the building, but that machine's still almost full. He scoops a few bucks out of the till, tops off the inventory, and moves on."

"How does he feel about that?"

"He's a bit pissed that he came all that way for basically nothing.

He hops back in the truck and heads across town. Still pissed about that full machine and the traffic, he's starting to feel like the traffic lights are conspiring against him. He gets to the next location, but has to double-park and gets honked at. He gets to the machine, opens the door, and sees that it's totally empty, in need of a full reload."

"How does he feel about that?"

"On one hand he feels like he's added a lot of value. But he also knows an empty machine's just a big electric paperweight. It's a dead asset that stopped making money days ago, and turned away a lot of potential customers since it ran out. Those machines pay his salary so that can't be good."

"So what's Phil's real problem with vending machines?"

"I guess it's timing. Across his loop, odds are he's either too early or too late getting to any given machine. Neither is good. If he's too early, his time and gas are wasted. If he's too late, the machine stopped making money, maybe days ago. And each too-early stop makes the too-late stops even later."

"Okay, but those are just symptoms. What's his real problem with vending machines?"

"He's flying blind. He can't tell which machines need him until he's already made the trip, turned the key, and yanked opened the door."

"Okay, let's make fixing that visibility problem part of the answer."

This foray into Phil's day is interesting on many levels. From a standpoint of technique, we're using storytelling as a method to put ourselves in the shoes of someone whose life we want to improve through the innovation we're working on. Harry Potter creator J. K. Rowling describes imagination as "the power that enables us to em-pathize with humans whose experiences we have never shared." Research is invaluable, but you don't need research to prescribe every step you take. Humans innovating for humans can get pretty far using their humanity.

Out of our narrative about Phil, we came to the realization that we could take a lot of stress out of his workday (and put a lot of money in his company's coffers) by making real-time data streaming and smart service dispatch features of a new interactive vending system—a whole new category of equipment we were imagining. By now you may have seen interactive vending machines in your hometown, down at the mall, selling anything from Coke to Wonka candy bars, ice cream, and even lipstick. What's interesting here is that Phil isn't the customer for the innovation we helped to create. He is not the hallowed end user that user-centered design methods tell us to obsess about.

So why be worried about Phil's tough day?

It's because business-to-business innovation (or B2B) is far more complex than its business-to-consumer (B2C) cousin. Consumer innovation usually involves a pretty lean business system—often just a manufacturer or service provider and an end user (by way of a retailer). B2B innovation, on the other hand, often involves broad ecosystems with a wide array of players you need to solve for if you want to see the innovation widely adopted and successful.

For example, as we map out the ecosystem for the new vending machines, there are no fewer than seven key players with meaningful roles in turning interactive vending machines from a hunch into a successful business. First, Samsung has to make the screens and microprocessors that make interactive vending machines tick. Their direct customers are the vending equipment manufacturers who, if we could convince them that interactive vending was an important innovation their business needs, would buy the raw components and assemble the machines. The equipment company in turn would sell the machines to consumer packaged goods companies who want to sell their drinks, snacks, ice cream, or whatever. The CPG companies would then put them in the hands of vending operating companies, with employees like Phil to service the machines. At the end of the food chain is the consumer, trying to grab something quick before hopping on a train.

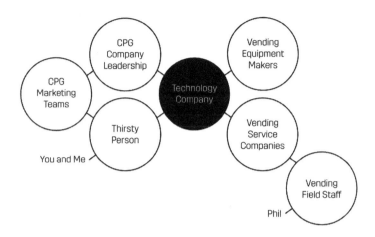

It doesn't take long to see that approaching this challenge with a singular focus on any one piece of this ecosystem will set you up for tough sledding. The needs of you and me—the end users—are important, but in a B2B play like this, they often have very limited influence on whether a new innovation like interactive vending will ever make it to market. The end user is asked to drop a buck or two on a snack or drink. In vending's case, we traditionally buy there only when there's no other option in proximity, so we're not picky about the nature of the equipment, we just want what it has. The other players in the ecosystem, meanwhile, are asked to shell out millions in capital investments and deploy their staff in new ways if they place a bet on interactive vending. It would be a problem if consumers were to reject it, but consumer appeal is just a box to tick. We can't assume consumers' enthusiasm will be enough to motivate everyone else who has to buy in. Said another way, consumers can say no, but they can't say yes to making it happen.

Where the Money & Magic way of thinking is so helpful to an undertaking like this is that deep down in its DNA, it is a multi-constituent approach to innovation. It says that for any innovation to work, it has to address the needs of all the key players in a business system. In B2C innovation, that typically means diagnosing and solving the needs of just two constituents, the consumer and the business, making the innovation challenge a two-sided problem. (The retailer is in the background, of course, but if you solve an unmet consumer need in a well-differentiated, profitable way, the retailer will usually come on board.) To win in complex B2B landscapes, however, B2B innovations need to simultaneously solve the needs of many different constituents. The moment we decided in our strategy phase that there was an opportunity to disrupt the languishing vending industry with a new interactive platform powered by Samsung technology, we signed up to solve a seven-sided problem.

In the vending machine scenario, instead of solving for the needs of *the* business, we needed to solve for *four different* businesses at once, and in turn a few different players within each of them. The four businesses were Samsung as a technology provider, the vending equipment maker, the CPG companies, and the vending machine operating companies.

What's true in this project and in the majority of B2B innovations of this scale is that the needs and motivations that bring one member of the ecosystem to the table are likely to be very different from the needs of the other players. In fact, they often have little or nothing to do with one another. This means each player in the ecosystem needs a value proposition all their own. One of the underlying mantras of our Money & Magic approach is "ideas at the crossroads"—that is, you have to understand the breadth of needs your innovation has to thread its way through, and build solutions at the crossroads where those needs can be served through a single product or innovation. The odds of a solution you build with only one constituent in mind working across all the others are astronomically small.

Maneuvering across these complex ecosystems demands resourcefulness. You rarely have open-ended amounts of time and money to do exhaustive exploratory research across a seven-part ecosystem, or anything close to it. Each part of the ecosystem could have scores of companies or players within it. One of our goals with interactive vending was to expand the footprint of industries in the vending arena, so we couldn't even confine our thinking to the companies that use vending today. Yet despite these constraints, we had to get to at least a solid hypothesis about what's keeping each constituent up at night.

Step one is to make assumptions about the pecking order among

When a fly looks at the world, it doesn't see one big picture but a series of discrete cells. In looking at B2B innovation challenges, we find that's a helpful way to look at the ecosystem you need to win over to get your idea to market. Each "cell" needs its own value proposition.

these players. There is always a pecking order, where some players are drivers, and others can be expected to fall in line if the key influencers buy in. While we're designing a value proposition for everyone involved, we're looking to identify the one player most capable of being the market maker, whose interest alone could ignite the rest. It's like tipping dominoes. You need to tip the right one first to tip the rest.

At Fahrenheit 212, the task of working out those levels of influence is led by Engagement Manager Nithya George, a former investment banker with a Wharton MBA. While the members of the Magic team are playfully putting themselves in Phil the truck driver's boots, Nithya is pounding the digital pavement, hunting for clues about what the business problems are that the companies in the vending ecosphere are most concerned about.

She starts her search with the vending equipment manufacturers. Scouring industry reports and financial analysts' assessments, she finds that the vending equipment business is in a deep hole with no obvious way out. With a lot of their equipment still wedded to lever and pulley technologies dating back to the seventies, they're facing a vicious cycle. The equipment business is sinking due to a lack of innovation, leaving their clientele (the packaged goods companies and vending operators who buy most of the machines) waiting for old machines to break down before they invest in new ones. The new machines they're selling are only marginally better than the old ones, so there's no motivation to replace machines sooner than necessary. The vending equipment companies' soft business performance leaves them starved for the investment capital they'd need to finance the kind of innovations capable of reinvigorating the market. Our value proposition to them is pretty clear early on. We'll win them over by getting other companies to write the check for the innovations they so desperately need.

Setting her sights next on the consumer packaged goods companies, Nithya plugs away for weeks hunting for insight on how these companies' senior executives see vending's role in their future. At one of our team work sessions, where we batted around dozens of questions we needed to answer across the complex B2B play, she vented frustration that she couldn't find any meaningful research on vending's role in CPG businesses' future. As we dug deeper, we understood why. Vending wasn't strategic for these companies. It was just something they did as a distribution tactic. Vending wasn't a big part of their business. The implication was that we couldn't get these companies excited by saying we were making vending better. A better version of a nonstrategic product or service is still nonstrategic, and a tough sell. We had to connect vending to things that were keeping these executives awake at night—core business problems where a reimagined approach to vending could be part of the answer.

Looking at the problem a whole new way—not hunting for CPG companies' issues with vending, but rather their core issues where we might be able to make vending a solution—Nithya found that issue. Facing a rapidly fragmenting media world, CPG leaders are deeply concerned about how to maintain and build their brands' relationships with consumers in the years ahead. In hindsight, this realization was the pivotal moment in the project that steered it down the path to success. A realization that the value proposition of interactive vending wouldn't be about a vending machine that looked cool and sold a few more units of whatever, but about something bigger. Interactive vending represented the opening up of a new communication channel between brands and the consumers on the streets. Picturing an end state of millions of machines around the world, talking to headquarters and to one another, there was something quite profound here. The world's first media network owned by the marketers who use it. A network that by the way would sell a lot of product, more than twice as much as the old machines, but that wasn't the big selling point. We were giving the world's best marketers a dynamic new, proprietary media platform of their own.

After we had mapped the ecosystem, found the pain points of

all the industries involved, worked out the ecosystem pecking order, and begun to sketch out the value propositions we'd offer each of them, the last key step was to work out what kind of product, system, and user experience it would take to make all this happen. We'd go deep into the functional features, tech specs, economics of equipment and business model, and user experience that consumers would encounter. As we were out to make interactive vending a platform innovation leaving room for hundreds of companies to create their own innovations on top of it over time (much as Apple approached the apps business), we were not out to define a prescriptive user experience, but rather to strategically define the key platform characteristics to guide and inspire other innovators using the platform for years to come. The direction we mapped out was that this should not be seen as a TV on the street, but a whole new medium, blending the push capability of broadcast television and the one-to-one, two-way interactivity of the internet. Interactive vending was born.

A big vivid touchscreen would dominate the front of each machine. The screen would have multiple roles. When no consumers were close by, it had a passive role in displaying dynamic branded content—not running TV commercials, though it could, but rather engaging new content purpose-built for this new medium, provoking, amusing, and attracting consumers from a distance. This was important to the business proposition. It was helping brands engage consumers and build valuable impressions, even if they weren't approaching the machines and buying.

Once consumers step up to the machines, the screen plays two new roles. First, it allows various forms of one-to-one interactions, from entertaining experiences to pulling up product information. Taps of the screen can access nutritional information, or hidden surprises waiting in the interface. Tapping the screen is also the way you select and buy a product. This allows a machine to stop promoting what it has run out of, rather than always having a button for each item, whether it's in stock or not.

In the end, we found the win-win times seven, solving for each part of this complex B2B ecosystem:

- For our client Samsung, the value proposition was that they could open and lead a big whitespace market, providing LCD screens and microchips to transform a market of almost 20 million stand-alone vending machines worldwide into interactive vending networks.

- For those consumer packaged goods executives, the value proposition was that while these new machines would deliver higher sell-through rates than current vending machines, the real value was that we're transforming these multimillion-dollar arrays of vending machines from a bunch of passive, dumb, disconnected assets into the world's first media network owned by the marketer who uses it.

- For brand leaders within those CPG companies, we were giving them a dynamic new brand-building tool, letting them connect their brands to consumers in a whole new interactive way, right at the point of consumption.

- To the vending equipment makers, the value proposition was that we were accelerating upgrade cycles, opening vending to new product categories, and bringing other companies' capital to the table to put into effect the innovation the equipment industry so desperately needed.

- To consumers, we were replacing an antiquated machine of last resort with a dynamic, fun, engaging, and social experience.

- For the vending operating companies, we were offering a way to drive down the out-of-stock rates that are the bane of their business model.

- And for good old Phil, driving his weekly rounds, we were

taking away the frustration of battling his way across town for nothing.

Coca-Cola became the first mover to jump on the new platform, jointly unveiling it with Samsung at the Beijing Olympics. Huge crowds lined up to play with the machines, which allowed them to twirl bottles around in explosive graphics.

Unilever was the next high-profile company to move into interactive vending, using it to sell ice cream, adding an overlay of facial recognition software to the system so that a customer with a big enough smile could get a free ice cream; images captured by the machine could be doctored up and sent straight from the machine to Facebook. Kraft picked it up next and used mood recognition software to recommend meals to potential customers. Nestlé jumped into interactive machines for its highly experiential Wonka candy brand. Even L'Oréal saw the potential, realizing that the interactive platform allowed image-conscious brands that never would have touched a vending machine in the past to bring exciting high-end experiences to a selling platform that never had them before. Called the Intelligent Color Experience, the L'Oréal machine deployed in the New York subway scans a woman's look as she stands in front of its built-in mirror, makes suggestions for makeup ideas that would work with her outfit, and filters the seven hundred products in the machine based on whether they'd match or clash with her look.

Our ambition to open a whole new category of vending equipment had been realized, with huge amounts of new revenue flowing across all corners of the ecosystem. Kraft reported sales velocity twice that of conventional machines. The *Financial Times* reported that while interactive vending machines cost roughly three times more than the traditional non-networked machines, they deliver ten times the return on investment.

But the crowning moment of interactive vending's journey, at least so far, came in 2013. The idea that vending could be transformed from a dumb machine of last resort into a networked platform for building customer relationships was initially just a strategic hunch. But Coca-Cola and its communications agencies put an exclamation point on it by using the system to do something amazing.

India and Pakistan share national borders and a great deal of cultural heritage. But for the past sixty years they've been bitterly divided. Since the borders were drawn in 1947, simmering political tensions have obscured the centuries-old cultural connections. Generations of young people have grown up without realizing how close the people on opposite sides of these relatively new borders had been all along. Coke took a small but intensely emotional step toward bridging that divide.

With considerable fanfare, they set up one interactive vending machine in a mall in the Indian city of New Delhi, and another three hundred miles away in the Pakistani city of Lahore. Each machine had a camera beaming a live feed of the scene in front of it for display on the machine on the other side of the border. A welcoming animated interface invited passersby in India to say hi and make a friend in Pakistan, and vice versa.

Timidly at first, a thirtyish Pakistani woman approached the machine, nervously smiled, and offered a little wave. On the other end, a fifty-something man in New Delhi waved back. They both beamed. The ice was broken. As the crowds built and more people stepped up, the machine, activated by the wave, egged them on to do things together. The digital suggestion, "Trace a Happy Picture," set in motion the tracing of dynamic sparkling hearts and peace signs. The tracing only worked when two individuals' hands, three hundred miles apart but digitally "touching," moved together in mirror image along the trace line.

As everyone grew more comfortable and excited, a prompt from the machine to "Do a Little Dance" unleashed a charismatic old white-haired Pakistani man into a freewheeling boogie that provoked the Indian onlookers into wild cheers, exhorting a local elder to keep up. Interviewed as they watched it unfold, an onlooker commented, "We're so much the same, but the drawing of these borders has made us feel like enemies. It's good to laugh and smile together and remember how close we are." Coke captured this magic moment in a deeply moving documentary video. Creating togetherness has been a core brand equity of Coca-Cola for as long as anyone at the company can remember. It's always your hope when you invent a new platform that smart people will find potential in it that's in line with what you imagined, yet far beyond it. The belief that something as unemotional as vending, long a dumb distribution tool of last resort, could be transformed into a dynamic tool for building brands and consumer relationships had been realized.

So what can we take away from all this and put to work on other B2B innovation challenges?

There are some helpful lessons in the way we came at it.

First, try to look at multiple needs rather than focusing only on the end user.

Dissect what those needs are.

Figure out the priorities—which needs do you need to address and solve for first?

Look for a solution at the crossroads of those different needs.

Principles of user-centered design have to be applied with care and appropriate context in B2B innovation, particularly in a case like this, opening a whole new category that disrupts everything about a given market. Here, all the players in the ecosystem are "users" in one way or another, and the literal end user turns out to be the least influential player in whether this vision gets to market. You need a multilayered approach to nail the value proposition for the different market makers who will make or break you.

A LESSON IN B2B COMPLEXITIES

Google is an amazing company that gets most things right. A rare and expensive misfire has been Google Wallet. Attempting to replace your cowhide billfold with an all-digital alternative, digitizing all your credit cards and loyalty cards on a phone-based application, it's been an ambitious attempt at winning across an immensely complex ecosystem. *Bloomberg Businessweek* estimates that the company spent more than $300 million acquiring digital payment startups to abet the effort, and committed hundreds of developers to the program for several years. But it's been a failure by all public accounts, with the leaders of the Google Wallet team having left the company, and with expected enhancements to the service having been canceled or delayed. Google Wallet is perhaps an idea ahead of its time, though some of the structural factors impeding its success will be hard to ever overcome. But for now, it's a great case study in what can go wrong if you don't solve for each cell of a complex B2B ecosystem.

The goal of Google Wallet wasn't to step into the payments business and make money on transaction fees, but rather to open new commercial capillaries through which it could use customer data to sell targeted advertising. Clearly this would be good for Google, as it fell right in line with their core business model. And if it functioned properly, it would offer new convenience to consumers. The problem was the litany of businesses sitting in the ecosystem between Google and the consumer, each of whom would need a big value proposition to overcome structural reasons why they wouldn't readily want to come aboard. Credit card companies demanded such high fees to participate in the program that Google reportedly lost money on every transaction. Phone carriers, believing that mobile payments are a gold mine and a future revenue stream they want a piece of, blocked Google Wallet in favor of their own similar service. Few mobile handset makers embedded the near-field communication (NFC) technology Google Wallet needed for ease of use as a payment tool at retail. Carrier resistance and the lack of NFC-enabled handsets meant Google Wallet could work on very few phones. And the retail sector, an extremely fragmented part of the ecosystem with hundreds of thousands of decision makers and touch points required for large-scale penetration, was slow to install NFC systems.

Marry up very few phones with very few merchants and you quickly undermine the convenience-driven consumer proposition. You would still need your old wallet to make it through your day. Each intermediary player needed a powerful value proposition to make it worth their trouble. It's not obvious that Google Wallet had a slam-dunk value prop for anyone in the B2B ecosystem standing between it and the end user. It appears to have underwhelmed, or run counter to the motivations of, many of the constituents that needed to be won over.

The lesson here: in B2B, you need a multi-constituent approach, shaping a winning value proposition for everyone that can block your innovation in its tracks.

Chapter 14

A Little Myth Busting

Some myths about innovation we're better off leaving behind.

The lessons thrown off by the experiences of tens of thousands of innovators working on radically different tasks have one thing in common: they are situation specific.

Applying the right approach to the wrong context is like using a flyswatter to paddle a canoe. In working on innovations across a wide body of activity, a particular type of myth tends to take hold. Things are held up as truisms or principles that are not untrue, but that are true in only in particular situations. Innovation is hard enough. Keeping the myths at bay is important to any team's pursuit of innovation success. Here are a set of myths that too often are held up as universal truths, when they aren't.

MYTH #1: IF YOU SOLVE FOR THE NEEDS OF THE MARKETPLACE, THE NEEDS OF YOUR BUSINESS WILL TAKE CARE OF THEMSELVES.

Experience has shown this to be one of the more expensive myths in innovation, and the root cause of vast troves of ingenious ideas coming to nothing. Like all the myths I'll call out here, the problem is a "sometimes true" thing being held up as universally true. The circumstance where it is consistently true is very narrow: when you're just iterating on existing products or well-established businesses. If you're just working on this year's version of last year's thing, and making your money out of the same economic engines you always have, all you need to worry about is understanding market needs and honing your next new-and-improved iteration. But if you're working on entering new businesses you're not in today, transforming the value chain, opening new tiers of an existing market, or creating new ones, this mantra of "solve for the needs of the market and the business will take care of itself" is often fatal. The business will rarely solve itself. This is not to say back off on the intensity you apply to solving those consumer needs, but that applying inadequate intensity to the other side of the equation will be an expensive omission.

The other context where "solve for the consumer, the business will take care of itself" can sometimes be true is in tech startups. But there's an irony here. The oft-repeated mantra in tech startups is that if you build a consumer base, the money will eventually come. The quiet truth, though, is that most successes born this way eventually make their money selling advertising. The advertising business model didn't need inventing. It was always there. So, yes, if success just requires building an audience of users, where you aren't selling those users something—you're selling other companies the eyeballs of your users—you can just worry about solving the needs of the marketplace.

But as a general rule, if you're tasking an innovation team with creating something new, assuming the business will sort itself out is the single best way to tilt the odds against your ambitions coming to fruition.

MYTH #2: THINKING ABOUT HOW TO MAKE MONEY IS TOXIC TO CREATIVITY.

This is another narrow situational truth that's been given universal status. I've found that talking about how money will be made kills creativity in just two specific situations.

One is where you leave those profitability concerns to the back end—when your creative thinkers have shaped a vision in a commercial vacuum, and the introduction of profitability questions late in the game cuts through the creative vision like a buzz saw. The best way to avoid that is to work out the profitability levers at the front of the process, so they become part of the creative toolbox. At the front end, understanding the levers of profitability doesn't mute creativity, it empowers it to use them, bend them, or stretch them.

The other circumstance where talk of profitability kills creativity is where the creative people tasked with shaping a vision for a big innovation haven't had enough exposure to the commercial factors to be comfortable doing their best work in that context. Not enough attention has been given to getting highly creative people who've chosen career paths in innovation to be comfortable with the commercial factors that determine whether their vision gets to market, and incorporate them into the creative process. At Fahrenheit, we've had a chance to see what happens when you join creativity and commercial perspectives at the hip from the first day of a project to the last. Seeing this play out, I've reached the conclusion that there's a self-fulfilling prophecy at work here. The unfounded belief that talk of profitability kills creativity has fostered a tendency to shelter creative thinkers from commercial conversations. This has perpetuated their inability to make commercial factors part of the creative process. In our practice, the most creative minds in the company have become both adept and instinctive about empowering their visions with sound commercial foundations. This has not muted or diminished their creativity one bit. In fact, it has extended it, putting more colors on their palette.

Don't coddle or shelter creativity from the factors that decide whether visionary innovations make it to market or don't. Make them part of the vision. You'll drive up your success rates if you do.

MYTH #3: CREATIVITY WORKS BEST IN THE ABSENCE OF PRESSURE TO DELIVER.

This is another of these sometimes-true things that's been unhelpfully distorted, perhaps because it's been a godsend to people who prefer to skate along free of accountability. It has been debunked in any number of studies. Remember, it takes pressure to make a precious diamond.

Peak creativity does need windows of time with no pressure. But it also benefits from other windows where the pressure gets somewhat intense. It's the interplay of pressure-free periods of time and moments of intense pressure and interrogation that really drives peak creativity. Pressure moments ignite and engage a different part of the brain. Fierce time constraints force us to cast widely for answers without the filters or censors we usually apply. There's a freedom in these creative moments that doesn't appear in more relaxed situations.

Also, there is a difference between good pressure and bad pressure. Bad pressure is threatening to fire someone if they fail at the task. Fear doesn't inspire. Good pressure does, and it comes in several forms. Accountability is positive pressure. It means taking ownership of what you're doing and the outcomes that result from it. Setting high standards is another form of positive pressure. The same is true of peer-based pressure. At Fahrenheit 212, we hire highly creative, motivated people and give them a simple mission: amaze one another every day. The pressure to excite, provoke, and inspire their colleagues is an unparalleled form of positive pressure.

The right kind of pressure is a potent creative catalyst.

MYTH #4: IF YOU HAVE A VISIONARY IDEA, ANY SMART MANAGEMENT TEAM CAN FIGURE OUT ITS STRATEGIC VALUE, HOW TO MAKE IT, AND HOW TO MAKE MONEY FROM IT.

If the idea in question is even moderately disruptive relative to what you or your company knows how to do, assuming someone else will solve the hard unsolved questions is like mailing in your tax return on a paper airplane and hoping the breeze takes it in the right direction. If *you* can't articulate the answers to your sponsors and management, how can you expect someone else who is less familiar with the project to do it for you? It's just not true that if you crack the big idea anyone can work out the rest. So take ownership of the whole thing, especially the hardest questions. And know that the more disruptive an innovation is, the harder those questions will be.

MYTH #5: SOLVING CONSUMER PROBLEMS IS CREATIVE; THE BUSINESS SIDE IS JUST FIGURING OUT THE NUTS AND BOLTS.

When you obsess over outcomes and sweat the details of what it takes to get to market, you come to an important realization about where creativity matters: it matters everywhere. It often takes just as much imagination to tackle seemingly unsolvable questions on the commercial side of an innovation as it does to solve for the consumer need. Assuming that the commercial factors don't need as much lateral thinking is a big misconception. Yet too often, the cleverest minds on a project team are allowed to check out once the consumer proposition is defined. We worked that way, too, in our early years, until we learned better.

MYTH #6: INSIGHT IS SOMETHING YOU EXTRACT FROM RESEARCH.

Again, this is a sometimes-true situational thing that's taken on a life of its own, and been applied with unhelpful breadth. I prefer to look at insight as the result of human synapse, which lets us see new connections and deep underlying truths beneath what we see on the surface. I've found that perhaps half of the best innovation-igniting insights we've uncovered over the years have surfaced as direct outputs of research, where that synapse we're after happened in the mind of someone we spoke with in research, so we could essentially borrow their insight. But the other half have come about through deep contemplation, heavily informed by research, but going beneath and beyond the literal outputs of the research to find deeper meaning. Thinking of insight as a synaptic process rather than a research deliverable keeps people thinking deeply, continually asking "why," and not considering the insight generation process finished just because the research phase is finished.

MYTH #7: FLEDGLING IDEAS SHOULD BE EXPLORED IN A JUDGMENT-FREE ZONE.

Using a model that turns this view on its head—where instead of creating a judgment-free zone where every idea is celebrated, we deliberately fuse creativity and intensive constructive criticism in real time—has been a key piece of how we've transformed innovation hit rates. By rapidly drilling into the tough questions that an idea will eventually have to answer, we strengthen ideas, where judgment-free ideation doesn't bring those hard questions to the surface until it's too late to solve them. There's a big enough body of evidence, both academically and in our own experience, to cement our conviction that this is the better creative approach. For us at least, the value of creative debate is no longer debatable. As for how to avoid applying the principle to inappropriate situations, let's state the obvious: don't debate issues or ideas until you have something worth debating. But once you have the raw material, go at it. A healthy tension between points of view is a powerful creative force that's neutered by the old edict of "don't judge" when you hear an idea. Turn it loose. You'll see your team's imaginations soar. Just keep it positive.

MYTH #8: PROTOTYPING AS SOON AS POSSIBLE IS THE PATH TO GLORY.

I'm a huge fan of prototyping and we do a lot of it, but I'm consistently surprised that people leap to it as a reflex response when it's not what they really need. In the right situations, prototyping hits the fast-forward button on learning and getting something primed for market. But there are a lot of situations where it proves to be an expensive, time-consuming distraction, steering attention to the smaller issues around an innovation opportunity while leaving the big ones unattended. Working out the ideal form factor for a spoon to be cradled in a toddler's hand is great once you have a compelling strategic and commercial basis for how you're going to win in the toddler spoons business, but if you don't have one, it's premature. It's as if there's a tacit assumption that getting the perfect form factor will make the other issues go away or get solved by somebody else. Are your project's sponsors or investors losing any sleep over whether you'll get that diameter right, or are they still at the level of wondering whether this is a business they want to be in? Is your core consumer value proposition solid enough that people will ever get close enough to the product you're fine-tuning to care how artfully it's been finessed? And is that proposition solid enough to guide you through the prototyping journey so you know what true north looks like? In the right situation, the prototyper's mantra, "build to think," is powerful. But in many situations, it's only lucrative for the people paid to make the premature prototypes. "Think to think" is in many circumstances the better call.

MYTH #9: FAILURE IS AWESOME.

Of all the sometimes-true lessons taken out of context, this one is the poster child. It's been bent to the breaking point, bastardized, abused, and even monetized by people hoping to make their sponsors feel good about losing a fortune investing in programs that come to nothing. The goal in innovation is not failure, it is success—bringing a new concept or product to market and successfully helping to grow the business. It's time to turn the page on failure's odd newfound fashionability.

Chapter 15

The F Word

Is innovation failure the valuable result everybody says it is?

Of late, innovation failure has taken on lofty stature, garnering so much celebratory ink in books and articles about innovation that I feel compelled to lend a fresh perspective, and hopefully some tempering sanity, to the dialogue.

THE FEAR FACTOR

Like the X Games of modern business, a big innovation challenge sets us racing down a mountain of variables, carving and cutting our way through obstacles, jumps, and stage gates, negotiating questions that come at us one by one:

\what's the strategy\
/what's the insight/
\what's the target\
/what's the category/
\what's the value prop\
/what's the product/
\what's the value chain\
/what's the competitive advantage/
\what's the risk\

/what's the reward/
\what did we overlook?\

Leaning the wrong way at any turn can undo months of sweat equity, leaving your limbs akimbo and your ambitions scattered in pieces up and down the hill.

To get out of bed every morning and do this over and over takes fearlessness and bravery. Failure is an ever-present possibility. Fearlessness is undeniably essential to innovation success. Fearing failure dooms us to think small, to cling to the comfortable, and to stop growing—both as businesses and as people. The generation of kids that's grown up relatively sheltered from failure's lessons, where everybody gets a trophy and is told daily that they're gifted, may in the long run be worse off for not tasting struggle.

In Fahrenheit 212's chosen endeavor, deciding to take on something as ubiquitous as innovation failure certainly required a fearless streak. The irony wasn't lost on us that in taking on failure, we were almost certain to fail. Let me say then with a level of street cred that I get the need for fearlessness. But that still leaves a big question: is innovation failure as good a thing as it's made out to be?

Edward Hess, professor at the Darden Graduate School of Business, and distinguished author of ten books and scores of articles on growth, played back much of the conventional wisdom around innovation failure in a recent *Forbes* piece. "My colleague Professor Jeanne Liedtka and I have spent combined over 17 years studying innovation leaders, systems and processes. What we found is that innovation requires a mindset that rejects the fear of failure and replaces that fear of failure with the joy of exploration and experimental learning. We also found that innovation organizations understand that failures are a necessity (. . . as much as 90% of the time) so long as the learning comes from small risk experiments. As one innovation leader stated: 'we celebrate success; we console failure; and we get rid of those who are afraid to try.'"

At the core, these are views I share, as would anyone living on innovation's front lines. A restless, exploratory spirit invigorates the chase and gives curious minds the freedom to probe the possible, extract the valuable, and abandon the fruitless.

But as right as all of this is, particularly for startups, I'm increasingly feeling like this celebration of failure has gone too far, and diverted attention from the real issues companies are facing today around their innovation challenges, investments, and returns.

Years on the front lines have taught me that there are two kinds of companies in the world: those that don't try enough innovation, and those that do.

For the companies that don't, the blitz of messaging about the value and nobility of failing is relevant and important. Their problem is they aren't failing enough.

But for the companies that do try a lot but fail a lot, which appear to be in the significant majority, the problem isn't the fear of failure, it's the reality of failure. They're trying plenty. Investing a fortune. Throwing their best and brightest at it. At times being bold and brave. They don't need more trying; they need more succeeding out of the vast amount of trying that they're already doing. Not by getting cautious or ducking risk, but by finding ways to make those brave moves pay out a lot more often.

For these companies, saying innovation failure's a great thing may make some people feel better about it, and perhaps help them persist. But let's be honest: failing at something you're relentlessly striving to succeed at sucks. It's bad for everyone involved: for the people trying to solve innovation problems, and for the people writing the checks for their explorations. We're overdue to bring the failure conversation in line with their reality.

I chatted recently with Luke Mansfield, Samsung's UK-based head of Innovation, on this subject of the nobility of failure. He's an innovation veteran who's worked in many different sectors and leads a high-performing team with a great success rate. Asked what he thinks when he hears someone stand up and say how great failing is, he pulls no punches. "The reality is that innovation has become a hot topic and a sexy career and has attracted a lot of people who are delivering little to no real value. They've rallied behind the nobility of failure as a great postrationalization for how little they've delivered. I'd liken it to a flood ravaging entire towns, leaving homes and lives in ruin, and someone raving about how all the silt washed in by the flood will be good for the crops. I'm sorry but it's not good."

Yes, fearing failure is an impediment. But celebrating it isn't helpful, either. What these companies need isn't palliative rhetoric, it's an actionable remedy.

So ask yourself one question: is my company trying enough big brave new things? If the answer is no, give innovation failure a hug, embrace its nobility, get past the fear, and go try big, brave stuff. But if, like at most companies, the answer is yes, we're trying a lot but not succeeding as often as our growth goals demand, then for God's sake don't put innovation failure on a pedestal. For you, innovation failure isn't a noble hero. It's a bully lurking by the water cooler, looking to steal your lunch money, your shareholders' dividends, your next promotion, and your kids' college fund. Don't fear it. But don't hug it. Find a way to beat it. Change the way you're approaching your projects and work tirelessly to drive up your hit rate. Raising the flag to celebrate innovation failure won't raise your hit rate.

A QUESTION OF FREQUENCY

After thinking about whether you're not failing enough or failing too much, we can add the missing modifier: innovation failure is a great thing . . . *only in moderation.*

In 2005, on the way to winning skiing's World Cup, Bode Miller fell or failed to finish more often than anyone else on the circuit, crashing out in about 30 percent of his runs. That was a sign that he was going for it, operating at the cusp of maximum speed and control, continuing to push the envelope. That's where you want to be in innovation: failing often enough to know that you're testing the limits, but succeeding a lot, too. What won Bode the title wasn't falling down, but going fast while staying upright 70 percent of the time. Professor Hess's big point is right, but it's a sign that something's very wrong when a 90 percent failure rate can be a parenthetical aside. In any other business pursuit, a failure rate that high would be the headline. Show me a ski racer who falls 90 percent of the time and I'll show you a racer bounced from his team.

Innovation is hard. But there's no shortage of pursuits in human endeavor that are really hard. Brain surgery is hard. Fighting terrorism is hard. Rocket science really *is* rocket science. But in none of these hard things is failure a celebrated thing. It shouldn't get the blanket praise it's getting in innovation, either. Failing is *only* great in moderation. But that's not where most companies find themselves today. They're failing too often, too slowly, and at a very high price.

THE BLURRY LINES

When you look closely, a lot of the celebration of innovation failure is predicated on an unhelpful blurring of lines between iteration and failure.

Iteration is great, fundamental, and part of every innovation success story I've ever heard or been part of. Swapping out version 1.0 of whatever you're working on for version 2.0 isn't failure. It's iteration.

Getting to version 2.0, running out of time and money, then being told by your sponsors they're shutting you down and there's no revenue to show for it, that's project failure.

Stop lumping iteration and failure together like they're the same thing. One's unequivocally good. The other is usually not.

ITERATION ≠ FAILURE

THE GREAT TEACHER

Another big theme in the glorification of innovation failure is its purported great educational value.

Spending years working with scores of the world's great companies, my observation is that innovation failure comes with a very high tuition bill, but the lessons don't take hold very well. The problem is human nature, particularly where it intersects with careers and company politics. Successes get very noisy. Failures keep a relatively low profile. If the value of a lesson learned in a company is a function of how well it travels, failure's lessons struggle to deliver as much value as those of success.

An illustration of this came from the widely read website InnovationExcellence.com, which has a great series called Failure Forums. One recent piece described Best Buy's ambitious but unsuccessful attempt at becoming a vertically integrated entertainment business by launching its own record label, called Redline Entertainment, signing its own recording artists, and getting rival retailers to carry them (a wishful assumption that didn't play out). What was striking about the piece was that its focus was less on the project itself than on the fact that the failure was actually documented and circulated in a white paper. Author Matt Hunt described it this way: "What makes [project leader J. J. Schaidler's] story unique is that she not only was willing to own her mistakes but she was willing to document them and share them with others inside the organization. Many executives would cower from this idea as career suicide, but not JJ."

The innovation world needs a lot more J. J. Schaidlers. But they're rare, and so is the circulation of failure's epiphanies.

I saw a similar pattern in my ten years of conducting new product work with P&G. Well-documented success stories from all corners of the globe flew across my desk on a regular basis. But lessons from failed efforts were rarely shared. P&G in my experience doesn't fear failure, and is one of the business world's greatest learning organizations. That combination of a learning culture and no fear of failure should foster an ideal climate for failure's lessons to spread far and wide. Yet the success stories were so abundant and noisy you couldn't miss them. If the failures were circulating at all, it was in relative stealth. They rarely crossed my path.

Yes, let's celebrate what failure can teach us. But let's not over-cook it. Failure doesn't have a monopoly on teaching. Success's lessons are no less profound, and far more viral. And since successes make money, those lessons pay their own tuition.

LESS CELEBRATION, MORE DISSECTION

There's good failure and bad failure. Half the battle is looking close enough to spot the difference.

From a project leader's standpoint, there are two kinds of failure you want to parse—avoidable, and unavoidable.

Unavoidable project failure is the better breed. Maybe your idea was just ahead of its time. It was strategically smart and potentially lucrative, but consumers weren't ready to go there. This happens and it's healthy. There's no way to know that until you try it. Or maybe unforeseeable external factors derailed your ambitions.

We've certainly tasted our share of these "unforeseeables." For Gucci's venerable French jewelry house Boucheron, we created a breakthrough concept in luxury retail. It was a sensual acrobatic spectacle called Desir, built around the 150-year history of the brand—spanning Napoléon's mistress and a Persian maharaja— surrounded by an intimate bar and jewelry boutique we designed and built out of moveable freight containers. It was mobile luxury retail, the first concept of its kind, built around the lure of a unique entertainment experience. The show and the business would migrate among America's most affluent cities, actively bringing the brand's story and its exquisite jewels to our well-heeled prospects, rather than hoping for them to come to us. To make the show happen, we partnered with the ingenious troupe of Spiegelworld, which serves up its performances in a nineteenth-century tent of mirrors (built for portability from the get-go), and, in parallel, worked on the formidable task of translating the retail concept from a vision to a reality.

Through a year of intense planning and development, we fine-tuned the business model for the world's first mobile high-end jewelry-selling concept, worked out solutions to killer issues like how to manage security around a million dollars' worth of jewelry in a public space, created design concepts for a new gem collection to accompany the show, forged the partnership between Boucheron and Spiegelworld, and oversaw construction.

As the opening approached, we pulled out all the stops to be ready when the curtain went up. Designers Jared Richardson and Hannah Aubrey honed details on the elaborate invitations, programs, and even the bar menu for the grand opening of this store with a show wrapped around it. Another of our designers, Nedjelco Karlovich, grew so passionate about the project that he took a new Boucheron logo concept he was working on and had it tattooed on his arm, where it sits to this day. Concerned that we might be slipping behind schedule, one of our original partners, Harry Smail, famously grabbed a paintbrush and climbed up on the roof of the freight container being transformed into a boutique, working shirtless in the blaring August sun to apply finishing touches in the final days. It was a testament to our culture of stopping at nothing to get to the desired outcome.

Opening night arrived with great fanfare for the show's first location—strategically chosen as New York's South Street Seaport, blocks from Wall Street. In the months ahead, thousands of financiers, flush with year-end bonuses, would enjoy a fabulous, highly sensual entertainment experience with their love interests, have a few drinks, and go home with expensive baubles funded by those bonus checks.

The *New York Times* theater critic Ben Brantley waxed poetic

about the show: "Désir summons a time when nightclub and bur-
lesque shows were less a matter of show-and-tell than tantalizing promise." The migration of guests from the show to the bar
to the boutique was seamless. The cash register was ringing. Our
thoughts were racing ahead to how to fine-tune the execution for
the next four cities where this pioneering luxury retail concept was
headed.

Nineteen days after the concept debuted in Wall Street's shadow,
Lehman Brothers collapsed, dragging down the entire global economy with it. Fat bonuses were replaced with mass firings. Nearly
every corner of the economy was fraught with uncertainty. Over-
night, the Wall Street wallets we'd designed the experience to coax
open were riveted shut for the foreseeable future. The investment
required and the expected payout of success hadn't changed, but the
risk had exponentially increased. The only sane decision was to say
the show can't go on. The national expansion had to be canceled.

Was this a failure? By our definition, yes: it was a big, ambitious
vision, and a sizable investment of our client's resources and ours,
derailed before its intended commercial impact was realized. Was
it noble, heroic, or wonderful? We didn't think so. We were deeply
upset. It was clearly, however, in that realm of unavoidable failure,
caused not by any omission or the ducking of important questions,
but by something truly beyond the innovation team's control.

On this subject of avoidable vs. unavoidable innovation failures, Luke lends further perspective: "You hear a lot of innovators
whose visions unravel describe the result in a fatalistic way. More
often than not, the things that went wrong were actually within
their control. But it's easier to blame fate. It's a form of ducking accountability. When you look closely, most failures are failures of risk
management."

The avoidable project failures are less okay, because they usually
fall into the category of things you didn't do. You didn't articulate
a compelling commercial proposition to the company stakeholders

whose support you needed. Or you didn't manage the risk/reward ratio. Or you ignored the limitations of company capability. Or you put forward a product that couldn't actually be made. Or you had a great product but a flawed economic model. Or you put something forward that was at odds with the strategic imperatives of the company. These failures are avoidable. They aren't good.

If you're a serial project leader, separate the unavoidable failures from the avoidable ones. The avoidable ones are the ones to obsess about fixing through reworking your methods, models, and capabilities. Or going back and iterating those ideas until you get them right.

If you lead the company rather than the projects, you probably want to bucket the failures a different way. You want to include three things in your tracking metrics:

Project Success Rates—the frequency with which individual innovation projects deliver (or don't deliver) ideas into company pipelines in preparation for launch. If very few projects are failing, you're being too cautious. If the project failure rate is extremely high, there's probably something wrong with your methodologies, strategies, or capabilities.

In-Market Hit Rates are the frequency with which initiatives that made it through your innovation pipeline succeed in market.

Aggregate Pipeline Impact is the combined performance of company-wide or division-wide innovation efforts in delivering revenue and profit growth to the business, relative to growth requirements.

By looking at innovation success or failure through all three of these lenses you can start to separate the good from the bad and the ugly.

Let's take them on in reverse order.

Aggregate Pipeline Impact is the measure that matters most. It says that overall you are driving enough profitable innovation revenue to deliver the growth the business needs. While a healthy mix of small wins and an occasional big bang are the more common way to get there, delivering a few blockbuster successes amid a lot of smaller failures can work, as well. Venture capital works this way. Some companies do, too.

In-Market Hit Rates measure what happens when your ideas make it through the company gauntlet and reach the street. Does the street salute, or spit them back at you? Different businesses view failures in this bucket in different ways. As these failures are more public than projects that run aground within the company halls, there's a lot of concern around them. Beyond trying to "fail quickly and cheaply," companies have a strong preference to *fail privately rather than publicly*, which is why in-market failures are rarely desired. When a big high-profile launch bombs, execs will tend to externally praise the value of trying and failing as a sign of the company's dynamism, but the internal conversations will typically have a more heated pitch. Some companies view launch miscues as innovation failures and hold the innovation team responsible for execution. Some see them as a failure of research, where weak propositions weren't caught at the stage gates. Some view them as marketing miscues, saying it was a great innovation poorly communicated. Some find that a paucity of big ideas leads to launching marginal ones that probably shouldn't have been launched at all. Launching something is seen in the moment as better than launching nothing, but regretted later.

Project Hit Rates are probably the cleanest measure of whether you're trying enough, and failing at a healthy rate, or have a lot of fixing to do.

By looking at your company's innovation efforts in these buckets, and assessing the relationship among them, you can start to see how you're doing and what needs to be improved or fixed. There are other metrics that matter, of course. Is the average size of a successful innovation getting bigger, smaller, or holding steady? What's your speed from blank page to shelf? And above all, what's your innovation ROI?

The big point here is that not all failures are created equal. Some are good, some aren't. Knowing the difference is an important step to getting higher success rates. Saying innovation failure is wonderful won't get you where you need to be.

THE A-WORD

If the F-word is *failure*, there's an equally loaded A-word sitting right behind it: *accountability*. Where does accountability for the success or failure of a specific innovation program reside? Innovation is a team effort, of course. Yet innovation accountability is surprisingly elusive for something of such great importance.

Lack of accountability is a barrier to transforming success rates in any endeavor, from elementary school education to federal government to your favorite football team to the mission-critical functions within your company. It is not unique to innovation. If someone doesn't step up and embrace accountability, little will change.

Part of the accountability void in innovation is caused by the gap described in Chapter 11, where the authors of innovation strategy and the creators of demand-building innovation solutions are rarely the same people. The strategist can fault the ideas and their execution. The idea developers can fault the strategy.

But the dilution of accountability also traces to structural issues in today's widely used models. Building innovation with heightened focus on consumer needs has generated a lot of insight, learning, and value over the years. But it has inadvertently contributed to the deflection of accountability—not out of anything less than great intentions among its practitioners, but in a structural way. Using models weighted so heavily to the needs of the end user, overtly keeping the needs of the business at bay until the back end of the process, has the effect of saying we're showing your company things consumers would like to have; if you can't make them work or can't make money out of them, we've still done a great job. It's a structural reality of the model. The model can do exactly what it set out to do—teasing out consumer needs and building product ideas that can meet them—yet leave the project sponsors without the growth they need.

Part of what has driven the higher success rates that come with using our two-sided model (which have run between 60 percent and 80 percent over the last few years) is the structural way the model transforms accountability. It assumes accountability for solving both sides of the equation—the needs of the consumer and the business—not just one. If the model delivers an idea that works for consumers but not the business, or vice versa, it has failed at what it set out to do. It's helpfully binary. To close the loop on accountability, we chose to back this model with a contingent compensation structure, so if the outcome isn't successful for our client, we leave money on the table. We did this not out of certainty that we'd solve every challenge and get paid in full, but out of certainty that lack of accountability was a key driver of high failure rates. Turning your hit rates around is impossible without clear lines of accountability for tangible outcomes.

Luke Mansfield believes that leading his team at Samsung to extraordinarily high success rates is due in part to bringing accountability down to an individual level. "Unless it's personal, it won't work. Self-interest will always be one of the most powerful motivations there are. Taking personal ownership of delivering the objective is where it starts."

POPPING THE BUBBLE WRAP

There's been a great deal written about how bank bailouts have affected the psychology and behavior of bankers. If failing doesn't bring the house down, why worry about whether what you're doing is fundamentally sound?

The dynamics of innovation are very different, but it's naive to assume that a mantra of "failure is okay" won't over time have its own effect on the psychology and behavior of people tasked with delivering innovation. Having seen how important an outcome-driven environment has been to our hit rate, part of me worries that hearing "failure is great" over and over will eventually compromise the intensity that innovators bring to bear on overcoming the litany of barriers we need to clear to succeed. Innovators are human.

Chucking around half-baked ideas is exciting, fun, and happy-go-lucky. We've seen some clever young people apply for jobs in our practice, and when we ask why they want to join us, they say they just love lobbing ideas around. We've come to recognize that as a red flag. We all love riffing on ideas, but leaning back and tossing ideas around is not what real innovation is or what makes it work. There's scintillating alchemy in getting that first spark of the idea, but that's the easy first 5 percent of what it takes to make stuff happen. Making big innovations real is really hard.

If we keep singing the virtues of failure, how long before we say, if failure is fine, let's fill the pasture with unicorns—beautiful, far-out, fantastical ideas that are destined to never improve people's lives or grow the businesses out to serve those people, because they've been built in a vacuum, and protected in bubble wrap from the realities of how products and money get made.

If failure's fine, let's only worry about the fun part—the wow—and ignore the tough part—that long list of how questions. If failure's fine, let's not take skin in the game. Let's just lob out cleverness and let someone else worry about the rest. If failure's fine, no one is accountable for fixing it.

Look, the possibility of failing is something innovators live with every day.

But let's replace the grand celebrations of failure with a more honest dialogue.

Let's be humble enough to admit that hit rates are deeply broken and that failing more than once in a while isn't awesome.

In fact it sucks.

Fixing it will send ROI through the roof.

There's plenty of trying.

Companies need more succeeding.

Chapter 16

Making It Work

Theories come easy. Robust models that work in the real world do not.

ENERGIZING TENSIONS

Some of life's most compelling ideas and experiences result from the sparks that fly when two seemingly opposing forces are flung together and forced to coexist.

Take democracy. Democracy sprang from a fundamental tension between the forces of freedom and governance. Before the invention of democracy, the question of how you could be both free *and* governed would be met with a scratch of the head. These things were polar opposites. Create a new political structure where these opposing forces coexist and you change the course of history.

This dynamic of what we call *energizing tensions* shows up

FREEDOM   DEMOCRACY   GOVERNANCE

everywhere, from the seismic to the lucrative to the merely engaging. Apple's vision was powered by the tension between technology and humanity, Virgin's by the tension between stodgy institutional businesses and a spirit of rebellion. The genius of the Grateful Dead's music lay in the tension between structured conventional song forms and unstructured improvisations. HBO's *The Sopranos* fed off the tension between unfathomable gangster brutality and mundane family challenges, like a dad giving his daughter's boyfriend the once-over.

The first step to unlocking their potential lies in seeing these tensions not as conflicts to avoid, but as catalysts to embrace in the pursuit of new possibilities.

The martial art of jujitsu offers some inspiration here. One of its tenets is that when a formidable opposing force is coming at you, pushing back against it leaves you spent in a stalemate. So don't push against it—use it. Redirect that force coming at you toward your intended purpose. On his mission to humanize technology, Steve Jobs had a unique perspective—using the *addition* of new technologies as a way to *reduce* or streamline the overtly technological dimensions of the product experience, stripping away buttons and complex commands. That's jujitsu.

If the first step is to see these tensions as sources of usable power, the second is finding effective structures and techniques to put that power to work. Democracy needed the mechanism of checks and balances. Apple needed intuitive design as the link between technology and humanity. The Grateful Dead needed a new technique where all five instruments were essentially soloing simultaneously and sympathetically. Whatever the endeavor, it takes structure and technique to make the power of these tensions usable, valuable, repeatable, and scalable.

So what does all this have to do with innovation?

Getting to the broad concept of Money & Magic wasn't that hard. It simply required the realization that there was a factionalized divide, with free-flowing user-focused creative inventiveness on one

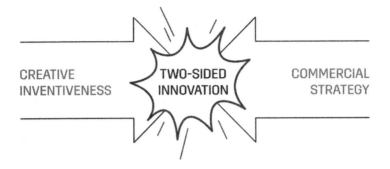

CREATIVE
INVENTIVENESS

TWO-SIDED
INNOVATION

COMMERCIAL
STRATEGY

side and commercial acumen on the other. In the pursuit of profitable innovation breakthroughs, each side needed what the other side had, but there wasn't a company or model out there facilitating this potentially awkward marriage. It felt like an idea whose time had come.

We saw design thinking as a better approach than the models that had come before. But in pushing the pendulum from a commercially centered orientation to a user-centered orientation, it had replaced one problem with another. The old models tended to deliver innovations that fit company strategies and operations but that consumers didn't necessarily need, want, or get excited by. Design thinking tended to generate ideas that consumers wanted, but businesses couldn't make, couldn't make money out of, or had a hard time rallying behind because they lacked the necessary strategic and commercial foundations. It was clearly better than the old way, but no more reliable. It left a lot of disappointment in its wake among companies and designers alike.

Some ascribe the misfire to the attempt at codifying lateral thinking to make it a plug-and-play corporate process. Author Bruce Nussbaum, an early vocal advocate of design thinking, reflected that view in a *Fast Company* piece headlined "Design Thinking Is a Failed Experiment": "Design consultancies that promoted Design Thinking were, in effect, hoping that a process trick would produce significant cultural and organizational change. . . . As practitioners of design thinking in consultancies now acknowledge, the success rate for the process was low, very low." Former *Bloomberg Business-week* editor Helen Walters, now ideas editor at TED, took a similar stance: "Coating a veneer of design processes on the top of innovation initiatives that will promptly be stymied by internal bureaucracy or politics doesn't help anyone. In fact, as we've seen, it'll frustrate designers, who find themselves with the unfulfilling role of making Post-it notes look pretty, and it'll disappoint executives, who feel like they've been sold a bill of goods."

While I agree with these views that trying to sell creativity under a veneer of process was part of the issue, there's another layer to it. Design thinking wasn't structurally set up for success, because it imposed an artificial hierarchy, saying, often quite explicitly, the consumer is all that really matters. The prior "business first" hierarchy was equally wrong, of course. But it's dead obvious, as only hindsight can be, that in trying to get innovations to market, neither the consumer nor the business can be satisfied without also satisfying the other. Fahrenheit's team simply said okay, design thinking has been rigorously prototyped, surfacing the issues that a more effective model would overcome. The only logical next step we could see was to take the best of consumer-centric innovation models, and the best of commercially robust strategic understanding of the needs and realities of a business, and fuse them together to better ends. We made this leap not as theorists, but as practitioners trying to get from point A to B.

Interestingly, as we reflect back on it now, what we were doing was more faithful to the concept of "Integrative Thinking" espoused by the brilliant Roger Martin, of Rotman School of Management, than design thinking was. Integrative thinking is not an innovation model, but a characteristic Martin spotted in studying high-performing company leaders: "When these outstanding leaders faced opposing models where it appeared they had to choose one or the other, and neither was satisfactory, rather than see their job as choosing, as most of us tend to do, they saw it as harnessing the tension creatively to try to evolve a better model that is superior to either. I call that pattern Integrative Thinking." In hindsight, design thinking, of which Martin has been an eloquent advocate, didn't quite do what integrative thinking points to. Design thinking took the bait and made the choice. It chose the needs of the consumer over those of the business. The right answer, for us at least, was not to choose, but to say we need both. In Martin's terms, we were harnessing the tension to evolve to a superior model.

MADNESS TO METHOD

Beginning as little more than a hypothesis wrapped in a hunch, the Money & Magic approach wasn't operational, let alone repeatable. In committing to it early on, we knew we were in uncharted waters. We had to figure it out for ourselves. There was no body of theory and no playbook to draw down on about how to fuse these disparate capabilities in a working model. What is now a workable, scalable model took shape by trying stuff, making mistakes, and figuring out what "better" looked like. That's why the principles I've discussed in the book are as much about what not to do as what to do.

Here are a handful of principles that emerged, usually through trial and error, to guide the translation of the Money & Magic model from a theory into a scalable process for developing breakthrough innovations. Think of it as a set of innovation rules, allowing unfettered creativity and the marketplace rigor of commercial need to make each other better.

It starts with an outcome-obsessed culture.
Our teams know that the impact of our outputs is all we measure ourselves by, and that neither Money nor Magic alone can get to the outcomes by which success is measured. We hold the entire team accountable for the net outcome of a project. This creates common ground and shared ambition across the more creative and more

analytical sides of any project team. It creates a massive desire to deliver *for* each other. Shared goals and interdependence cut through differences in orientation like a hot knife.

Not to be missed here is the importance of specificity about what the outcome is you're after. Saying your team is "goal oriented" is borderline useless if the goal itself is fuzzy. Across the innovation landscape, you'll hear many murky definitions of success, like "We're here to learn." "We're here to teach." "We're here to explore." "We're here to make consumers' lives better." "We're here to do what other people in the company can't." None of these is wrong. They're just not specific or comprehensive enough to separate good intentions from actual success. So we made it black-and-white:

> *The outcome we're after is getting brilliant two-sided solutions embedded in our clients' innovation pipelines, on their way to market.*

Our goal—building two-sided solutions our clients can success-fully bring to market—is clear and constantly reinforced through-out the company. Culture withers if you don't keep reinforcing it, from the top down and from the bottom up. As our cofounder Geoff Vuleta says, "Religion works because you get reminded every Sunday." Without that cultural fixation on outcomes, the fusion of the creative and the profitable would not have worked at Fahrenheit 212.

Process is really helpful, in its place.

We have a robust process that's been built through trial and error to a point where it's delivering successful project outcomes time after time. But despite this, we're leery of letting the running of the pro-cess ever be misconstrued as what we're here to do—it's about the outcomes, not the process of pursuing them. To drive home the point, we tell our teams to feel free to bend or break the process as needed. They almost never do, because the process works. But knowing they can reinforces the message that the process is no more than a means to an end, and it's the end that counts.

As for what that process is, I'll serve it up here with the broad brush.

Two-Track Immersion

You've picked this up by now, but we start with two concurrent intensive immersions, going on side by side in real time. We run a deep dive with consumers, via ethnographies or other appropriate quantitative or qualitative research techniques, plus an atypical and equally intensive second track of interrogating the realities of the business, as described earlier. Consumer and commercial insights are gathered, debated, and filtered in preparation for synthesis of strategy. In this part of the process, while Money ostensibly owns the commercial immersion and Magic the consumer immersion, there's a high degree of cross-fertilization, as the things we uncover on one side of the ledger often ignite new lines of inquiry on the other. We are typically joined at the hip with our clients through this part of the journey, which includes an exhaustive hunt through prior learning, gathering stakeholder perspectives, competitive context, analogues, and sources of inspiration.

Innovation Strategy Synthesis

Key consumer, company, category, and channel insights are distilled and extracted from the broad body of initial learning, giving us the four filters we'll use to significantly narrow the problem definition and the ground we'll be exploring in the subsequent idea development process. The innovation strategy is in essence an intersection between the problems, needs, and aspirations of consumers, and the problems, needs, capabilities, realities, and assets of the business. It makes big choices about where we will and won't play, connecting the intent of the project to overarching strategic imperatives of the company, and laying out the economic basis for the where-to-play decisions—namely, why we believe the choice of aiming our innovations in a particular area will deliver the kind of growth the business needs.

Concurrent with shaping the strategy definition, we define the three or four commercial hypotheses—the if/then statements that act as springboards between the strategy and creation of ideas.

Idea Development

Any innovation process has a window like this where preliminary answers are explored. There are several relatively unique aspects of the way we do it. First, rather than start the discussion with a blank whiteboard and piles of Post-it notes, we actually have each participant in the session (everyone on the team from Magic and from Money) independently accountable to develop ideas to bring into the work session and present to the group, ensuring we get breadth of perspectives rather than getting sucked into groupthink. The second unique aspect is that each fledgling idea pitched to the group is framed up by its presenter as an intersection between a consumer insight and a commercial insight, ensuring that from the get-go we're on a path toward creating win-win solutions that solve the needs of the consumer and the business. Third, as we go around sharing these fledgling ideas, we put them through a gauntlet of positive debate, drawing out the exciting aspects of the ideas, but also the important "what must be true?" factors and mission-critical questions that need answering for that idea to make it into the world. This will ignite a chain reaction of events in the weeks ahead after the session. An idea that's intriguing at this stage may raise questions like how much revenue there is today in a particular part of a market we're considering, whether anything similar has been done before, what the profitability of that market is today for the players in it, what the household penetration of that category is, and whether our client's technology has any particular advantages or disadvantages for that type of application. We've heard of no other innovation process where questions of that depth get surfaced on an idea that's literally five minutes old. Typically each idea in contention will leave the room with a host of consumer questions that the Magic team will set out to answer in the ensuing days, and a host of Money questions as well.

As for the quantity of ideas in play, as you've gathered by now, we've learned that profuse quantity isn't actually a driver of successful outcomes. In fact it's counterproductive since you end up going a mile wide and an inch deep, glossing over huge questions that need answering to get the innovation to market. There's no specific number of ideas we're after at this stage, but a typical session like this will see about twenty fledgling ideas come into the room for sharing, prepared ahead of time by all the participants through personal reflection. About a third of those ideas will emerge from the session largely intact, another third will be fundamentally elevated or redirected from their initial incarnations, and a third will die off, being replaced by new ideas arising through the exercises, riffing, and debate that go on through the course of the work session.

The team then heads off to answer the killer questions raised in the work session, periodically regrouping to share what they've learned and developed. We start filtering and mapping the ideas, elevating the big and doable with added dimensions and, yes, killing off some unicorns. These lead ideas are then brought to life for a client workshop, where we again debate, share areas of excitement and concern, surface potential killer issues, and look at them through the big/fast/doable framework. This workshop is typically followed soon after by field research exploring these ideas in concept form, allowing us to then blend the guidance from the marketplace and the guidance of the company. Based on all that learning, we will identify just three or four ideas from the pool that will migrate into the next phase of work, where these fledgling ideas are developed into what we call two-sided solutions.

Solution Development

The three or four ideas selected from the pool are then turned from ideas into what we call solutions—marrying the key dimensions that drive consumer appeal (consumer insight, benefits, reasons to believe, key product dimensions/features, user experience, design, identity, bull's-eye target, etc.) and the key dimensions of the commercial proposition (strategic fit, operational fit, addressable market size, financial assumptions, risk factors, right to win, trend alignment, etc.). Products are prototyped in some form, typically using video, as it's more nimble than physical prototyping, allowing more rapid iteration at the back end, though in cases where physical prototyping is right, we do it that way.

The solutions are shared with client leadership, and typically taken again to consumers. Once again, we do a Money & Magic blending of market guidance and company guidance across a spectrum of variables.

Iteration

While we've in a way been iterating from the first expression of each idea up to this point, in the remaining time of a typical initial engagement we continue to evolve the consumer and commercial proposition based on things we're learning. A big part of this is the tuning of assumptions around the commercial proposition, from economics to operational assumptions and risk assessments.

This is the core chassis of the process, though, as I've said, its power sources are our outcome-driven culture and talented team.

Protect the creative-commercial equilibrium.

Every company we compete with is presided over by a predominant creative or commercial orientation. Those origins are indelibly written in the organizational DNA. That bias affects the way they work in perpetuity. We've noticed that when those firms whose origins lean heavily one way or the other try to broaden their skill set by adding a noncore capability (design firms hiring MBAs; management consultancies hiring people with creative backgrounds), the body tends to reject the transplant, as these noncore capabilities aren't taken seriously. So we've obsessed over maintaining that equilibrium where Money & Magic have equal say and equal accountability in everything we do. I would postulate that the only way to get to a true fusion of creative and commercial capability is for those two sides to share the pedestal. Neither runs the place. Each is accountable to the other. That's the way our place works.

A creative/commercial model needs the right mix of "openers" and "closers."

In building a team capable of navigating the creative/commercial divide to get to two-sided solutions, we've found there are two personality types you need in the mix. We call them openers and closers.

Openers are people with a natural tendency to continually broaden the playing field, to keep expanding the range of possibilities. They tend to feel less constrained by decisions the team has made in the preceding weeks and will continually look at alternate paths that come into view. Their value to an innovation team is huge, both in their lateral thinking and their obsession with continually challenging whether the answer in hand is the best one available. To the opener, the clay never fully hardens.

The complementary opposite to the opener is the closer. In an outcome-driven practice aiming to solve for both the consumer and the business, closers are equally mission critical. What they bring to the table is an ability to lead the team to make the tough and timely decisions, often with an incomplete set of facts to support their decision, and lots of variables still in the air. Why is the closer so critical? You can't build out the strategic and commercial case behind an idea and a product until you put a stake in the ground and commit to what it is. There are key moments in our process where we need the closers to assert themselves and transition the team from exploration into execution.

Getting preliminary P&Ls on ideas you're putting forward means you need initial product specs and design specs. If it's a food product, what are your recipes, ingredient costs, and sizing assumptions? What are the operational risks? Can you get by on existing molds, or do you need new ones? What channels will you sell it in? What's your target price point, and how does that compare to the competition? What are your options for manufacturing? Whichever questions matter most to a given project, you can't answer them if you're still vacillating about what the product is. The closers on the team manage that pivot from exploration into zeroing in on the specifics. A project staffed with nothing but openers covers amazing amounts of interesting terrain but struggles to make timely decisions on which ideas to rally around. If decisions don't get made, you can't get past tossing vague ideas around. On the flip side, we saw that projects staffed primarily with closers tended to rush to answers without going as broad as you'd like to see in stretching the perimeter. Balance is everything.

When clients tell us they've tried to marry creative and commercial capability and it doesn't work, what we see on closer inspection is actually that they had teams full of closers. They had to pry so hard to get these closers to open up to new possibilities that the moment the team let commercial considerations come into play, those closers snapped shut like Venus flytraps.

Are there people capable of playing both the opener and the closer? Yes. In fact they're ideal for innovation work and we actively hunt for them. But they're rare. They have nimble minds, are able to change modes in a moment; they restlessly and broadly explore, then shift gears to lock in and build out the specifics at the pace the project demands.

Make the gauntlet inside your team tougher than the gauntlet outside.

Vision, optimism, and conviction are vital to innovation. But unless we're innovating with our own bankroll, we need people on board to write the check to make those ideas happen, be they company sponsors or investors. Those check writers usually aren't paid to be optimistic or naive. They're paid to be right. It's a very different orientation from the relentless belief in possibility that's required to turn a blank page into a big idea. You often hear these financial gatekeepers bemoaned. There's a passage I love in David Hansson and Jason Fried's bestselling book, *Rework*, about the depressing "real world."

> *Ignore the real world. "That would never work in the real world." You hear it all the time when you tell people about a fresh idea. This real world sounds like an awfully depressing place to live. It's a place where new ideas, unfamiliar approaches, and foreign concepts always lose. The only things that win are what people already know and do, even if those things are flawed and inefficient.*
>
> *Scratch the surface and you'll find these "real world" inhabitants are filled with pessimism and despair. They expect fresh concepts to fail. They assume society isn't ready for or capable of change. Even worse, they want to drag others down into their tomb. If you're hopeful and ambitious, they'll try to convince you your ideas are impossible. They'll say you're wasting your time.*

David's right. Optimism and conviction are fundamental to innovation. You have to expect the headwinds of naysayers every time you push the envelope. But we also owe it to our big ideas to go a step further. This doesn't mean we should dial down the ambition. It just means we can't stop at the broad vision. We need to drill deeper into the how. What David is describing is that moment when a big new vision appears. In our practice, this moment is happening every day on one of the dozens of projects we're working on. We're optimists by nature and by necessity. But we're realists about what must be true to get that vision to happen. So we're always leaning into the next question ahead of us.

It's easy to describe the gatekeepers who write the checks as lacking vision. The truth is that the gatekeepers can't afford to get too swept up in optimism. The people generating the creative ideas are paid to be smart and fearless. Management is paid to deliver growth. It's tempting to bemoan the structural cautiousness that surrounds the people in those executive gatekeeper roles. But success in innovation is measured in impact. People charged with running innovation projects can't win over the gatekeepers by burying their heads in the sand.

So what do you do? Make your own internal gauntlet tougher than theirs. Fearing the proverbial real world won't help make your idea happen. So outsmart it. Get ahead of it.

Make the gauntlet inside your immediate team every bit as tough as the gauntlet your idea will have to survive in the "real world" of your organization or backers. Obsess over the killer question: WMBT—*What Must Be True* for this idea to work as a consumer solution and a business?

Amazing things happen when you use the idea-generation time to get ready for the real world. Young guns like Melissa Tischler, Alex Bertha, Faiz Rashid, Alejandra Gomez-Gallardo, Nick Partridge, Sandra Steving Villegas, and Michael Stenclik at Fahrenheit 212 are able to stand up to the tough questions thrown at them by CEOs of Fortune 500 companies, because they've thought about these tough issues for weeks. We try to make it harder for an idea to make it out of the Fahrenheit 212 gauntlet than it is to make it into a client's innovation pipeline.

We score the ideas we're about to put in front of our clients on a host of risk factors like operational risk (how sure are we that this product can be made at speed and scale), financial risk (how big a capital and marketing investment is required), demand risk (how sure are we that people need and want what we're creating), capability risk (is this in the wheelhouse of what the organization knows how to do?), and brand risk (whether it comfortably aligns with brand equity or is borderline). Even a simple green/yellow/red scoring system on these risk factors is massively helpful. Not to steer all our energies to low-risk places, but to get ahead of what the gatekeepers will need to understand as they look at opportunities. We know that higher-risk ideas need deeper rationale. Why duck that? Run at it.

We don't nail it every time. But the effect on hit rates is huge. By the time we face the real world, the tough questions we expect to confront have already been addressed and often solved for. We don't have all the answers, and we're open about which answers we have and which we don't. Laying out a road map of how the big unknowns will get answered in the period ahead is highly reassuring to gatekeepers.

Make the internal gauntlet within your team harder than the one outside and watch your hit rate go through the roof.

Work like a double helix.
One of the ways we've achieved the integration of creative and commercial capabilities is through a model inspired by the double helix of DNA. Think of the creativity that solves for the needs of the consumer, and the commercial capability that solves for the needs of the business, as the two strands. Each has its own set of questions to answer over the course of creating and building an innovation and turning it into a two-sided solution. In DNA, those two strands are moving in the same direction independently, but connected at regular intervals from beginning to end.

What this means in innovation in practical terms is that in shaping innovation strategies, ideas, and solutions, our Money & Magic people alternate between real-time collaboration and going off separately to advance aspects of an idea or solve key questions. When they connect, they share ideas, debate their merits, ask challenging

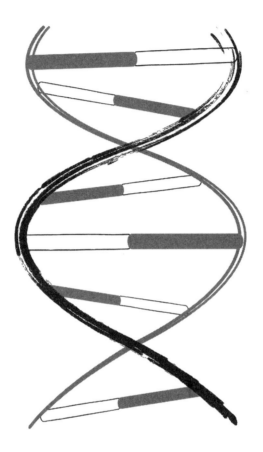

One of the keys to integrating creative and commercial capabilities is a helix interaction model, where the Money & Magic people work in parallel from the start of the project to the end, but alternate between working independently and connecting at regular intervals to share new thinking, swap perspectives, and challenge each other with tough questions.

questions about each other's efforts, and agree on what needs answering in the next interval of independent work. Converge. Diverge. Converge. Diverge.

This pulsing of individual and group work does two important things. First, it allows each side to do what it needs to do the way it needs it do it, without forcing it to work in a mode better suited to the other. Second, in our experience it is the best way to get big ideas from the people who work for us. This pulsing creates spikes of new stimulation when the group gathers, cross-fertilizes provocative thinking, surfaces transformational questions, and creates productive debate. Then in turn this pulsing leaves ample room for individual contemplation, which overcomes the limitations of in-the-moment brainstorming.

I recently saw a great talk by NASA's chief knowledge officer, Ed Hoffman. He talked about how one of his organization's greatest struggles is getting highly motivated, outcome-driven people to slow down and carve out time for reflective thinking. His experience had much in common with ours. That's why this pulsing of collaborative and individual work has become fundamental to the way we work.

There are practical and logistical factors in how you make that pulsing work. We have an open-plan office, which helps fuel collaboration and creative energy, yet noise-canceling headphones have become a critical tool to allow our people to retreat inside themselves to contemplate a project in the middle of all that energy and dynamism. Everyone knows that when you're wearing the headphones, you are thinking through ideas, and people try to respect that like a closed door.

So follow the double helix model. It's the key to connecting Money & Magic, and getting the best from all your people.

Rules are helpful, especially for rule breakers.
Having a set of innovation rules *is* important and helpful. Here are ours. I offer them with the caveat that they work in context of our culture, people, and process. Don't assume they'll be of value in every situation or on every team. That said, they're hugely important to us:

- Rule 1: Where you land matters. Where you start is irrelevant. Both the Money and the Magic sides of the team are empowered to ignite an idea, from any angle they see, starting with a consumer insight or a commercial insight. User-centered orthodoxy says the consumer has to come first. We say it absolutely can and often does, but it's not the only way. It's the endpoint that counts, not the starting point.

- Rule 2: Build ideas at the crossroads of creativity and commerce. Consciously set out to create the win-win by solving a big consumer problem and big business problem in one bold move.

- Rule 3: Be explicit about the transformation you've set out to achieve. It's easy to get seduced by product features and lose sight of the need for a clear, simple transformation.

- Rule 4: For each question you answer, look to the next one ahead. A blank page is a mass of critical questions written in invisible ink. What unmet customer and business needs am I out to solve for? What's the big innovation idea that's going to solve them? Who's my target consumer? What transformation am I out to deliver? What's the right lead product to do that? What are its benefits and features? What capabilities do I have and need to pull this off? What's the development path for products that will follow over time to make this a platform rather than a one-off? What's our right to win in the game this innovation opens up? How big can this be? Is the organization equipped to pull it off? Success hinges on answering as many of these key questions as possible in a fixed amount of time (in our case, usually three to twelve months). Answering them all isn't always necessary or doable, but you'll find over time that the more of them you're able to solidly answer, the more likely your innovation will come to fruition. So make it a reflex: the moment you answer one question, look for what's next.

My favorite thing about rules, even simple ones like ours, is that they make rogue thinkers better. Without rules you deny your contrarians the pleasure and power of standing up and saying that rule is stupid, so we broke it.

Respect the difference between innovation and design.

When the editors at *Fast Company* asked me to lend perspective to their special issue on "The United States of Design," the context of the issue was that design matters more to businesses and consumers now than it ever has. It's unequivocally true and massively exciting. Design's ascent has broadened and elevated what's possible for innovators, and the consumers and businesses that are served by innovation. Many businesses haven't yet figured out how to leverage design, but the pacesetters and startups are showing the way in highly contagious manifestations. The momentum is undeniable and deeply inspiring.

Beyond the thrill my colleagues and I feel every time we see our designers turn a fledgling idea into a gleaming, tangible thing you want in your life, it's also fascinating to see why and how this surge in design's importance has come about. It's not merely a case of the public getting exposed to higher-order design and acquiring better taste, though that's helped. It's also a matter of stark competitive necessity, as markets grow saturated with excessive choice, and the low-hanging fruit is long gone. As I expressed it in the *Fast Company* piece, in this hypercompetitive world *design is differentiation made visible, visceral, and experiential.* The products and brands that are winning in this crowded world aren't just functionally strong; they have differentiation you can spot from a distance, feel up close and connect with on a deep human level. Products designed with great empathy and humanism become part of us.

Passionate as all of us at Fahrenheit are about design's amazing power to broaden the way we solve problems, to move us as people and to move products off the shelves, I would attribute a great deal of Fahrenheit's success at transforming innovation hit rates to a realization we had that runs counter to the prevailing zeitgeist: design and innovation are not the same thing.

Understanding the ideal relationship between the two, and letting that inform the way we structure our model, has been a key to transforming innovation success rates.

AIR, FOOD, AND WATER

Design is as fundamental to innovation as air is to life. But as life requires not just air, but food and water, too, design is just one vital piece of innovation's bigger whole.

A successful two-sided innovation requires:

- *a great idea* that opens big new possibilities for both consumers and the companies that serve them,
- *a great product* (or better yet a family of them expanding over time) delivering on the possibilities and promises embedded in the idea, and
- *a great business* shaped around that idea and product.

Success requires getting all three of these things right. They're interdependent, but also independent to the extent that getting one right does not ensure the other two will fall into place. A great idea can't become a great business unless it becomes a great product. A brilliantly designed product born of a weak idea—that is, lacking a big strategic value proposition addressing a meaningful need and market gap—might win acclaim in the design community, but it won't ever be a great scaled business. And a weak business

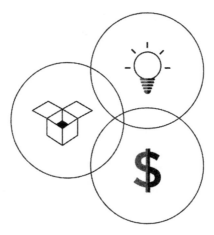

proposition will tend to either prevent that great product from ever making it to market, or hobble it by minimizing the resources thrown behind it, so it won't touch many lives.

Allowing the power of design to assert itself more broadly in innovation has been one of the most exciting developments of the past few decades, but with unforeseen side effects. Blurring of the lines between design and innovation has played an enabling role in allowing chronically high project failure rates to remain the norm. Design's impact has been profound and positive, though arguably less than many stakeholders had expected, hoped for, and counted on to drive growth.

The issue here, at least in my view, is that for many years, design was a product-centric discipline, focused primarily on iterative improvement of products and user experiences.

While the principles behind design processes are deeply powerful and exportable to many facets of life, the leap from designers designing products to designers taking the helm of commercial innovation projects and processes has by most assessments proved to be a wishful leap too far. What was sold was not the importance of design having a powerful voice, but design and its processes taking charge. It was a big ask, and a big departure from what designers were traditionally great at.

Deep down, many designers—not all, but many—have to this day an instinctive bias toward viewing innovation as the creation of products, rather than the creation of great businesses with products igniting them. It's a vital distinction. I expect that we'll see a generational shift in the decades ahead that could change this. It seems inevitable that more and more designers, particularly those throwing their imaginations at digital opportunities, will, through osmosis or new dimensions of design education, become far more adept at understanding the interactions of commercial innovation strategies, products, experiences, and business models. And perhaps more excited by them, too, which is another missing piece today. But for now, most designers and design firms only are in the earliest stages of migrating down that path. They're still perhaps too fixated on the product to see the business lurking behind it.

In a way, design thinking has in effect tried to pull innovation back to design's traditional comfort zone—solving for people and products—pushing the needs of the business into the background. What was left out was asking whether design itself needed to change its ways of thinking to adapt to this bigger responsibility it was stepping into. Saying that business needs should no longer drive the front end of the process was one thing, yet the business needs were still driving the decisions at the back end on what would go to market or be killed off, so downplaying them has spelled the demise of troves of projects, potentially great ideas, and the associated investments.

What has made our two-sided model more effective is that we've simply ended this tug-of-war between the old-world approach of putting commercial imperatives at the front of the process, and the design thinkers saying no, put the consumer there. We've reached the obvious conclusion that they both belong at the front, the middle, and the end.

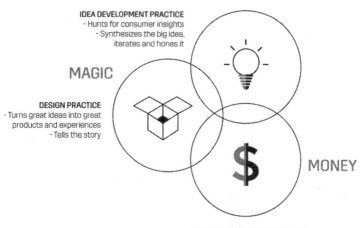

IDEA DEVELOPMENT PRACTICE
- Hunts for consumer insights
- Synthesizes the big idea,
  iterates and hones it

MAGIC

DESIGN PRACTICE
- Turns great ideas into great
  products and experiences
- Tells the story

MONEY

COMMERCIAL STRATEGY PRACTICE
- Hunts for commercial insights
- Sets strategy to guide idea development
- Hones the business proposition at the back

A big part of doing this has been finding a way to leverage design's potency without repeating the pitfalls. What we've done is not complicated. We've let design be great at the things it has always been great at.

We do this through a functional organization structure that creates separate but connected epicenters for the creation of those three things a successful innovation needs: a great idea, a great product, and a great business. Form follows function. So we structured our organization around those key functions. What we call "Money" is a commercial strategy team that leads the creation of strategy. What we call "Magic" is two discrete creative epicenters, each with an eponymous function. Idea Development leads the development of the idea. Design develops the design.

By asking Design to be great at design, we get all its power throughout the process.

An important piece of making it work is the way these three epicenters interact. All are active through every phase of work. Their responsibility levels step up at certain points and step back in others.

Yet all three are engaged, pushing and prodding, actively noisy every step of the way. Design is a pivotal piece of a bigger whole. It's the air that life requires, with strategy and idea development as the food and water.

RESPONSIBILITY LEVELS BY PHASE

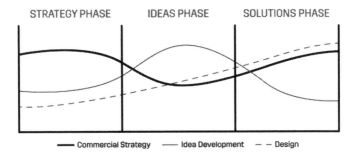

To sum it up, each of these eight things has been material to turning Money & Magic from an intriguing theory into a robust, repeatable process and organizational model that transforms success rates. Each has its own embedded lessons.

While I always urge caution to anyone hoping to export a set of lessons, processes, or practices from the host environment in which they're proven successful, the principles here are by now well tested and I hope they offer you some combination of guidance and inspiration as you head out the door Monday morning.

Chapter 17

Monday Morning

For us at Fahrenheit 212, and I suspect for anyone drawn to innovation as a calling, innovation asks all we have to give. All our senses. All our mental processing power. All our childlike curiosity. All our empathy. All our strategic savvy. All our ability to inspire. All our instincts. All our nimbleness. All our tenacity.

When we serve it well, innovation rewards us with a sense of accomplishment that few pursuits can match. The page that's beautifully yet dauntingly blank on day one gives way to a concrete vision. Able to stand proud as a product, an experience, and a business, and to make the leap from merely possible to thoroughly real.

Surviving the journey from the Post-it note to the street and the balance sheet, that vision creates value, and pushes human experience one humble degree forward. Successfully getting through the gauntlet of obstacles an idea has to clear inside and outside any organization is a labor of love.

I often tell friends that our work at Fahrenheit 212 is like giving birth every week. When I do, my wonderful wife, Elizabeth, an artist and designer whose work inspires me daily, smiles and calls me on it—reminding me that by dint of gender I'll never really know. But perhaps seeing our son Jacob blossom into so much more than I ever dreamed gives me license to say that the struggles, demands, and joys of the innovation journey follow a similar arc. Wishful open-ended hope and uncertainty at the journey's beginning. Awe and humble pride down the road.

It's often said that the journey is the reward. It's a powerful and ancient sentiment, attributed through the ages to the Tao, Homer, and more recently Steve Jobs.

Jobs's use of this as an innovation mantra was layered with meaning. A reflection of the guiding inspiration he drew from Zen, and his love of the innovation process—contemplating the inner nature of things, finding insight and inspiration, stretching, distilling, expressing, honing, paring back, and finally letting go.

But we can't forget that for all his love of the journey, Jobs was also unequivocally obsessed with the outcome. The finished thing. The vision made real. The flirtation with perfection. The tangible value.

Jobs was in a rare and wonderful position, one usually afforded only to startup entrepreneurs. He was both the holder of the product vision and the leader deciding what would go out the door and into the world. There was really no question about whether in the end there would be a tangible outcome, only about how long it would take and how close it could come to perfection.

Few of us wear both of those hats.

For the rest of us who aren't Steve Jobs, I'd suggest a variation on how we think about that great journey that starts Monday morning when we roll up our sleeves and have at it.

The joy of the journey is your only *certain* reward.

The other reward we hope to achieve is the outcome. That one we have to earn.

Innovation has soared in importance but the methods created to serve those ends remain hit-or-miss on even their best days.

It's time to transform the odds that you'll reach journey's end with more than the joy of the journey in hand.

That's been the whole point of our own ten-year journey at Fahrenheit 212.

As Monday morning approaches, do these things. Be optimistic. Use the creative power of debate. Define both sides of the problem.

Solve them both. Hunt for transformational questions. Vet, then vet again. Dream big and swing for the fences, not Mars. Bend, don't break. Aim for big-fast-doable. Identify the unicorns, then cut them loose. Don't ever fear failure, but don't let it steal your lunch money, either. Take ownership. Treat capabilities as canvas. Put your money where your mouth is. Treat every dollar a sponsor invests in your talent and vision like it's your own. Don't fear the real world, out-smart it. Use the advantage you have to blow away the doubters. Turn every stone. Move the hardest questions from the back of the process to the front. Ruthlessly ask, *What must be true?* Don't mistake learning for success. Separate avoidable from unavoidable failures. Don't covet failure's lessons; success will teach you as much or more, at a more attractive tuition. Match risk and reward. Fill the room with amazing people, tell them to go amaze one another, and get out of the way. Don't let the process ever be the point. Know when to open and when to close. Disrupt the marketplace more than you dis-rupt your company. Set the bar high and keep raising it. And never waver in saying the outcome is the thing.

Money & Magic is nothing more than an innovation aimed at innovation—a new way of thinking, assembling talent, solving prob-lems, and turning visions into genuine outcomes.

Whether our model is a revelation, a revolution, a project-saving prescription, or a dead-obvious iteration standing on the shoulders of all the smart thinking, design thinking, forward thinking, and strategic thinking that's come before, is best judged by others. This book is written on behalf of everyone involved in our journey—those of us who founded Fahrenheit, the partners who joined us, the clients who've pushed us as hard as we've pushed their sense of the possi-ble, and the hundreds of brilliant, committed staff and partners who have reached, stretched, hoped, burned midnight oil, tried, failed, and ultimately nailed it.

The spectacular group of people I have written about have defied the inevitable gravitational pull of innovation toward failure.

Not by turning down the flame of their ambition, but by raising it higher and torching obstacles.

None of this would have been possible without the loving support of their families and friends who tolerated our restless curiosity, our late nights, and our repeated abuse of their willingness to be sounding boards.

We first started talking about the Money & Magic model seven years ago as I write this. The ensuing attention our approach has received has been gratifying. Between scribbling "Strategy + Creativity" on a piece of paper and building a scalable, repeatable model that made it work was a long journey. The linguistics came easy, the logistics less so. The greatest reward was seeing a vision become a reality. Powered by inspiration. But measured in realization.

It is our hope that *How to Kill a Unicorn* will make a difference, great, small, or somewhere between, in ensuring that you, too, reach the end of your innovation journey with much more than the joy of the journey to show for it.

Onward and upward.

Acknowledgments

I could easily fill several volumes with thanks, kudos, and credits for the leaps that made the stories and the body of knowledge they contain possible.

But I'll endeavor to do justice on a page, in loosely chronological order, with apologies to anyone I've left out.

Thanks to Marcia Roosevelt for the spark that lit the way. To AG Lafley and Kevin Roberts for seeing the potential. To Geoff Vuleta for taking us from zero to sixty, and making us believe when belief was all we had. To Derek Lockwood for that can-do Kiwi genius. To John McCabe for showing us the power of a big idea. To Harry Smail, debater without peer. To Thom Middlebrook, our Keith Moon in a tux. To Matt Low, always part of the family. To Diana Poveromo. the soul of the company. To Jared Richardson, Viresh Chopra, Hannah Aubrey, Julie Regina, Andrea Pagliughi, Michael Pollack, Marty Williams, Jason Martin, Jen Garran, Drew Beam, Craig Knowles, and Barbara Nurenberger. Thanks to Sean Ferry, Meg Paradise, Faun Chapin, Jonathan Goldblatt, Abby Brewster, and Agi Moraskawa. And to Lily Q. Jolly for making it less of a secret.

Thanks to Elizabeth, Sarah, Ro, Bridget, Grant, and Taylor for putting up with your spouses' madness.

To Larry Chu, John Kennedy, and Bob Dennen for sage guidance in moments where it made all the difference.

Thank you to all our clients past and present for betting on us, pushing us, and letting us push you back.

To the contributors whose stories and insights make this worth reading: Yoon Lee, Reed Howlett, Ralph Erenzo, Brian Lee, Willson

Overend, Rachel Antalek, RA Farouknia, David Flueck, Debby Hopkins, Beth Comstock, and Chris Trimble.

Thank you to the Eames Foundation and Black Swan cooperage.

Thank you to super-agent Steve Ross for coaxing Fahrenheit 212 into bottling up what we've learned so others could benefit, and to the Crown Business team for patiently enduring a rookie author: to our wonderful editor, the ever-patient great simplifier Roger Scholl, publisher Tina Constable, Campbell Wharton, Cindy Berman, Barbara Sturman, Ayelet Gruenspecht, and Megan Perritt.

Last and certainly not least, let me extend a very special shout-out to the brilliant Carlo Espiritu, whose deft illustrations have become my favorite part of this book. And to Chris Cook, for lending his inspiration and craft to the cover and inserts that bring it all to life.

Index

288   Index   BC 6|15